Who We Are
ASIANS

ASIANS

BY THE NEW STRATEGIST EDITORS

New Strategist Publications, Inc.
Ithaca, New York

New Strategist Publications, Inc.
P.O. Box 242, Ithaca, New York 14851
800/848-0842; 607/273-0913
www.newstrategist.com

ISBN 978-1-935775-31-7 (hardcover)
ISBN 1-935775-32-4 (paper)

Printed in the United States of America

Table of Contents

Chapter 6. Labor Force

Chapter 7. Living Arrangements

Chapter 8. Population

Chapter 9. Spending

Chapter 10. Time Use

List of Tables

Chapter 3. Health

Chapter 4. Housing

Chapter 5. Income

Chapter 6. Labor Force

Chapter 7. Living Arrangements

List of Illustrations

Introduction

The 2010 census surprised us: The population of the United States turned out to be even more diverse than the Census Bureau had anticipated. Fully 36 percent of the nation's residents are Asian, African American, Hispanic, or another minority. The count of minorities was 3 million people greater and 1 percentage point bigger than the Census Bureau had estimated.

The 2010 census counted 17 million Asians in the United States. Between 2000 and 2010, the Asian population expanded by 44 percent, making them the fastest-growing minority. Asians are also the most highly educated and affluent segment of the U.S. population. Two other minority groups are also central to the U.S. culture and economy: Blacks have made tremendous strides in education and earning power over the past few decades and become decidedly middle class. Hispanics are the largest minority and also growing rapidly. Only by understanding each of these increasingly important groups can policymakers and businesses hope to tailor their programs and products to the wants and needs of the more than 308 million Americans.

The second edition of *Who We Are: Asians* provides a comprehensive look at the characteristics of the fastest-growing minority population in the United States. In addition to detailed 2010 census counts of the numbers of Asians nationally and by state and metropolitan area, *Who We Are: Asians* includes the latest socioeconomic data on the Asian population. It also includes detailed spending data for Asian households. Results from the American Time Use Survey can be found here, profiling Asian time use and comparing it with the averages. Attitudinal data from the General Social Survey compare and contrast Asian attitudes with those of blacks, Hispanics, and whites on a whole range of issues.

Understanding the demographics and lifestyles of racial and ethnic groups is of vital importance to researchers and policymakers. *Who We Are: Asians* provides the key to understanding both the similarities and differences between Asians and other Americans. Regardless of race or ethnic origin, there is no doubt Americans are more alike than different, and *Who We Are: Asians* documents our many similarities. But there are also important differences among racial and ethnic groups that, if not taken into account, can derail public policy efforts and business strategies. Asians are much more educated than the average American, for example. They are more likely to postpone childbearing until their thirties, and many have children living in their home well into their fifties. These differences affect not only lifestyles but also consumer behavior and are of utmost importance to policymakers and business leaders.

Racial classification

The 2010 census used the same racial definitions that were first introduced in the 2000 census, which transformed racial classification in the United States. The 2000 census allowed Americans, for the first time in modern history, to identify with more than one racial group. This made the analysis of racial and ethnic diversity more complex, but also more rewarding.

To understand the federal government's racial classification system, you need to understand three terms: race alone, race in combination, and race alone or in combination. The "race alone" population consists of people who identify themselves as being of only one race. The "race in combination" population consists of people who identify themselves as being of more than one race, such as black and white. The "race, alone or in combination" population includes both those who identify themselves as being of one race and those who identify themselves as being of more than one race. For example, the "Asian, alone or in combination" population includes those who say they are Asian alone and those who say they are Asian and white and those who say they are Asian, white, and black, and so on.

While the new classification system is a goldmine for researchers, the numbers do not add up. This may frustrate some, but it provides a more accurate picture of each racial group than the old classification scheme did, which required the multiracial to align with only one race. Under the current methodology, however, tables that show the "race alone" population exclude the multiracial. Tables that show the "race in combination" population count some people more than once. To make matters even more complex, Hispanics are considered an ethnic group rather than a race and can be black, white, or Asian. Keep these factors in mind as you peruse the numbers.

Whenever possible, the tables in *Who We Are: Asians* show the "race alone or in combination" populations. We prefer this classification because it includes everyone who identifies with a particular racial group and does not exclude the multiracial. In some instances, the "race alone or in combination" population figures are not available. In these cases, the "race alone" population is shown. The racial classification used is noted at the bottom of each table, if the information is available. Note that some data sources do not define their racial classifications.

How to use this book

Who We Are: Asians is designed for easy use. It is divided into 10 chapters arranged alphabetically: Attitudes, Education, Health, Housing, Income, Labor Force, Living Arrangements, Population, Spending, and Time Use. Descriptive text and charts accompany most of the tables, highlighting the important trends.

Most of the tables in *Who We Are: Asians* are based on data collected by the federal government, in particular the Census Bureau, the Bureau of Labor Statistics, the National Center for Education Statistics, the National Center for Health Statistics, and the Federal Reserve Board. The federal government continues to be the best source of up-to-date, reliable information on the changing characteristics of Americans.

Several government databases are of particular importance to *Who We Are: Asians.* One is the 2010 census, the findings of which are included here if they were available at the time of publication. Another important source is the Census Bureau's Current Population Survey. The CPS is a nationally representative survey of the civilian noninstitutional population aged 15 or older. The Census Bureau takes the CPS monthly, collecting information from 50,000 households on employment and unemployment. Each year, the March survey includes a demographic supplement that is the source of most national data on the characteristics of Americans, such as their educational attainment, living arrangements, and incomes. CPS data appear in many tables of this book.

The American Community Survey is another important source of data for *Who We Are: Asians*. The ACS is an ongoing nationwide survey of 250,000 households per month, providing detailed demographic data at the community level. Designed to replace the census long-form questionnaire, the ACS includes more than 60 questions that formerly appeared on the long form, such as queries about language spoken at home, income, and education. ACS data are available for the nation, regions, states, counties, metropolitan areas, and smaller geographic units.

The Consumer Expenditure Survey is the data source for the Spending chapter. Sponsored by the Bureau of Labor Statistics, the CEX is an ongoing study of the day-to-day spending of American households. The data collected by the survey are used to update prices for the Consumer Price Index. The CEX includes an interview survey and a diary survey administered to two separate, nationally representative samples. The average spending figures shown in the Spending chapter of this book are integrated data from both the diary and interview components of the survey. For the interview survey, about 7,500 consumer units are interviewed on a rotating panel basis each quarter for five consecutive quarters. For the diary survey, another 7,500 consumer units keep weekly diaries of spending for two consecutive weeks.

The Bureau of Labor Statistics' American Time Use Survey is the source of data for the Time Use chapter. Through telephone interviews with a nationally representative sample of noninstitutionalized Americans aged 15 or older, ATUS collects information in minute detail about what survey respondents did during the previous 24 hours—or diary day. Time use data allow social scientists to better understand our economy and lifestyle and how policy decisions affect our lives.

To compare and contrast the attitudes of Asians with those of blacks, Hispanics, and whites, New Strategist extracted custom data from the nationally representative General Social Survey of the University of Chicago's National Opinion Research Center. NORC conducts the biennial GSS through face-to-face interviews with an independently drawn, representative sample of 3,000 to 4,000 noninstitutionalized people aged 18 or older in the United States. The GSS is the best source of data on American attitudes available today.

Note: There are no wealth data for Asians.

The outsourcing of trend analysis

Most of the tables in *Who We Are: Asians* are based on data collected by the federal government, which continues to be the best, if not the only, source of up-to-date, reliable information on the changing characteristics of Americans. For those who need to know the trends, there is no better source than the government's massive demographic and socioeconomic databases. But searching, downloading, and analyzing information from these databases can be time consuming. Essentially, the government has outsourced the job of uncovering the trends to bloggers, market researchers, students, and library visitors, many of whom may feel overwhelmed by computer screens filled with numbers. In short, it has become more time consuming than ever to track the trends.

In *Who We Are: Asians*, New Strategist has done the work for you. Although the government collected most of the data presented here, each table in *Who We Are: Asians* was handcrafted by New Strategist's demographers. Our editors have spent hundreds of hours scouring government web sites, extracting numbers, creating tables that reveal trends, and producing indexes, percent distributions, and other calculations that provide context. *Who We Are: Asians* has the numbers and the stories behind them. Thumbing through its pages, you can gain more insight into the dynamics of the Asian population than you could by spending all afternoon surfing databases on the Internet. By having *Who We Are: Asians* on your computer (with links to the Excel version of each table) or on your bookshelf, you can get the answers to your questions faster than you can online—no calculator required. Researchers who want to go further can use the source listed at the bottom of each table to explore the original data. The book contains a comprehensive table list to help readers locate the information they need. For a more detailed search, use the index at the back of the book. Also in the back of the book is the glossary, which defines most of the terms commonly used in the tables and text.

Who We Are: Asians gives you the opportunity to discover and become familiar with the large and rapidly growing Asian population and its many unique characteristics. Armed with such knowledge, you will be closer to understanding what the future holds for our vast and complex nation.

Executive Summary

What You Need to Know about Asians

The United States is no longer about to be transformed into a multicultural melting pot. It already has been transformed. In 2010, 36 percent of the population—more than 100 million people—were Asian, black, Hispanic, or another minority. Keeping track of the changing racial and ethnic makeup of the nation requires more than hearsay and hunches. It requires more than cursory attention to media reports—which are often wrong. To seize the opportunity, you need to know the facts about the country's growing minority populations. Whether you are a marketer, retailer, manufacturer, politician, policymaker, or social service provider, the nation's Asians, blacks, and Hispanics are a growing share of your customers and constituents.

Unfortunately, many Americans know little about the racial and ethnic makeup of the population. The public often wildly overestimates the size of minority groups while at the same time underestimating or even ignoring their powerful influence. In these difficult times, getting it wrong can mean the difference between profit and loss, winning and losing, successful programs and failures. To keep you informed, the summary charts below highlight the most important facts you need to know about the nation's Asian population. More details are available in the chapters that follow. Use these charts as a starting point for generating product ideas, developing marketing insights, and creating innovative policies.

1. Asians are still a small percentage of Americans

Asians account for only 6 percent of U.S. residents, a much smaller proportion than the black or Hispanic share of the population. Although few in number, Asians are highly influential because they are more affluent and educated than any other group. (For more information, see the Population chapter.)

Six percent of Americans are Asian

(percent of population by race and Hispanic origin, 2010)

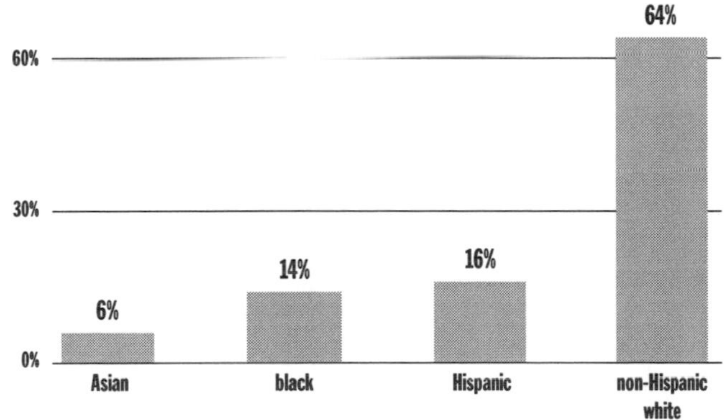

2. Most Asians were born in another country

The majority of Asians are citizens, but only because many have been naturalized. Only one in three Asians was born in the United States. A larger 39 percent are naturalized citizens. The remaining 28 percent of Asians are not citizens. (For more information, see the Population chapter.)

More than one-third of Asians are naturalized citizens

(percent distribution of Asians by place of birth and citizenship status, 2009)

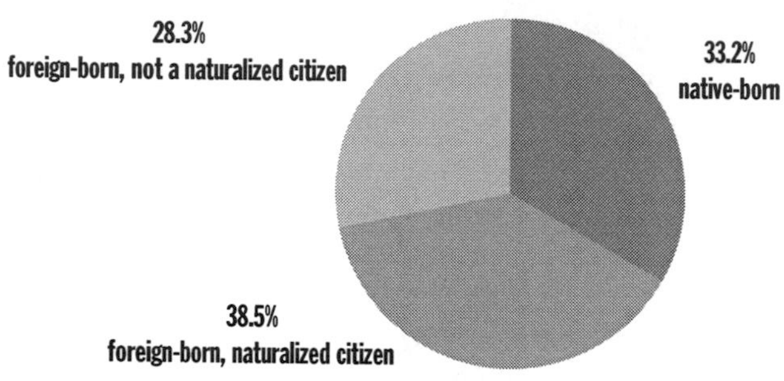

3. Nearly one-third of Asians live in California

The 57 percent majority of Asians live in just five states. Those five states can be found in three of the nation's four regions—the West, Northeast, and South. (For more information, see the Population chapter.)

Nine percent of Asians live in New York State

(percent of the Asian population living in the five states with the most Asians, 2010)

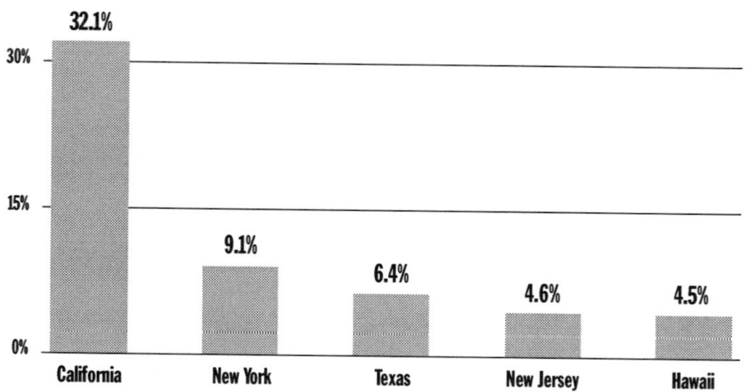

4. One in seven California residents is Asian

California is the most-populous state in the country, and one in seven state residents is Asian. The political and economic power of California amplifies the Asian influence in the rest of the United States. In San Jose, 31 percent of the population is Asian. In San Francisco, the figure is 23 percent. (For more information, see the Population chapter.)

In Hawaii, Asians are in the majority

(Asian share of population in the five states in which Asians account for the largest share of the population, 2010)

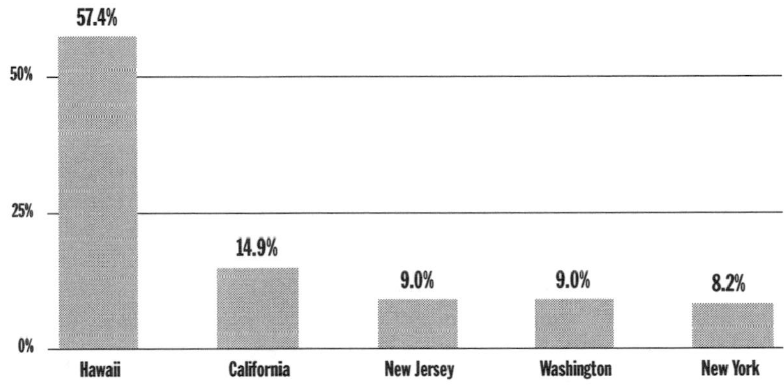

5. Asians have the highest incomes

Asian household incomes are far above average for two reasons: Asians are highly educated, and their households are more likely to have two or more earners. Nearly half (49 percent) of Asian households have two or more earners compared with a smaller 41 percent of all households. (For more information, see the Income and Labor Force chapters.)

Asian household income is 31 percent above average

(median income of total and Asian households, 2009)

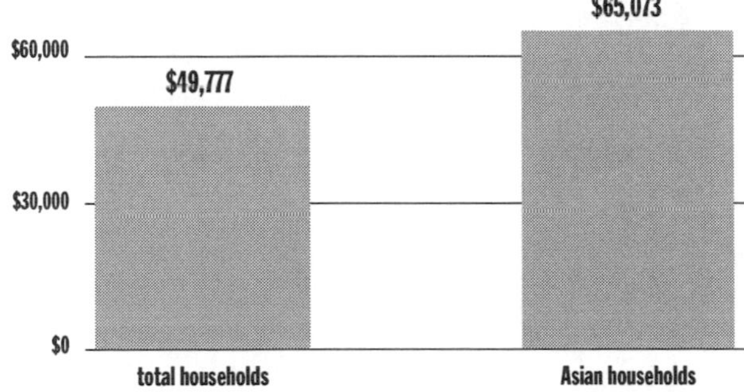

Asian households have more earners

(percent of total and Asian households with two or more earners, 2010)

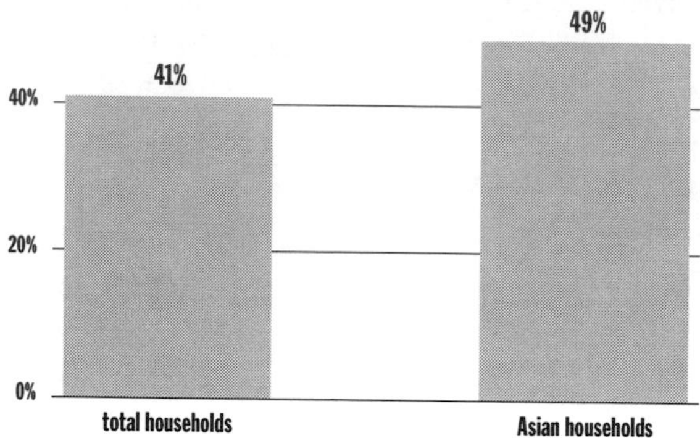

6. Asians are the most highly educated Americans

Asians are far better educated than the average American. More than half of Asians have a bachelor's degree, compared with only 30 percent of adults nationwide. Their high educational level results in better paying jobs and larger incomes for Asian men and women. (For more information, see the Education chapter.)

Half of Asians have a bachelor's degree

(percent of total people and Asians aged 25 or older who have a bachelor's degree, 2010)

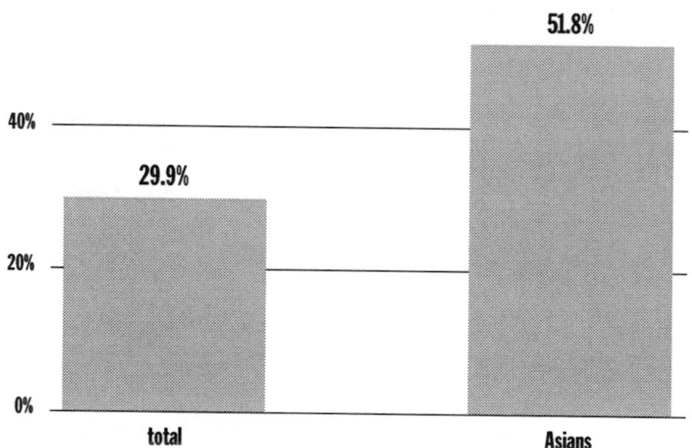

7. Most Asian women postpone childbearing until aged 30 or older

Asians have children later than blacks, Hispanics, or non-Hispanic whites. Behind their postponed childbearing is their educational attainment. With men and women remaining in school well into their twenties, most Asians delay starting a family until after they have earned a degree and established a career. (For more information, see the Health chapter.)

Few Asian births are to women under age 25

(percent distribution of Asian births by age of mother, 2009)

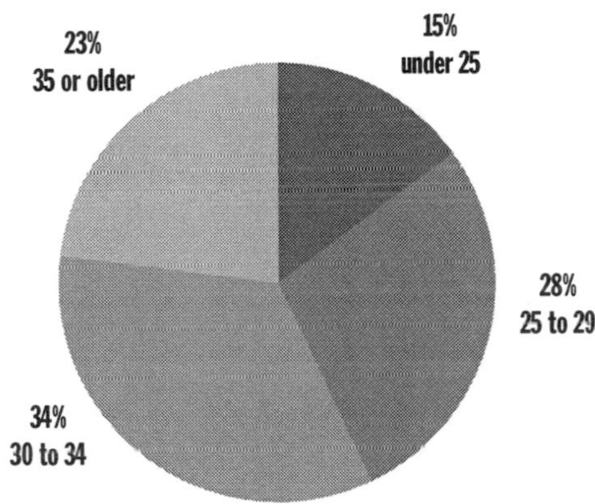

8. Asians spend more than other households

The spending of Asian households is 15 percent above average because their incomes are relatively high. Asians spend 70 to 71 percent more than the average household on lunch and dinner at full-service restaurants. They spend 50 percent more than average on mortgage interest, and their spending on college tuition is more than twice the average. (For more information, see the Spending chapter.)

Asians spend 15 percent more than the average household

(average annual spending of total and Asian households, 2009)

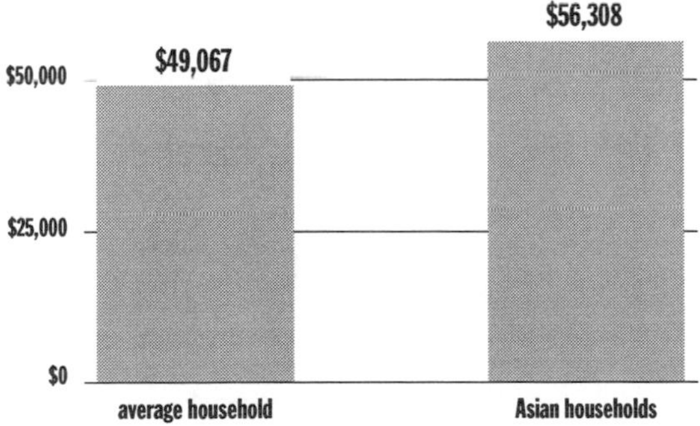

9. Married couples head most Asian households

Another reason why Asian household incomes are so high is that married couples—the most affluent household type—head a larger than average share of Asian households. Among all households, married couples head just under 50 percent. Among Asian households, the figure is 60 percent. Most Asian couples are dual earners. (For more information, see the Living Arrangements chapter.)

Sixty percent of Asian households are headed by married couples

(percent of total and Asian households headed by married couples, 2010)

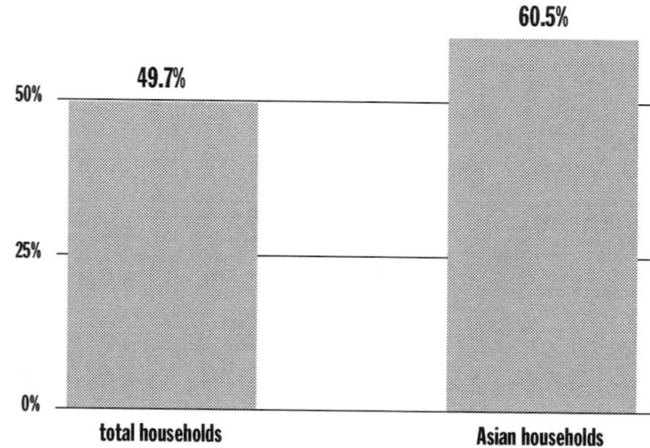

10. Asians spend more time working

On a typical day, Asians spend more time working than the average person. They also spend more time caring for children and eating and drinking. Asians spend less time watching television than the average person. (For more information, see the Time Use chapter.)

Asians spend less time watching television

(indexed hours per day Asians aged 15 or older spend doing selected activities compared with the average person, 2009)

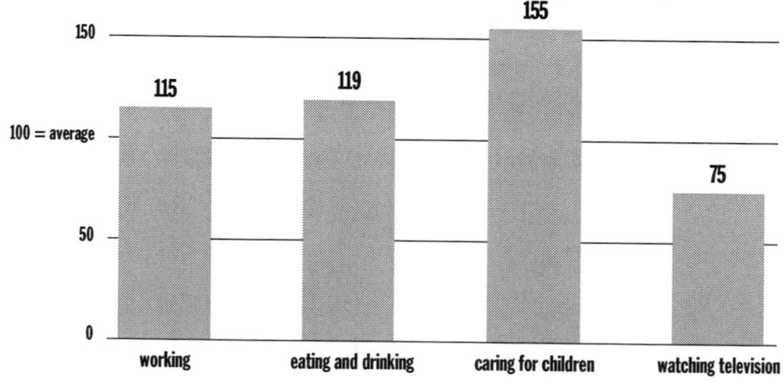

CHAPTER

1

Attitudes

- The 51 percent majority of Asians think life is exciting.

- Only 34 percent of Asians say most people can be trusted. While this is not a large number, Asians are far more trusting than blacks or Hispanics.

- Asians are more likely than blacks, Hispanics, or whites to think their family income is above average. Twenty-nine percent said their income was above average in 2010.

- Twenty-six percent of Asians are satisfied with their personal financial situation, a greater share than the proportions among blacks (17 percent), Hispanics (11 percent), or whites (25 percent).

- Sixty percent of Asians say their standard of living is much better than their parents' was at the same age.

- Asians are more likely than any other racial or ethnic group to believe in evolution. Eighty-two percent of Asians say it is true that humans developed from earlier species of animals.

- Asians are more supportive of same-sex marriage than any other racial or ethnic group. Seventy-one percent of Asians support the right of gays and lesbians to marry.

- Asians, blacks, and Hispanics favor the Democratic party. Fifty-three percent of Asians identify themselves as Democrats, while only 20 percent say they are Republicans.

Most People Say They Are Pretty Happy

But few trust others.

By race and Hispanic origin, the 52 to 64 percent majority of each racial and ethnic group feels pretty happy. But a substantial 20 to 21 percent of Asians, blacks, and Hispanics admit that they are not too happy, far above the 12 percent of whites who feel that way.

Most husbands and wives say they are very happily married. The proportion is above 50 percent for blacks, Hispanics, and whites. Among Asians, however, the figure is slightly below the 50 percent mark.

The share of Americans who say life is exciting (52 percent) substantially tops the percentage saying it is pretty routine (43 percent). The majority of Asians, Hispanics, and whites think life is exciting. Among blacks, the figure is slightly below 50 percent. Nine percent of blacks say life is dull.

Few believe most people can be trusted. Only 32 percent of the total public agrees that most people can be trusted. Blacks and Hispanics are far less trusting than Asians or whites.

■ The low levels of trust among blacks and Hispanics is a problem for marketers who need to convince potential customers of the value of their products or services.

Blacks and Hispanics are less trusting

(percent of people aged 18 or older who think most people can be trusted, by race and Hispanic origin, 2010)

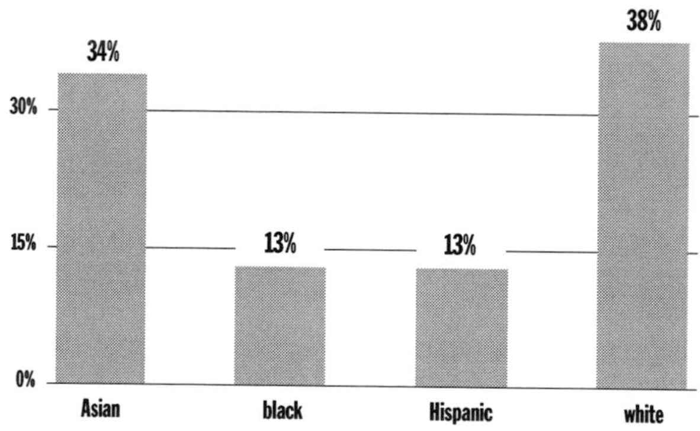

Table 1.1 General Happiness, 2010

"Taken all together, how would you say things are these days—would you say that you are very happy, pretty happy, or not too happy?"

(percent of people aged 18 or older responding by race and Hispanic origin, 2010)

	very happy	pretty happy	not too happy
Total people	**28.8%**	**57.0%**	**14.2%**
Asian	14.8	64.1	21.1
Black	24.6	55.3	20.1
Hispanic	27.9	52.4	19.7
White	30.8	57.0	12.2

Note: Hispanics may be of any race.
Source: Survey Documentation and Analysis, Computer-assisted Survey Methods Program, University of California, Berkeley, General Social Surveys, 1972–2010 Cumulative Data Files, Internet site http://sda.berkeley.edu/cgi-bin32/hsda?harcsda+gss10; calculations by New Strategist

Table 1.2 Happiness of Marriage, 2010

"Taking all things together, how would you describe your marriage?"

(percent of married people aged 18 or older responding by race and Hispanic origin, 2010)

	very happy	pretty happy	not too happy
Total people	**63.0%**	**34.3%**	**2.6%**
Asian	49.8	47.6	2.5
Black	54.7	41.9	3.4
Hispanic	50.5	47.2	2.3
White	64.9	32.6	2.5

Note: Hispanics may be of any race.
Source: Survey Documentation and Analysis, Computer-assisted Survey Methods Program, University of California, Berkeley, General Social Surveys, 1972–2010 Cumulative Data Files, Internet site http://sda.berkeley.edu/cgi-bin32/hsda?harcsda+gss10; calculations by New Strategist

Table 1.3 Life Exciting or Dull, 2010

"In general, do you find life exciting, pretty routine, or dull?"

(percent of people aged 18 or older responding by race and Hispanic origin, 2010)

	exciting	pretty routine	dull
Total people	**52.1%**	**43.3%**	**4.6%**
Asian	51.4	45.2	3.4
Black	49.5	41.4	9.1
Hispanic	51.9	45.1	3.1
White	52.5	43.8	3.7

Note: Hispanics may be of any race.
Source: Survey Documentation and Analysis, Computer-assisted Survey Methods Program, University of California, Berkeley, General Social Surveys, 1972–2010 Cumulative Data Files, Internet site http://sda.berkeley.edu/cgi-bin32/hsda?harcsda+gss10; calculations by New Strategist

Table 1.4 Trust in Others, 2010

"Generally speaking, would you say that most people can be trusted or that you can't be too careful in life?"

(percent of people aged 18 or older responding by race and Hispanic origin, 2010)

	can trust	cannot trust	depends
Total people	**32.2%**	**62.5%**	**5.3%**
Asian	34.3	55.5	10.2
Black	12.7	81.2	6.0
Hispanic	13.5	84.9	1.6
White	37.6	57.3	5.1

Note: Hispanics may be of any race.
Source: Survey Documentation and Analysis, Computer-assisted Survey Methods Program, University of California, Berkeley, General Social Surveys, 1972–2010 Cumulative Data Files, Internet site http://sda.berkeley.edu/cgi-bin32/hsda?harcsda+gss10; calculations by New Strategist

Most Think Hard Work Leads to Success

Many Asians, blacks, and Hispanics doubt that private enterprise can solve U.S. problems.

How do people get ahead? Nearly 70 percent of Americans say it is through hard work, and another one-fifth cite a combination of hard work and luck. By race and Hispanic origin, the majority of blacks, Hispanics, and whites believe hard work is the answer. Among Asians, only 43 percent feel this way. A larger 44 percent of Asians believe it is a combination of hard work and luck that leads to success.

There are large differences in the lifetime geographic mobility of Americans by race and Hispanic origin. In 2010, nearly half of Asians and Hispanics said they had lived outside their current state of residence at age 16. Many probably lived outside the United States when they were teenagers. Among blacks and whites, only 30 to 34 percent say they lived outside their current state of residence at age 16. Half of blacks are in the same city they lived in at age 16.

Forty-five percent of the public thinks private enterprise will solve our problems. Among Asians, blacks, and Hispanics, the figure is much smaller. Just 24 percent of blacks think private enterprise will come to our rescue. The figure is 35 percent among Asians and 38 percent among Hispanics. In contrast, nearly half (49 percent) of whites see private enterprise as the answer. The 62 percent majority of blacks agree that we worry too much about the environment and too little about the economy. Nearly half of Hispanics agree. Among Asians and whites, the figures are a smaller 35 and 39 percent, respectively.

■ Anxiety about the economy is making many people question their stance on environmental issues.

Blacks doubt that private enterprise will solve our problems

(percent of people aged 18 or older who agree that private enterprise will solve U.S. problems, by race and Hispanic origin, 2010)

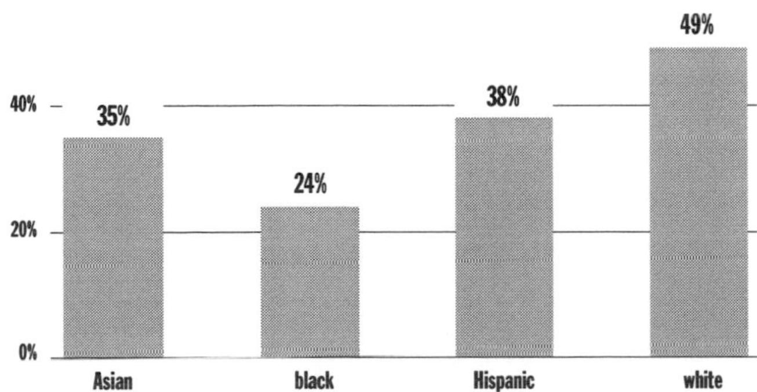

Table 1.5 How People Get Ahead, 2010

"Some people say that people get ahead by their own hard work; others say that lucky breaks or help from other people are more important. Which do you think is most important?"

(percent of people aged 18 or older responding by race and Hispanic origin, 2010)

	hard work	both equally	luck
Total people	**69.6%**	**20.4%**	**10.0%**
Asian	42.6	44.1	13.3
Black	64.8	21.0	14.2
Hispanic	84.0	9.3	6.7
White	71.5	19.8	8.7

Note: Hispanics may be of any race.
Source: Survey Documentation and Analysis, Computer-assisted Survey Methods Program, University of California, Berkeley, General Social Surveys, 1972–2010 Cumulative Data Files, Internet site http://sda.berkeley.edu/cgi-bin32/hsda?harcsda+gss10; calculations by New Strategist

Table 1.6 Geographic Mobility since Age 16, 2010

"When you were 16 years old, were you living in this same (city/town/county)?"

(percent of people aged 18 or older responding by race and Hispanic origin, 2010)

	same city	same state different city	outside state
Total people	**39.4%**	**25.7%**	**34.9%**
Asian	35.2	16.8	48.0
Black	50.4	19.7	29.9
Hispanic	34.6	15.7	49.7
White	37.6	28.0	34.4

Note: Hispanics may be of any race.
Source: Survey Documentation and Analysis, Computer-assisted Survey Methods Program, University of California, Berkeley, General Social Surveys, 1972–2010 Cumulative Data Files, Internet site http://sda.berkeley.edu/cgi-bin32/hsda?harcsda+gss10; calculations by New Strategist

Table 1.7 Private Enterprise Will Solve Problems, 2010

"Private enterprise will solve U.S. problems. Do you agree or disagree?"

(percent of people aged 18 or older responding by race and Hispanic origin, 2010)

	strongly agree	agree	neither agree nor disagree	disagree	strongly disagree
Total people	**14.4%**	**30.2%**	**27.5%**	**22.8%**	**5.1%**
Asian	13.4	21.7	25.1	36.9	2.9
Black	8.2	15.4	24.7	40.3	11.3
Hispanic	8.4	29.3	35.8	20.0	6.4
White	15.8	33.6	27.8	18.9	3.9

Note: Hispanics may be of any race.
Source: Survey Documentation and Analysis, Computer-assisted Survey Methods Program, University of California, Berkeley, General Social Surveys, 1972–2010 Cumulative Data Files, Internet site http://sda.berkeley.edu/cgi-bin32/hsda?harcsda+gss10; calculations by New Strategist

Table 1.8 Environment versus Economy, 2010

"We worry too much about the environment, too little about the economy. Do you agree or disagree?"

(percent of people aged 18 or older responding by race and Hispanic origin, 2010)

	strongly agree	agree	neither agree nor disagree	disagree	strongly disagree
Total people	**10.2%**	**32.3%**	**18.1%**	**31.7%**	**7.7%**
Asian	11.8	23.1	30.4	29.5	5.3
Black	21.3	40.4	11.4	23.5	3.3
Hispanic	8.6	40.3	20.6	23.8	6.7
White	8.0	30.6	18.9	33.7	8.9

Note: Hispanics may be of any race.
Source: Survey Documentation and Analysis, Computer-assisted Survey Methods Program, University of California, Berkeley, General Social Surveys, 1972–2010 Cumulative Data Files, Internet site http://sda.berkeley.edu/cgi-bin32/hsda?harcsda+gss10; calculations by New Strategist

Blacks and Hispanics Call Themselves Working Class

Asians and whites are most likely to identify themselves as middle class.

Among all Americans in 2010, only 42 percent identified themselves as middle class while a larger 47 percent said they were working class. Hispanics are least likely to put themselves in the middle class (25 percent) and most likely to identify as working class (66 percent). Among blacks, the 55 percent majority says they are working class and 28 percent call themselves middle class. Asians are more likely than whites to call themselves middle class (49 percent versus 46 percent).

Thirty-six percent of Americans say their family income is below average. By race and Hispanic origin, blacks and Hispanics are most likely to say their income is below average (47 and 46 percent, respectively). Asians are most likely to say their family income is above average (29 percent).

Only 23 percent of the public is satisfied with their present financial situation. The figure is smallest among Hispanics (11 percent) and largest among Asians and whites (26 and 25 percent, respectively). Blacks are most likely to say they are not at all satisfied with their finances, 44 percent feeling that way.

■ Asians are most satisfied with their finances because their incomes are higher than those of blacks, Hispanics, or whites.

Hispanics are least likely to say they are satisfied with their financial situation

(percent of people aged 18 or older who are satisfied with their present financial situation, by race and Hispanic origin, 2010)

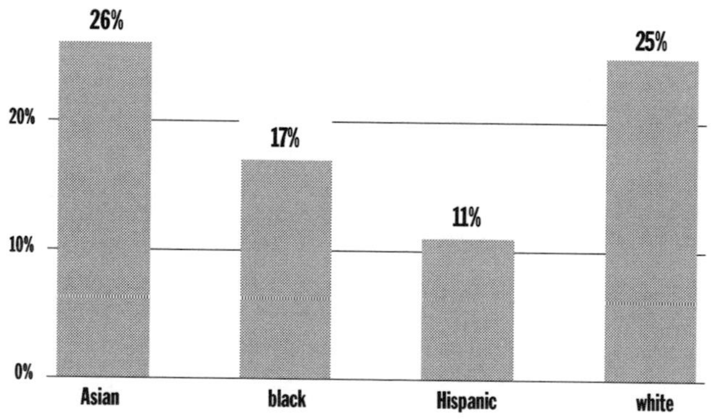

Table 1.9 Social Class Membership, 2010

"If you were asked to use one of four names for your social class, which would you say you belong in: the lower class, the working class, the middle class, or the upper class?"

(percent of people aged 18 or older responding by race and Hispanic origin, 2010)

	lower	working	middle	upper
Total people	**8.2%**	**46.8%**	**42.4%**	**2.5%**
Asian	7.2	42.5	48.9	1.3
Black	14.2	55.1	28.1	2.6
Hispanic	9.0	65.5	25.3	0.2
White	7.0	44.0	46.4	2.6

Note: Hispanics may be of any race.
Source: Survey Documentation and Analysis, Computer-assisted Survey Methods Program, University of California, Berkeley, General Social Surveys, 1972–2010 Cumulative Data Files, Internet site http://sda.berkeley.edu/cgi-bin32/hsda?harcsda+gss10; calculations by New Strategist

Table 1.10 Family Income Relative to Others, 2010

"Compared with American families in general, would you say your family income is far below average, below average, average, above average, or far above average?"

(percent of people aged 18 or older responding by race and Hispanic origin, 2010)

	far below average	below average	average	above average	far above average
Total people	**6.8%**	**28.8%**	**43.5%**	**18.4%**	**2.5%**
Asian	2.6	22.7	45.6	25.5	3.7
Black	10.9	36.0	45.3	7.6	0.2
Hispanic	7.9	37.9	47.4	5.3	1.5
White	6.0	26.8	42.8	21.5	2.9

Note: Hispanics may be of any race.
Source: Survey Documentation and Analysis, Computer-assisted Survey Methods Program, University of California, Berkeley, General Social Surveys, 1972–2010 Cumulative Data Files, Internet site http://sda.berkeley.edu/cgi-bin32/hsda?harcsda+gss10; calculations by New Strategist

Table 1.11 Satisfaction with Financial Situation, 2010

"We are interested in how people are getting along financially these days. So far as you and your family are concerned, would you say that you are pretty well satisfied with your present financial situation, more or less satisfied, or not satisfied at all?"

(percent of people aged 18 or older responding by race and Hispanic origin, 2010)

	satisfied	more or less satisfied	not at all satisfied
Total people	**23.3%**	**45.2%**	**31.5%**
Asian	26.2	49.9	23.8
Black	17.0	38.9	44.1
Hispanic	11.0	57.2	31.8
White	25.4	45.5	29.1

Note: Hispanics may be of any race.
Source: Survey Documentation and Analysis, Computer-assisted Survey Methods Program, University of California, Berkeley, General Social Surveys, 1972–2010 Cumulative Data Files, Internet site http://sda.berkeley.edu/cgi-bin32/hsda?harcsda+gss10; calculations by New Strategist

Many Think Their Standard of Living Is Falling

Fewer Americans believe they are better off than their parents.

When comparing their own standard of living now with that of their parents when they were the same age, 59 percent of respondents say they are better off. The figure was a higher 67 percent 10 years ago. Asians and Hispanics are more likely than blacks or whites to say they are doing better than their parents.

When asked whether they think they have a good chance of improving their present standard of living, only 58 percent of Americans agree. A decade earlier, fully 77 percent felt optimistic. By race and Hispanic origin, whites are least likely to feel like they will be able to get ahead. Only 53 percent of whites think they have a good chance of improving their standard of living.

Fifty-nine percent of parents believe their children will have a better standard of living when they reach their age. The share was a larger 69 percent 10 years earlier. Hispanics are most likely to think things will improve for their children, 81 percent feeling that way.

■ Americans who have the least are most likely to believe that things will get better.

Most think their children will be better off

(percent of parents who think their children's standard of living will be better than theirs is today, by race and Hispanic origin, 2010)

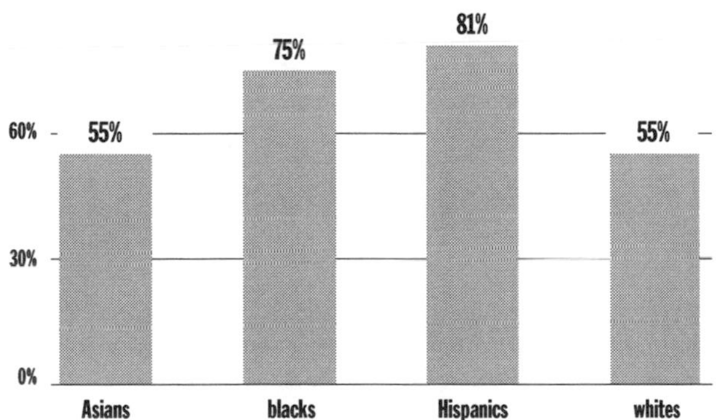

Table 1.12 Parents' Standard of Living, 2010

"Compared to your parents when they were the age you are now, do you think your own standard of living now is much better, somewhat better, about the same, somewhat worse, or much worse than theirs was?"

(percent of people aged 18 or older responding by race and Hispanic origin, 2010)

	much better	somewhat better	about the same	somewhat worse	much worse
Total people	**29.2%**	**29.7%**	**24.8%**	**12.1%**	**4.2%**
Asian	60.0	18.4	14.0	7.6	0.0
Black	29.8	28.6	25.6	8.9	7.1
Hispanic	35.4	37.7	14.5	7.0	5.4
White	27.3	30.1	26.2	12.8	3.6

Note: Hispanics may be of any race.
Source: Survey Documentation and Analysis, Computer-assisted Survey Methods Program, University of California, Berkeley, General Social Surveys, 1972–2010 Cumulative Data Files, Internet site http://sda.berkeley.edu/cgi-bin32/hsda?harcsda+gss10; calculations by New Strategist

Table 1.13 Standard of Living Will Improve, 2010

"The way things are in America, people like me and my family have a good chance of improving our standard of living. Do you agree or disagree?"

(percent of people aged 18 or older responding by race and Hispanic origin, 2010)

	strongly agree	agree	neither	disagree	strongly disagree
Total people	**13.1%**	**44.9%**	**16.2%**	**21.6%**	**4.2%**
Asian	18.6	50.6	18.4	10.4	2.0
Black	25.6	50.5	9.9	11.6	2.4
Hispanic	20.0	56.3	11.7	9.4	2.6
White	9.5	43.6	17.3	24.9	4.7

Note: Hispanics may be of any race.
Source: Survey Documentation and Analysis, Computer-assisted Survey Methods Program, University of California, Berkeley, General Social Surveys, 1972–2010 Cumulative Data Files, Internet site http://sda.berkeley.edu/cgi-bin32/hsda?harcsda+gss10; calculations by New Strategist

Table 1.14 Children's Standard of Living, 2010

"When your children are at the age you are now, do you think their standard of living will be much better, somewhat better, about the same, somewhat worse, or much worse than yours is now?"

(percent of people aged 18 or older with children responding by race and Hispanic origin, 2010)

	much better	somewhat better	about the same	somewhat worse	much worse
Total people	**27.4%**	**32.0%**	**20.6%**	**15.0%**	**5.1%**
Asian	15.9	39.3	31.1	11.4	2.1
Black	44.3	31.1	12.6	7.7	4.4
Hispanic	48.1	32.5	10.4	7.6	1.4
White	21.7	32.9	22.8	17.2	5.5

Note: Hispanics may be of any race.
Source: Survey Documentation and Analysis, Computer-assisted Survey Methods Program, University of California, Berkeley, General Social Surveys, 1972–2010 Cumulative Data Files, Internet site http://sda.berkeley.edu/cgi-bin32/hsda?harcsda+gss10; calculations by New Strategist

The Two-Child Family Is Most Popular

Most Asians and whites say two children are ideal.

Among all Americans, the 48 percent plurality thinks two is the ideal number of children. Among Asians and whites, the figures are even higher. Fifty-six percent of Asians and 51 percent of whites think two children is the ideal number. A smaller 46 percent of Hispanics think two are ideal. Among blacks, only 34 percent think two are ideal. Slightly more than half of blacks say three or more children are ideal.

The great majority of the public believes children should get a good, hard spanking when they misbehave. By race and Hispanic origin, the figure ranges from 80 percent among blacks to 61 percent among Asians.

Traditional sex roles—defined as the man being the breadwinner and the woman caring for the home—are spurned by most Americans today. In 2010, only 35 percent of the public thought traditional sex roles were best. Asians are least likely to favor traditional sex roles, with only 21 percent saying they are best. Regardless of race or Hispanic origin, few think work harms a mother's relationship with her children.

Forty-seven percent of all Americans think the federal government should help people pay their medical bills. A larger 55 to 69 percent majority of Asians, blacks, and Hispanics think the government should help. In contrast, only 42 percent of whites support government involvement.

■ Few Asians, blacks, Hispanics, or whites regard one child as ideal.

Whites are least likely to think the government should help with medical bills

(percent of people aged 18 or older who agree that the government should help people pay for their doctor and hospital bills, by race and Hispanic origin, 2010)

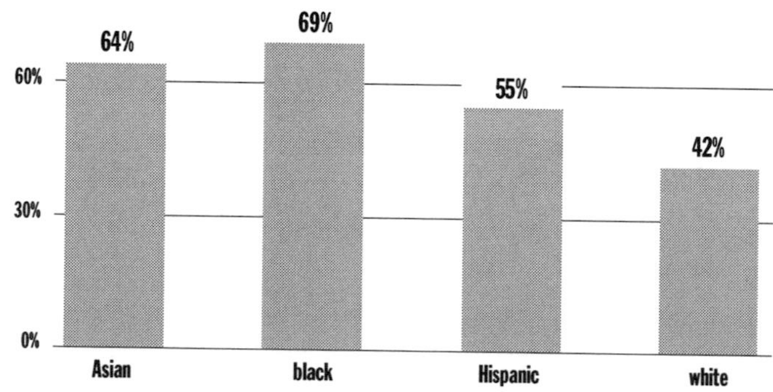

Table 1.15 Ideal Number of Children, 2010

"What do you think is the ideal number of children for a family to have?"

(percent of people aged 18 or older responding by race and Hispanic origin, 2010)

	none	one	two	three	four or more	as many as want
Total people	**0.3%**	**2.5%**	**48.4%**	**26.3%**	**12.0%**	**10.5%**
Asian	0.0	1.9	56.7	32.0	9.4	0.0
Black	0.2	1.8	33.8	23.4	27.0	13.8
Hispanic	0.0	0.8	46.4	30.8	16.7	5.3
White	0.4	2.9	51.5	25.8	8.5	10.9

Note: Hispanics may be of any race.
Source: Survey Documentation and Analysis, Computer-assisted Survey Methods Program, University of California, Berkeley, General Social Surveys, 1972–2010 Cumulative Data Files, Internet site http://sda.berkeley.edu/cgi-bin32/hsda?harcsda+gss10; calculations by New Strategist

Table 1.16 Spanking Children, 2010

"Do you strongly agree, agree, disagree, or strongly disagree that it is sometimes necessary to discipline a child with a good, hard spanking?"

(percent of people aged 18 or older responding by race and Hispanic origin, 2010)

	strongly agree	agree	disagree	strongly disagree
Total people	**23.6%**	**45.4%**	**23.5%**	**7.5%**
Asian	27.6	33.1	31.0	8.3
Black	35.4	44.2	16.3	4.0
Hispanic	22.7	42.2	27.7	7.4
White	21.1	47.0	23.9	8.0

Note: Hispanics may be of any race.
Source: Survey Documentation and Analysis, Computer-assisted Survey Methods Program, University of California, Berkeley, General Social Surveys, 1972–2010 Cumulative Data Files, Internet site http://sda.berkeley.edu/cgi-bin32/hsda?harcsda+gss10; calculations by New Strategist

Table 1.17 Better for Man to Work, Woman to Tend Home, 2010

"Do you strongly agree, agree, disagree, or strongly disagree with the statement: It is much better for everyone involved if the man is the achiever outside the home and the woman takes care of the home and family?"

(percent of people aged 18 or older responding by race and Hispanic origin, 2010)

	strongly agree	agree	disagree	strongly disagree
Total people	**6.8%**	**28.6%**	**43.5%**	**21.2%**
Asian	2.8	18.4	60.5	18.4
Black	7.2	28.8	44.0	20.0
Hispanic	8.9	29.9	43.5	17.7
White	7.0	28.1	42.5	22.4

Note: Hispanics may be of any race.
Source: Survey Documentation and Analysis, Computer-assisted Survey Methods Program, University of California, Berkeley, General Social Surveys, 1972–2010 Cumulative Data Files, Internet site http://sda.berkeley.edu/cgi-bin32/

Table 1.18 Working Mother's Relationship with Children, 2010

"Do you strongly agree, agree, disagree, or strongly disagree with the statement: A working mother can establish just as warm and secure a relationship with her children as a mother who does not work?"

(percent of people aged 18 or older responding by race and Hispanic origin, 2010)

	strongly agree	agree	disagree	strongly disagree
Total people	**28.8%**	**45.9%**	**20.1%**	**5.1%**
Asian	36.4	32.0	24.2	7.4
Black	28.3	47.7	15.2	8.8
Hispanic	27.3	44.3	23.5	4.9
White	29.0	46.3	20.6	4.1

Note: Hispanics may be of any race.
Source: Survey Documentation and Analysis, Computer-assisted Survey Methods Program, University of California, Berkeley, General Social Surveys, 1972–2010 Cumulative Data Files, Internet site http://sda.berkeley.edu/cgi-bin32/hsda?harcsda+gss10; calculations by New Strategist

Table 1.19 Should Government Help the Sick, 2010

"Some people think that it is the responsibility of the government in Washington to see to it that people have help in paying for doctors and hospital bills; they are at point 1. Others think that these matters are not the responsibility of the federal government and that people should take care of these things themselves; they are at point 5. Where would you place yourself on this scale?"

(percent of people aged 18 or older responding by race and Hispanic origin, 2010)

	government should help 1	2	agree with both 3	4	people should help themselves 5
Total people	**30.5%**	**16.4%**	**31.9%**	**11.1%**	**10.1%**
Asian	38.6	25.1	25.0	9.2	2.1
Black	53.1	15.7	26.9	1.9	2.4
Hispanic	38.6	16.6	36.1	5.3	3.4
White	24.7	16.9	32.9	13.1	12.5

Note: Hispanics may be of any race.
Source: Survey Documentation and Analysis, Computer-assisted Survey Methods Program, University of California, Berkeley, General Social Surveys, 1972–2010 Cumulative Data Files, Internet site http://sda.berkeley.edu/cgi-bin32/hsda?harcsda+gss10; calculations by New Strategist

Religion Is Important to Most Americans

The majority of blacks, Hispanics, and whites say they are at least moderately religious.

Asked whether science makes our way of life change too fast, the 52 to 53 percent majority of blacks and whites disagree. But most Asians and Hispanics agree that science is making things change too fast.

Most Asians, Hispanics, and whites believe in evolution, with Asians especially likely to believe (82 percent). Among blacks, only 42 percent believe human beings developed from earlier species of animals.

Fifty-eight percent of all Americans identify themselves as at least moderately religious. Religiosity is especially high among blacks (68 percent) and Hispanics (63 percent). In contrast, only 33 percent of Asians say they are at least moderately religious.

Religious preference varies widely by race and Hispanic origin. Blacks are most likely to identify themselves as Protestant (65 percent). Hispanics are most likely to be Catholic (63 percent). Asians are most likely to identify themselves as Buddhists (18 percent) or to say they have no religious preference (36 percent). Blacks are the only race/Hispanic origin group in which the majority believes the Bible is the actual word of God (56 percent).

■ Asians are the only ones in which the majority approves of the Supreme Court ruling banning Bible reading in public schools.

Religious preference varies greatly by race and Hispanic origin

(percent of people aged 18 or older by selected religious preference, by race and Hispanic origin, 2010)

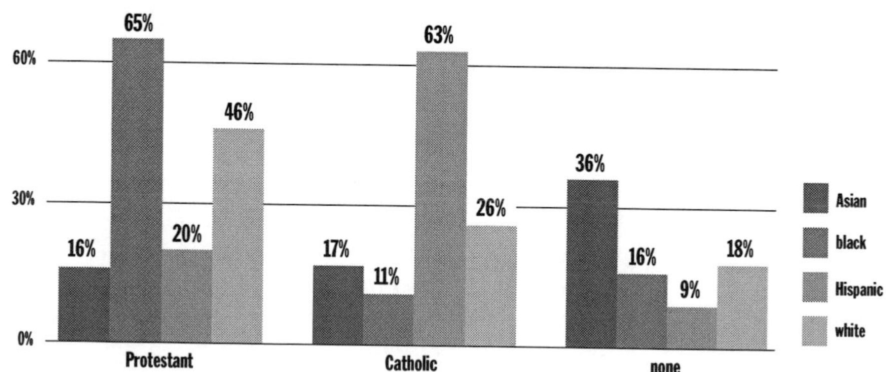

Table 1.20 Attitude toward Science, 2010

"Do you strongly agree, agree, disagree, or strongly disagree with the statement: Science makes our way of life change too fast?"

(percent of people aged 18 or older responding by race and Hispanic origin, 2010)

	strongly agree	agree	disagree	strongly disagree
Total people	**7.2%**	**41.5%**	**43.2%**	**8.1%**
Asian	23.5	38.6	23.5	14.4
Black	10.5	36.5	44.7	8.3
Hispanic	7.7	58.1	29.2	5.1
White	5.8	41.7	44.7	7.8

Note: Hispanics may be of any race.
Source: Survey Documentation and Analysis, Computer-assisted Survey Methods Program, University of California, Berkeley, General Social Surveys, 1972–2010 Cumulative Data Files, Internet site http://sda.berkeley.edu/cgi-bin32/hsda?harcsda+gss10; calculations by New Strategist

Table 1.21 Attitude toward Evolution, 2010

"True or false: Human beings, as we know them today, developed from earlier species of animals?"

(percent of people aged 18 or older responding by race and Hispanic origin, 2010)

	true	false
Total people	**55.7%**	**44.3%**
Asian	82.1	17.9
Black	42.5	57.5
Hispanic	61.5	38.5
White	57.0	43.0

Note: Hispanics may be of any race.
Source: Survey Documentation and Analysis, Computer-assisted Survey Methods Program, University of California, Berkeley, General Social Surveys, 1972–2010 Cumulative Data Files, Internet site http://sda.berkeley.edu/cgi-bin32/hsda?harcsda+gss10; calculations by New Strategist

Table 1.22 Religious Preference, 2010

"What is your religious preference?"

(percent of people aged 18 or older responding by race and Hispanic origin, 2010)

	Protestant	Catholic	Jewish	Buddhism	Hinduism	Moslem/Islam	other	none
Total people	**46.7%**	**25.2%**	**1.6%**	**0.9%**	**0.2%**	**0.6%**	**6.8%**	**18.0%**
Asian	15.9	17.2	3.6	18.2	4.0	2.6	2.7	35.8
Black	64.9	10.7	0.2	0.3	0.0	2.1	6.1	15.7
Hispanic	20.3	63.1	0.4	0.0	0.0	0.0	7.0	9.2
White	46.4	25.9	1.9	0.4	0.0	0.3	7.0	18.1

Note: Hispanics may be of any race.
Source: Survey Documentation and Analysis, Computer-assisted Survey Methods Program, University of California, Berkeley, General Social Surveys, 1972–2010 Cumulative Data Files, Internet site http://sda.berkeley.edu/cgi-bin32/hsda?harcsda+gss10; calculations by New Strategist

Table 1.23 Degree of Religiosity, 2010

"To what extent do you consider yourself a religious person?"

(percent of people aged 18 or older responding by race and Hispanic origin, 2010)

	very religious	moderately religious	slightly religious	not religious
Total people	**16.8%**	**41.6%**	**23.6%**	**18.1%**
Asian	12.5	20.1	46.5	20.9
Black	28.5	39.3	16.8	15.5
Hispanic	11.5	51.8	26.3	10.3
White	14.6	42.5	23.9	19.0

Note: Hispanics may be of any race.
Source: Survey Documentation and Analysis, Computer-assisted Survey Methods Program, University of California, Berkeley, General Social Surveys, 1972–2010 Cumulative Data Files, Internet site http://sda.berkeley.edu/cgi-bin32/hsda?harcsda+gss10; calculations by New Strategist

Table 1.24 Belief in the Bible, 2010

"Which of these statements comes closest to describing your feelings about the Bible? 1) The Bible is the actual word of God and is to be taken literally, word for word; 2) The Bible is the inspired word of God but not everything in it should be taken literally, word for word; 3) The Bible is an ancient book of fables, legends, history, and moral precepts recorded by men."

(percent of people aged 18 or older responding by race and Hispanic origin, 2010)

	word of God	inspired word	book of fables	other
Total people	**34.1%**	**43.6%**	**20.6%**	**1.7%**
Asian	12.5	35.2	49.6	2.7
Black	55.8	29.7	12.8	1.7
Hispanic	41.9	40.6	16.9	0.6
White	29.8	47.6	21.0	1.7

Note: Hispanics may be of any race.
Source: Survey Documentation and Analysis, Computer-assisted Survey Methods Program, University of California, Berkeley, General Social Surveys, 1972–2010 Cumulative Data Files, Internet site http://sda.berkeley.edu/cgi-bin32/hsda?harcsda+gss10; calculations by New Strategist

Table 1.25 Bible in the Public Schools, 2010

"The United States Supreme Court has ruled that no state or local government may require the reading of the Lord's Prayer or Bible verses in public schools. What are your views on this? Do you approve or disapprove of the court ruling?"

(percent of people aged 18 or older responding by race and Hispanic origin, 2010)

	approve	disapprove
Total people	**44.1%**	**55.9%**
Asian	59.8	40.2
Black	38.3	61.7
Hispanic	43.6	56.4
White	44.9	55.1

Note: Hispanics may be of any race.
Source: Survey Documentation and Analysis, Computer-assisted Survey Methods Program, University of California, Berkeley, General Social Surveys, 1972–2010 Cumulative Data Files, Internet site http://sda.berkeley.edu/cgi-bin32/hsda?harcsda+gss10; calculations by New Strategist

Most Asians Support Same-Sex Marriage

Hispanics and blacks are least supportive.

Fifty-three percent of Americans believe premarital sex is not wrong at all. Among Asians, the 66 percent majority feels this way. A smaller 54 percent of whites agree. Blacks and Hispanics are more conservative. Less than half of blacks and Hispanics think premarital sex is not wrong at all.

When it comes to sexual relations between adults of the same sex, 43 percent of all Americans say homosexuality is not wrong at all. Asians are much more accepting than the average person, with 60 percent saying homosexual relations are not wrong at all. Only 25 percent of blacks and 30 percent of Hispanics agree.

On the issue of whether gays and lesbians should have the right to marry, 47 percent of the public thinks they should. Support is greatest among Asians (71 percent). Only 34 percent of Hispanics and 37 percent of blacks believe same-sex marriage should be legal.

■ American attitudes toward sexuality have been changing as younger, more tolerant generations replace older generations with less tolerance.

Only about one-third of Hispanics support same-sex marriage

(percent of people aged 18 or older who agree with the statement, "Homosexual couples should have the right to marry one another," by race and Hispanic origin, 2010)

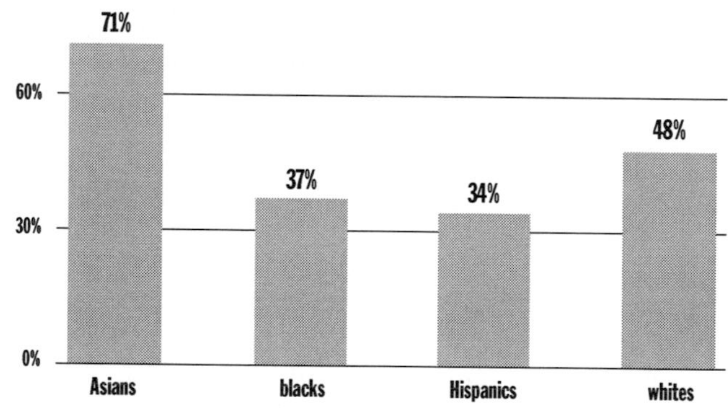

Table 1.26 Premarital Sex, 2010

"If a man and woman have sex relations before marriage, do you think it is always wrong, almost always wrong, wrong only sometimes, or not wrong at all?"

(percent of people aged 18 or older responding by race and Hispanic origin, 2010)

	always wrong	almost always wrong	sometimes wrong	not wrong at all
Total people	**21.3%**	**7.8%**	**17.8%**	**53.1%**
Asian	5.5	6.8	21.2	66.4
Black	28.2	11.1	11.3	49.4
Hispanic	23.9	4.6	23.1	48.5
White	20.9	7.3	18.3	53.5

Note: Hispanics may be of any race.
Source: Survey Documentation and Analysis, Computer-assisted Survey Methods Program, University of California, Berkeley, General Social Surveys, 1972–2010 Cumulative Data Files, Internet site http://sda.berkeley.edu/cgi-bin32/hsda?harcsda+gss10; calculations by New Strategist

Table 1.27 Homosexual Relations, 2010

"What about sexual relations between two adults of the same sex?"

(percent of people aged 18 or older responding by race and Hispanic origin, 2010)

	always wrong	almost always wrong	sometimes wrong	not wrong at all
Total people	**45.7%**	**3.7%**	**7.9%**	**42.7%**
Asian	20.1	4.8	15.5	59.6
Black	66.6	3.7	4.3	25.5
Hispanic	59.1	4.3	6.3	30.3
White	42.8	3.7	7.8	45.7

Note: Hispanics may be of any race.
Source: Survey Documentation and Analysis, Computer-assisted Survey Methods Program, University of California, Berkeley, General Social Surveys, 1972–2010 Cumulative Data Files, Internet site http://sda.berkeley.edu/cgi-bin32/hsda?harcsda+gss10; calculations by New Strategist

Table 1.28 Gay Marriage, 2010

"Do you agree or disagree? Homosexual couples should have the right to marry one another."

(percent of people aged 18 or older responding by race and Hispanic origin, 2010)

	strongly agree	agree	neither agree nor disagree	disagree	strongly disagree
Total people	**21.1%**	**25.4%**	**12.8%**	**15.6%**	**25.1%**
Asian	21.1	49.6	3.4	16.9	8.9
Black	13.4	23.2	13.9	22.5	26.9
Hispanic	11.4	23.0	26.6	16.6	22.3
White	23.6	24.4	11.4	14.3	26.4

Note: Hispanics may be of any race.
Source: Survey Documentation and Analysis, Computer-assisted Survey Methods Program, University of California, Berkeley, General Social Surveys, 1972–2010 Cumulative Data Files, Internet site http://sda.berkeley.edu/cgi-bin32/hsda?harcsda+gss10; calculations by New Strategist

Television News Is Most Important

Asians, blacks, and Hispanics are particularly dependent on TV for news.

Asians, blacks, and Hispanics are much more likely than whites to get most of their news from television. Sixty percent of Asians, 69 percent of blacks, and 71 percent of Hispanics depend primarily on television for news. In contrast, only 44 percent of whites say television is number one. Asians and whites are much more likely than blacks or Hispanics to get their news from the Internet. Whites are more likely than other groups to get their news from newspapers.

When asked about their political leanings, liberals outnumber conservatives among Asians, blacks, and Hispanics. In particular, Asians are much more liberal (40 percent) than conservative (26 percent). In contrast, whites are more conservative (36 percent) than liberal (27 percent). Political party identification is even more tilted than political leanings. The majority of Asians, blacks, and Hispanics identify themselves as Democrats (near to strong). Blacks are particularly likely to be Democrats (72 percent). In contrast, whites are about evenly split between Democrats (40 percent) and Republicans (39 percent).

■ Democrats could win more elections if Asians and Hispanics were more likely to vote.

Democrats are heavily favored by Asians, blacks, and Hispanics

(percent of people aged 18 or older who identify themselves as near to strong Democrats or Republicans, by race and Hispanic origin, 2010)

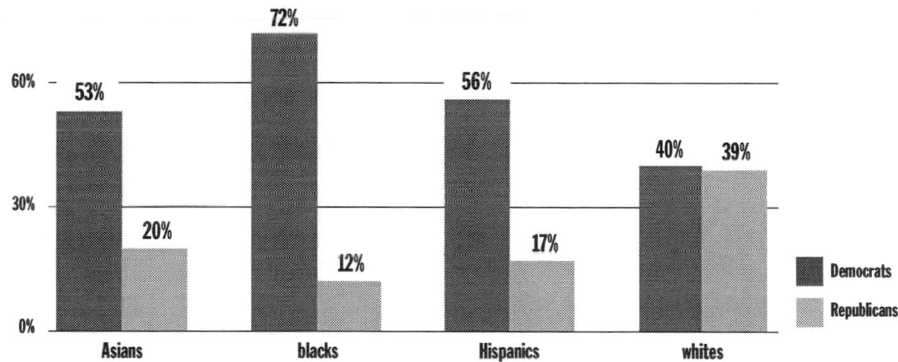

Table 1.29 Main Source of Information about Events in the News, 2010

"We are interested in how people get information about events in the news. Where do you get most of your information about current news events?"

(percent of people aged 18 or older responding by race and Hispanic origin, 2010)

	television	Internet	newspapers	radio	family, friends, or colleagues	books, other printed	government agencies	magazines
Total people	**49.1%**	**21.6%**	**17.7%**	**7.7%**	**2.2%**	**0.8%**	**0.6%**	**0.3%**
Asian	60.0	25.0	10.0	5.0	0.0	0.0	0.0	0.0
Black	68.7	6.0	13.4	0.0	7.1	0.0	4.8	0.0
Hispanic	71.2	14.8	7.0	0.0	7.0	0.0	0.0	0.0
White	44.0	24.2	19.4	9.7	1.4	0.8	0.0	0.4

Note: Hispanics may be of any race.
Source: Survey Documentation and Analysis, Computer-assisted Survey Methods Program, University of California, Berkeley, General Social Surveys, 1972–2010 Cumulative Data Files, Internet site http://sda.berkeley.edu/cgi-bin32/hsda?harcsda+gss10; calculations by New Strategist

Table 1.30 Political Leanings, 2010

"We hear a lot of talk these days about liberals and conservatives. On a seven-point scale from extremely liberal (1) to extremely conservative (7), where would you place yourself?"

(percent of people aged 18 or older responding by race and Hispanic origin, 2010)

	1 extremely liberal	2 liberal	3 slightly liberal	4 moderate	5 slightly conservative	6 conservative	7 extremely conservative
Total people	**3.8%**	**12.9%**	**11.9%**	**37.6%**	**12.8%**	**16.6%**	**4.4%**
Asian	1.4	22.5	16.5	33.9	14.8	5.9	5.0
Black	7.1	16.7	10.3	38.4	8.3	13.6	5.6
Hispanic	2.8	10.2	18.4	44.4	11.5	9.3	3.3
White	3.2	11.6	11.8	37.3	13.7	18.3	4.0

Note: Hispanics may be of any race.
Source: Survey Documentation and Analysis, Computer-assisted Survey Methods Program, University of California, Berkeley, General Social Surveys, 1972–2010 Cumulative Data Files, Internet site http://sda.berkeley.edu/cgi-bin32/hsda?harcsda+gss10; calculations by New Strategist

Table 1.31 Political Party Affiliation, 2010

"Generally speaking, do you usually think of yourself as a Republican, Democrat, independent, or what?"

(percent of people aged 18 or older responding by race and Hispanic origin, 2010)

	strong Democrat	not strong Democrat	independent, near Democrat	independent	independent, near Republican	not strong Republican	strong Republican	other party
Total people	**16.5%**	**15.7%**	**13.5%**	**18.8%**	**10.0%**	**13.4%**	**9.6%**	**2.6%**
Asian	16.3	19.3	17.0	21.9	6.6	10.3	3.2	5.3
Black	40.0	19.1	13.3	14.0	4.2	7.0	1.1	1.3
Hispanic	13.0	22.7	19.9	26.0	6.7	8.0	2.0	1.8
White	12.2	14.9	12.5	18.6	11.8	15.1	12.2	2.7

Note: Hispanics may be of any race.
Source: Survey Documentation and Analysis, Computer-assisted Survey Methods Program, University of California, Berkeley, General Social Surveys, 1972–2010 Cumulative Data Files, Internet site http://sda.berkeley.edu/cgi-bin32/hsda?harcsda+gss10; calculations by New Strategist

Most Support Right to Die, Gun Permits

Blacks are against capital punishment, while others support it.

Americans have long been in support of the death penalty for convicted murderers. In 2010, 68 percent of the public was in favor of the death penalty. Blacks are the only demographic segment in which the majority (52 percent) opposes the death penalty. Sixty-five percent of Asians, 53 percent of Hispanics, and 73 percent of whites favor the death penalty for people convicted of murder.

Most Americans favor requiring a permit for gun ownership. In 2010, fully 74 percent favored requiring a permit before buying a gun. By race and Hispanic origin, support ranges from a low of 71 percent among whites to a high of 94 percent among Asians.

Among racial and ethnic groups, Hispanics are least likely to support abortion. Only 26 percent think abortion should be allowed for any reason. Nevertheless, the great majority of Hispanics support abortion if a woman's health is endangered, if she has been raped, or if there is a serious defect in the baby. Asians are most supportive of abortion rights, with 60 percent saying women should be able to obtain a legal abortion for any reason.

More than two-thirds of Americans support the right of the terminally ill to die with a doctor's assistance. Support ranges from a low of 54 percent among blacks to a high of 92 percent among Asians.

■ Although a growing number of states are outlawing the death penalty, the public continues to overwhelmingly support it.

Asians support abortion rights for any reason

(percent of people aged 18 or older who responded "yes" to the question, "Should a woman be able to obtain a legal abortion for any reason?" by race and Hispanic origin, 2010)

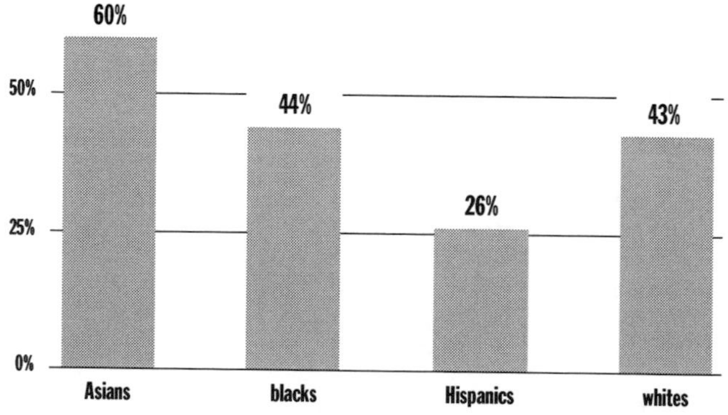

Table 1.32 Favor or Oppose Death Penalty for Murder, 2010

"Do you favor or oppose the death penalty for persons convicted of murder?"

(percent of people aged 18 or older responding by race and Hispanic origin, 2010)

	favor	oppose
Total people	**67.8%**	**32.2%**
Asian	64.5	35.5
Black	47.8	52.2
Hispanic	53.2	46.8
White	72.9	27.1

Note: Hispanics may be of any race.
Source: Survey Documentation and Analysis, Computer-assisted Survey Methods Program, University of California, Berkeley, General Social Surveys, 1972–2010 Cumulative Data Files, Internet site http://sda.berkeley.edu/cgi-bin32/hsda?harcsda+gss10; calculations by New Strategist

Table 1.33 Favor or Oppose Gun Permits, 2010

"Would you favor or oppose a law which would require a person to obtain a police permit before he or she could buy a gun?"

(percent of people aged 18 or older responding by race and Hispanic origin, 2010)

	favor	oppose
Total people	**74.3%**	**25.7%**
Asian	93.8	6.2
Black	83.5	16.5
Hispanic	83.1	16.9
White	71.3	28.7

Note: Hispanics may be of any race.
Source: Survey Documentation and Analysis, Computer-assisted Survey Methods Program, University of California, Berkeley, General Social Surveys, 1972–2010 Cumulative Data Files, Internet site http://sda.berkeley.edu/cgi-bin32/hsda?harcsda+gss10; calculations by New Strategist

Table 1.34 Support for Legal Abortion by Reason, 2010

"Please tell me whether or not you think it should be possible for a pregnant woman to obtain a legal abortion if the woman wants it."

(percent of people aged 18 or older responding yes by race and Hispanic origin, 2010)

	her health is seriously endangered	pregnancy is the result of rape	there is a serious defect in the baby	she cannot afford more children	she is married, but does not want more childen	she is single and does not want to marry the man	for any reason
Total people	**86.4%**	**79.1%**	**73.9%**	**44.9%**	**47.7%**	**41.9%**	**42.9%**
Asian	92.5	85.0	81.2	67.3	73.7	58.7	60.0
Black	83.9	79.9	69.8	48.6	50.7	41.8	43.9
Hispanic	75.4	62.8	63.7	31.1	37.3	24.3	25.8
White	87.2	79.7	75.1	44.2	46.7	42.6	43.3

Note: Hispanics may be of any race.
Source: Survey Documentation and Analysis, Computer-assisted Survey Methods Program, University of California, Berkeley, General Social Surveys, 1972–2010 Cumulative Data Files, Internet site http://sda.berkeley.edu/cgi-bin32/hsda?harcsda+gss10; calculations by New Strategist

Table 1.35 Allow Patients with Incurable Disease to Die, 2010

"When a person has a disease that cannot be cured, do you think doctors should be allowed by law to end the patient's life by some painless means if the patient and his family request it?"

(percent of people aged 18 or older responding by race and Hispanic origin, 2010)

	yes	no
Total people	**68.4%**	**31.6%**
Asian	92.4	7.6
Black	54.3	45.7
Hispanic	61.2	38.8
White	71.3	28.7

Note: Hispanics may be of any race.
Source: Survey Documentation and Analysis, Computer-assisted Survey Methods Program, University of California, Berkeley, General Social Surveys, 1972–2010 Cumulative Data Files, Internet site http://sda.berkeley.edu/cgi-bin32/hsda?harcsda+gss10; calculations by New Strategist

CHAPTER

2

Education

■ Asians are much more likely to have a bachelor's degree than the American population as a whole. In 2010, 52 percent of Asians aged 25 or older were college graduates.

■ Many Asians are in school through their twenties. Among Asians aged 22 to 24, the 53 percent majority are in school. The figure is a substantial 19 percent among 25-to-29-year-olds.

■ The number of Asians enrolled in the nation's colleges has climbed from less than 200,000 in 1976 to more than 1 million.

■ Among Asians enrolled in college, 48 percent attend a four-year school and 31 percent are in graduate school, where they account for 10 percent of students.

■ Asians earned 7 percent of bachelor's degrees awarded in 2008–09, but their share of degrees awarded in biology is a much higher 17 percent.

■ Asians account for more than one in five degrees awarded in dentistry, medicine, optometry, and pharmacy.

Asians Are Far Better Educated than the Average American

Most have a college degree.

Asians are much more likely to be college graduates than the American population as a whole. In 2010, the 52 percent majority of Asians aged 25 or older had a bachelor's degree. This compares with a much smaller 30 percent of the total population. Twenty percent of Asians have an advanced degree. Asians account for 12 percent of the 3 million people aged 25 or older in the United States with a doctoral degree.

The educational attainment of Asians varies by age. Among Asians aged 25 to 44, fully 59 to 60 percent have a bachelor's degree. Among those aged 65 or older the proportion is 35 percent. Even among the oldest Asians, however, the share with a college degree surpasses the figure for the American population as a whole.

■ Although Asian men are somewhat more educated than Asian women overall, in the 25-to-34 age group Asian women are more likely than Asian men to have a bachelor's degree.

Asian educational attainment is well above average

(percent of total people and Asians aged 25 or older by educational attainment, 2010)

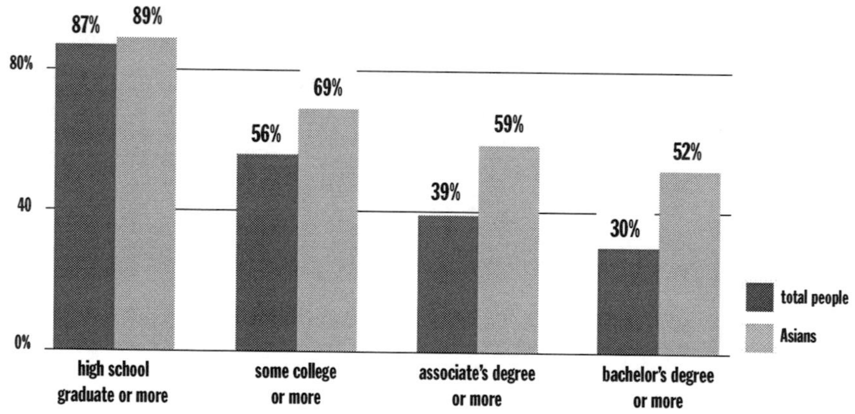

Table 2.1 Educational Attainment of Total People and Asians, 2010

(number and percent distribution of total people and Asians aged 25 or older by educational attainment, Asian share of total, and Asian percent distribution indexed to total, 2010; numbers in thousands)

		Asians	
	total	number	share of total
Total people	**199,928**	**9,882**	**4.9%**
Not a high school graduate	25,711	1,077	4.2
High school graduate only	62,456	2,015	3.2
Some college, no degree	33,662	951	2.8
Associate's degree	18,259	719	3.9
Bachelor's degree	38,784	3,163	8.2
Master's degree	15,203	1,321	8.7
Professional degree	3,074	295	9.6
Doctoral degree	2,779	342	12.3
High school graduate or more	174,217	8,806	5.1
Some college or more	111,761	6,791	6.1
Associate's degree or more	78,099	5,840	7.5
Bachelor's degree or more	59,840	5,121	8.6
	total	total	index, Asian to total
PERCENT DISTRIBUTION			
Total people	**100.0%**	**100.0%**	–
Not a high school graduate	12.9	10.9	85
High school graduate only	31.2	20.4	65
Some college, no degree	16.8	9.6	57
Associate's degree	9.1	7.3	80
Bachelor's degree	19.4	32.0	165
Master's degree	7.6	13.4	176
Professional degree	1.5	3.0	194
Doctoral degree	1.4	3.5	249
High school graduate or more	87.1	89.1	102
Some college or more	55.9	68.7	123
Associate's degree or more	39.1	59.1	151
Bachelor's degree or more	29.9	51.8	173

Note: Asians are those who identify themselves as being of the race alone or as being of the race in combination with other races. The index is calculated by dividing the Asian percentage by the total percentage and multiplying by 100. "–" means not applicable.
Source: Bureau of the Census, 2010 Current Population Survey Annual Social and Economic Supplement, Detailed Tables, Internet site http://www.census.gov/hhes/www/cpstables/032010/perinc/toc.htm; calculations by New Strategist

Table 2.2 Educational Attainment of Asians by Age, 2010

(number and percent distribution of Asians aged 25 or older by educational attainment and age, 2010; numbers in thousands)

	total	25 to 34	35 to 44	45 to 54	55 to 64	65 or older
Total Asians	**9,882**	**2,514**	**2,470**	**2,032**	**1,487**	**1,378**
Not a high school graduate	1,077	135	193	188	199	362
High school graduate only	2,015	367	424	496	361	367
Some college, no degree	951	319	210	193	127	101
Associate's degree	719	205	163	156	125	70
Bachelor's degree	3,163	915	835	625	461	327
Master's degree	1,321	422	449	230	134	85
Professional degree	295	73	83	69	35	34
Doctoral degree	342	76	112	76	45	34
High school graduate or more	8,806	2,377	2,276	1,845	1,288	1,018
Some college or more	6,791	2,010	1,852	1,349	927	651
Associate's degree or more	5,840	1,691	1,642	1,156	800	550
Bachelor's degree or more	5,121	1,486	1,479	1,000	675	480
PERCENT DISTRIBUTION						
Total Asians	**100.0%**	**100.0%**	**100.0%**	**100.0%**	**100.0%**	**100.0%**
Not a high school graduate	10.9	5.4	7.8	9.3	13.4	26.3
High school graduate only	20.4	14.6	17.2	24.4	24.3	26.6
Some college, no degree	9.6	12.7	8.5	9.5	8.5	7.3
Associate's degree	7.3	8.2	6.6	7.7	8.4	5.1
Bachelor's degree	32.0	36.4	33.8	30.8	31.0	23.7
Master's degree	13.4	16.8	18.2	11.3	9.0	6.2
Professional degree	3.0	2.9	3.4	3.4	2.4	2.5
Doctoral degree	3.5	3.0	4.5	3.7	3.0	2.5
High school graduate or more	89.1	94.6	92.1	90.8	86.6	73.9
Some college or more	68.7	80.0	75.0	66.4	62.3	47.2
Associate's degree or more	59.1	67.3	66.5	56.9	53.8	39.9
Bachelor's degree or more	51.8	59.1	59.9	49.2	45.4	34.8

Note: Asians are those who identify themselves as being of the race alone or as being of the race in combination with other races.

Source: Bureau of the Census, 2010 Current Population Survey Annual Social and Economic Supplement, Detailed Tables, Internet site http://www.census.gov/hhes/www/cpstables/032010/perinc/toc.htm; calculations by New Strategist

Table 2.3 Educational Attainment of Asian Men by Age, 2010

(number and percent distribution of Asian men aged 25 or older by educational attainment and age, 2010; numbers in thousands)

	total	25 to 34	35 to 44	45 to 54	55 to 64	65 or older
Total Asian men	**4,605**	**1,215**	**1,169**	**965**	**680**	**576**
Not a high school graduate	404	67	79	83	67	107
High school graduate only	886	189	191	225	149	132
Some college, no degree	476	175	96	98	61	46
Associate's degree	318	107	47	78	62	24
Bachelor's degree	1,437	414	396	261	213	153
Master's degree	683	187	243	123	71	59
Professional degree	165	34	38	40	27	27
Doctoral degree	235	43	79	56	29	28
High school graduate or more	4,200	1,149	1,090	881	612	469
Some college or more	3,314	960	899	656	463	337
Associate's degree or more	2,838	785	803	558	402	291
Bachelor's degree or more	2,520	678	756	480	340	267
PERCENT DISTRIBUTION						
Total Asian men	**100.0%**	**100.0%**	**100.0%**	**100.0%**	**100.0%**	**100.0%**
Not a high school graduate	8.8	5.5	6.8	8.6	9.9	18.6
High school graduate only	19.2	15.6	16.3	23.3	21.9	22.9
Some college, no degree	10.3	14.4	8.2	10.2	9.0	8.0
Associate's degree	6.9	8.8	4.0	8.1	9.1	4.2
Bachelor's degree	31.2	34.1	33.9	27.0	31.3	26.6
Master's degree	14.8	15.4	20.8	12.7	10.4	10.2
Professional degree	3.6	2.8	3.3	4.1	4.0	4.7
Doctoral degree	5.1	3.5	6.8	5.8	4.3	4.9
High school graduate or more	91.2	94.6	93.2	91.3	90.0	81.4
Some college or more	72.0	79.0	76.9	68.0	68.1	58.5
Associate's degree or more	61.6	64.6	68.7	57.8	59.1	50.5
Bachelor's degree or more	54.7	55.8	64.7	49.7	50.0	46.4

Note: Asians are those who identify themselves as being of the race alone or as being of the race in combination with other races.
Source: Bureau of the Census, 2010 Current Population Survey Annual Social and Economic Supplement, Detailed Tables, Internet site http://www.census.gov/hhes/www/cpstables/032010/perinc/toc.htm; calculations by New Strategist

Table 2.4 Educational Attainment of Asian Women by Age, 2010

(number and percent distribution of Asian women aged 25 or older by educational attainment and age, 2010; numbers in thousands)

	total	25 to 34	35 to 44	45 to 54	55 to 64	65 or older
Total Asian women	**5,277**	**1,299**	**1,301**	**1,068**	**807**	**802**
Not a high school graduate	672	69	114	103	132	254
High school graduate only	1,129	178	233	271	212	235
Some college, no degree	475	144	115	95	66	55
Associate's degree	401	98	117	77	63	46
Bachelor's degree	1,726	501	440	364	247	174
Master's degree	638	236	206	107	63	27
Professional degree	129	39	45	30	9	7
Doctoral degree	107	33	32	20	16	5
High school graduate or more	4,605	1,229	1,188	964	676	549
Some college or more	3,476	1,051	955	693	464	314
Associate's degree or more	3,001	907	840	598	398	259
Bachelor's degree or more	2,600	809	723	521	335	213
PERCENT DISTRIBUTION						
Total Asian women	**100.0%**	**100.0%**	**100.0%**	**100.0%**	**100.0%**	**100.0%**
Not a high school graduate	12.7	5.3	8.8	9.6	16.4	31.7
High school graduate only	21.4	13.7	17.9	25.4	26.3	29.3
Some college, no degree	9.0	11.1	8.8	8.9	8.2	6.9
Associate's degree	7.6	7.5	9.0	7.2	7.8	5.7
Bachelor's degree	32.7	38.6	33.8	34.1	30.6	21.7
Master's degree	12.1	18.2	15.8	10.0	7.8	3.4
Professional degree	2.4	3.0	3.5	2.8	1.1	0.9
Doctoral degree	2.0	2.5	2.5	1.9	2.0	0.6
High school graduate or more	87.3	94.6	91.3	90.3	83.8	68.5
Some college or more	65.9	80.9	73.4	64.9	57.5	39.2
Associate's degree or more	56.9	69.8	64.6	56.0	49.3	32.3
Bachelor's degree or more	49.3	62.3	55.6	48.8	41.5	26.6

Note: Asians are those who identify themselves as being of the race alone or as being of the race in combination with other races.
Source: Bureau of the Census, 2010 Current Population Survey Annual Social and Economic Supplement, Detailed Tables, Internet site http://www.census.gov/hhes/www/cpstables/032010/perinc/toc.htm; calculations by New Strategist

Many Asians Are in School Well into Adulthood

Asians account for a disproportionate share of older students.

Asians are much more likely than black, Hispanic, or non-Hispanic whites to go to college. Consequently a large proportion of Asian men and women are in school well into their twenties. Among Asians aged 18 to 19, fully 90 percent are in school. The proportion stands at 74 percent among those aged 20 to 21. More than half (53 percent) of Asians aged 22 to 24 are still in school, as are nearly one-fifth of those aged 25 to 29.

The Asian share of public elementary and secondary students has climbed from 3.9 percent in 1998 to 5.0 percent in 2008. Asians are the majority of public elementary and secondary students in Hawaii. They account for 12 percent of students in California.

■ The National Center for Education Statistics projects that the Asian share of the nation's public high school graduates will rise from 5.5 percent in 2009–10 to 7.3 percent in 2019–20.

Many Asians remain in school through their twenties

(percent of Asians aged 18 to 34 enrolled in school, by age, 2009)

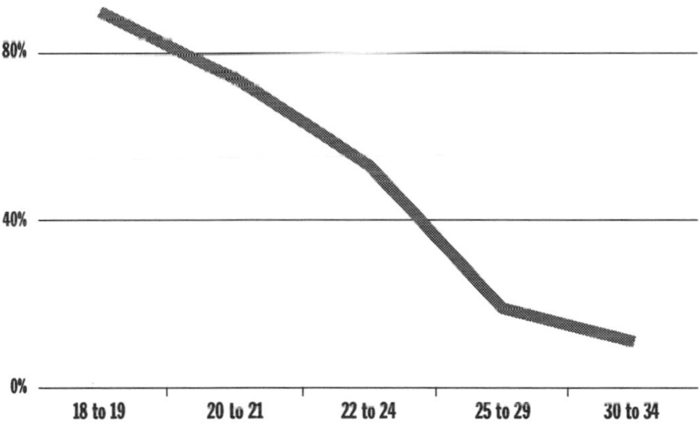

Table 2.5 Total and Asian School Enrollment by Age, 2009

(total number of people aged 3 or older enrolled in school, number of Asians enrolled, and Asian share of total, by age, October 2009; numbers in thousands)

		Asian	
	total	number	share of total
Total aged 3 or older	**77,288**	**4,117**	**5.3%**
Aged 3 to 4	4,475	287	6.4
Aged 5 to 6	7,783	450	5.8
Aged 7 to 9	11,921	611	5.1
Aged 10 to 13	15,688	704	4.5
Aged 14 to 15	7,789	313	4.0
Aged 16 to 17	7,939	330	4.2
Aged 18 to 19	5,935	346	5.8
Aged 20 to 21	4,163	253	6.1
Aged 22 to 24	3,818	330	8.6
Aged 25 to 29	2,819	207	7.3
Aged 30 to 34	1,576	131	8.3
Aged 35 to 44	1,927	120	6.2
Aged 45 to 54	1,064	24	2.3
Aged 55 or older	393	12	3.1

Note: Asians are those who identify themselves as being of the race alone or as being of the race in combination with other races.

Source: Bureau of the Census, School Enrollment—Social and Economic Characteristics of Students: October 2009, Internet site http://www.census.gov/population/www/socdemo/school/cps2009.html

Table 2.6 School Enrollment of Asians by Age and Sex, 2009

(number and percent of Asians aged 3 or older enrolled in school, by age and sex, October 2009; numbers in thousands)

	total		female		male	
	number	percent	number	percent	number	percent
Total Asians enrolled	**4,117**	**29.0%**	**2,014**	**27.7%**	**2,103**	**30.5%**
Aged 3 to 4	287	55.3	127	55.8	160	54.9
Aged 5 to 6	450	95.6	223	95.9	227	95.3
Aged 7 to 9	611	97.2	292	97.8	319	96.6
Aged 10 to 13	704	95.8	367	96.3	337	95.3
Aged 14 to 15	313	96.8	120	95.2	193	97.8
Aged 16 to 17	330	97.0	156	98.1	174	96.1
Aged 18 to 19	346	90.1	174	88.8	172	91.4
Aged 20 to 21	253	73.6	131	73.0	122	74.3
Aged 22 to 24	330	53.5	165	55.6	165	51.5
Aged 25 to 29	207	18.7	109	19.5	98	17.9
Aged 30 to 34	131	10.8	74	11.9	57	9.7
Aged 35 to 44	120	4.7	58	4.3	62	5.1
Aged 45 to 54	24	1.2	13	1.2	11	1.1
Aged 55 or older	12	0.4	5	0.3	7	0.5

Note: Asians are those who identify themselves as being of the race alone or as being of the race in combination with other races.
Source: Bureau of the Census, School Enrollment—Social and Economic Characteristics of Students: October 2009, Internet site http://www.census.gov/population/www/socdemo/school/cps2009.html

Table 2.7 Asian Enrollment in the Nation's Public Elementary and Secondary Schools by State, 1998 and 2008

(percentage of students enrolled in public elementary and secondary schools who are Asian, by state, 1998 and 2008; percentage point change, 1998–2008)

	2008	1998	percentage point change
Total enrolled	**5.0%**	**3.9%**	**1.0**
Alabama	1.2	0.7	0.5
Alaska	7.2	5.1	2.2
Arizona	3.0	1.9	1.1
Arkansas	1.6	0.8	0.8
California	11.7	11.1	0.6
Colorado	3.6	2.7	0.9
Connecticut	4.2	2.6	1.6
Delaware	3.4	2.0	1.4
Dist. of Columbia	1.6	1.6	0.0
Florida	2.6	1.8	0.7
Georgia	3.3	2.0	1.3
Hawaii	72.9	71.7	1.2
Idaho	1.7	1.2	0.5
Illinois	4.2	3.2	1.0
Indiana	1.5	0.9	0.6
Iowa	2.2	1.7	0.5
Kansas	2.8	2.1	0.7
Kentucky	1.1	0.4	0.7
Louisiana	1.4	1.3	0.1
Maine	1.6	0.9	0.6
Maryland	5.9	4.0	1.8
Massachusetts	5.2	4.2	1.1
Michigan	2.7	1.7	1.0
Minnesota	6.2	4.7	1.5
Mississippi	0.9	0.6	0.3
Missouri	1.9	1.1	0.8
Montana	1.2	0.8	0.3
Nebraska	2.1	1.4	0.7
Nevada	8.1	5.1	3.0
New Hampshire	2.4	1.2	1.2
New Jersey	8.5	5.8	2.6
New Mexico	1.4	1.0	0.4
New York	7.7	5.6	2.1
North Carolina	2.5	1.7	0.8
North Dakota	1.1	0.7	0.3
Ohio	1.7	1.1	0.7
Oklahoma	2.1	1.4	0.8
Oregon	5.0	3.7	1.3
Pennsylvania	2.9	1.9	1.1

	2008	1998	percentage point change
Rhode Island	3.2%	3.3%	–0.1
South Carolina	1.6	0.9	0.7
South Dakota	1.3	0.9	0.4
Tennessee	1.6	1.0	0.7
Texas	3.6	2.5	1.0
Utah	3.3	2.5	0.7
Vermont	1.5	1.0	0.4
Virginia	5.9	3.7	2.1
Washington	8.9	7.1	1.8
West Virginia	0.7	0.3	0.4
Wisconsin	3.7	3.1	0.6
Wyoming	1.1	0.8	0.3

Source: National Center for Education Statistics, Digest of Education Statistics: 2010, Table 43, Internet site http://nces .ed.gov/programs/digest/d10/

Table 2.8 Projections of Total and Asian Public High School Graduates, 2009–10 to 2019–20

(projected number of total people and Asians graduating from public high schools, 2009–10 to 2019–20; percent change 2009–10 to 2019–20; numbers in thousands)

	total graduates	Asian graduates	
		number	share of total
2009–10	2,991	165	5.5%
2010–11	2,937	168	5.7
2011–12	2,906	173	5.9
2012–13	2,891	178	6.2
2013–14	2,868	184	6.4
2014–15	2,872	189	6.6
2015–16	2,906	192	6.6
2016–17	2,933	197	6.7
2017–18	2,989	213	7.1
2018–19	2,985	215	7.2
2019–20	2,953	215	7.3
Percent change			
2009–10 to 2019–20	–1.3%	30.7%	–

Note: "–" means not applicable.
Source: National Center for Education Statistics, Projections of Education Statistics to 2019, Internet site http://nces.ed.gov/programs/projections/projections2019/tables.asp; calculations by New Strategist

More than One Million College Students Are Asian

Asians account for 6 percent of college students.

The number of Asians enrolled in the nation's colleges has climbed sharply over the past few decades. In 1976, fewer than 200,000 college students were Asian. The figure surpassed 1 million in 2001 and has increased every year since then.

Of the 1.2 million Asians enrolled in college in 2009, nearly half (48 percent) attend a four-year school, 21 percent are in a two-year school, and 31 percent are in graduate school. Asians account for 10 percent of graduate students.

■ The number of Asian college students will continue to grow along with the Asian population.

Asian students are more likely to be in graduate school than a two-year college

(number of Asians enrolled in college, by type of school, 2009)

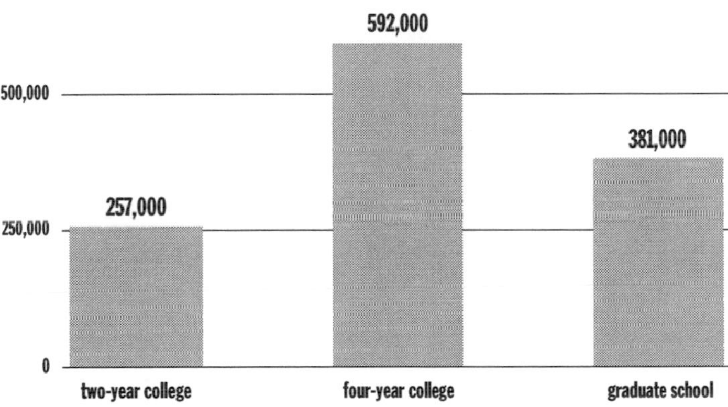

Table 2.9 Total and Asian College Enrollment, 1976 to 2009

(number of total people and Asians aged 15 or older enrolled in institutions of higher education, and Asian share of total, selected years 1976 to 2009; numbers in thousands)

		Asian	
	total enrolled	number	share of total
2009	20,428	1,338	6.5%
2008	19,103	1,303	6.8
2007	18,248	1,218	6.7
2006	17,759	1,165	6.6
2005	17,488	1,134	6.5
2004	17,272	1,109	6.4
2003	16,901	1,076	6.4
2002	16,612	1,074	6.5
2001	15,928	1,019	6.4
2000	15,312	978	6.4
1999	14,791	910	6.2
1998	14,507	901	6.2
1997	14,502	859	5.9
1996	14,368	828	5.8
1995	14,262	797	5.6
1990	13,819	572	4.1
1980	12,087	286	2.4
1976	10,986	198	1.8

Note: Enrollment figures are based on a survey of institutions of higher education. They differ from enrollment figures in other tables, which are based on household surveys.

Source: National Center for Education Statistics, Digest of Education Statistics: 2010, Table 236, Internet site http://nces.ed.gov/programs/digest/d10/

Table 2.10 Total and Asian College Enrollment by Age, 2009

(total number of people aged 15 or older enrolled in college, number of Asians enrolled, and Asian share of total, by age, October 2009; numbers in thousands)

		Asian	
	total	number	share of total
Total enrolled in college	**19,765**	**1,231**	**6.2%**
Under age 20	4,495	254	5.7
Aged 20 to 21	4,034	216	5.4
Aged 22 to 24	3,749	308	8.2
Aged 25 to 29	2,769	197	7.1
Aged 30 to 34	1,524	114	7.5
Aged 35 to 44	1,848	110	6.0
Aged 45 to 54	998	22	2.2
Aged 55 or older	347	9	2.6

Note: Asians are those who identify themselves as being of the race alone.
Source: Bureau of the Census, School Enrollment—Social and Economic Characteristics of Students: October 2009, Internet site http://www.census.gov/population/www/socdemo/school/cps2009.html; calculations by New Strategist

Table 2.11 Asian Share of College Enrollment by Attendance Status and Type of School, 2009

(total number of people aged 15 or older enrolled in college, number of Asians enrolled, and Asian share of total, by attendance status and type of school, October 2009; numbers in thousands)

		Asians	
	total	number	share of total
Total enrolled in college	**19,765**	**1,231**	**6.2%**
Two-year college	5,551	257	4.6
Four-year college	10,461	592	5.7
Graduate school	3,753	381	10.2
Enrolled full-time	**14,364**	**972**	**6.8**
Two-year college	3,633	175	4.8
Four-year college	8,685	516	5.9
Graduate school	2,046	281	13.7
Enrolled part-time	**5,401**	**259**	**4.8**
Two-year college	1,918	82	4.3
Four-year college	1,776	76	4.3
Graduate school	1,707	100	5.9

Note: Asians are those who identify themselves as being of the race alone.
Source: Bureau of the Census, School Enrollment—Social and Economic Characteristics of Students: October 2009, Internet site http://www.census.gov/population/www/socdemo/school/cps2009.html; calculations by New Strategist

Table 2.12 College Enrollment of Asians by Type of School and Attendance Status, 2009

(number and percent distribution of Asians aged 15 or older enrolled in college by type of school and attendance status, October 2009; numbers in thousands)

	total	full-time	part-time
Total Asians enrolled	**1,231**	**972**	**259**
Two-year college	257	175	82
Four-year college	592	516	76
Graduate school	381	281	100
PERCENT DISTRIBUTION BY ATTENDANCE STATUS			
Total Asians enrolled	**100.0%**	**79.0%**	**21.0%**
Two-year college	100.0	68.1	31.9
Four-year college	100.0	87.2	12.8
Graduate school	100.0	73.8	26.2
PERCENT DISTRIBUTION BY TYPE OF SCHOOL			
Total Asians enrolled	**100.0%**	**100.0%**	**100.0%**
Two-year college	20.9	18.0	31.7
Four-year college	48.1	53.1	29.3
Graduate school	31.0	28.9	38.6

Note: Asians are those who identify themselves as being of the race alone.
Source: Bureau of the Census, School Enrollment—Social and Economic Characteristics of Students: October 2009, Internet site http://www.census.gov/population/www/socdemo/school/cps2009.html; calculations by New Strategist

Many Asian Students Earn Math and Science Degrees

Asians account for more than one in five newly minted physicians.

Asians earned 7 percent of bachelor's degrees granted in 2008–09, according to the National Center for Education Statistics. The Asian share of bachelor's degrees awarded in biology is much higher, however. In 2008–09, Asians earned 17 percent of bachelor's degrees awarded in biological and biomedical sciences. They also earned 13 percent of engineering degrees.

At the master's degree level, Asians continue to be disproportionately represented in biology (12 percent) and engineering (12 percent). At the first-professional degree level, Asians accounted for one-fifth or more of the degrees awarded in dentistry, medicine, and optometry, and pharmacy.

■ The strong math and science background of many Asian students allows them to pursue lucrative careers, which boosts Asian household incomes.

Asians account for a disproportionate share of students who earn degrees in medical fields

(Asian share of first-professional degrees awarded, 2008–09)

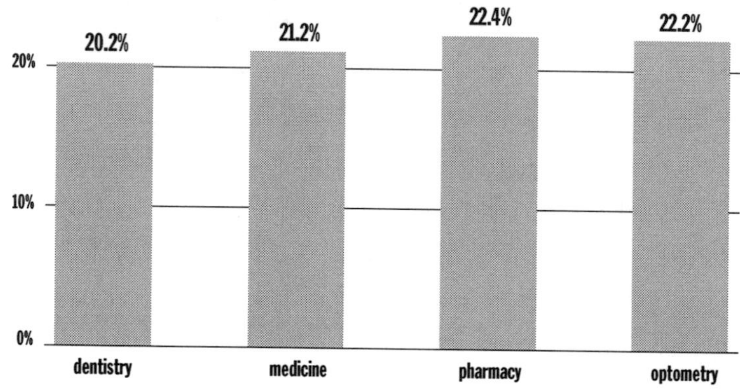

Table 2.13 Associate's Degrees Earned by Total People and Asians by Field of Study, 2008–09

(total number of associate's degrees conferred and number and percent earned by Asians, by field of study, 2008–09)

	total	earned by Asians number	earned by Asians share of total
Total associate's degrees	**787,325**	**40,914**	**5.2%**
Agriculture and natural resources	5,724	54	0.9
Architecture and related services	596	39	6.5
Area, ethnic, cultural, and gender studies	173	10	5.8
Biological and biomedical sciences	2,364	359	15.2
Business	127,848	7,270	5.7
Communications, journalism, and related programs	2,722	85	3.1
Communications technologies	4,803	186	3.9
Computer and information sciences	30,006	1,496	5.0
Construction trades	4,252	97	2.3
Education	14,123	267	1.9
Engineering	2,181	183	8.4
Engineering technologies	30,434	1,213	4.0
English language and literature/letters	1,525	167	11.0
Family and consumer sciences	9,020	336	3.7
Foreign languages, literatures, and linguistics	1,627	41	2.5
Health professions and related clinical sciences	165,163	8,662	5.2
Legal professions and studies	9,062	208	2.3
Liberal arts and sciences, general studies, and humanities	263,853	13,914	5.3
Library science	116	6	5.2
Mathematics and statistics	930	138	14.8
Mechanics and repair technologies	16,066	670	4.2
Military technologies	721	36	5.0
Multi/interdisciplinary studies	15,459	1,891	12.2
Parks, recreation, leisure, and fitness studies	1,587	57	3.6
Philosophy and religious studies	191	10	5.2
Physical sciences and science technologies	3,617	391	10.8
Precision production	2,126	58	2.7
Psychology	3,949	180	4.6
Public administration and social service professions	4,178	87	2.1
Security and protective services	33,033	778	2.4
Social sciences and history	9,142	801	8.8
Theology and religious vocations	675	11	1.6
Transportation and materials moving	1,430	60	4.2
Visual and performing arts	18,629	1,153	6.2

Source: National Center for Education Statistics, Digest of Education Statistics 2010, Table 294, Internet site http://nces.ed.gov/programs/digest/d10/; calculations by New Strategist

Table 2.14 Bachelor's Degrees Earned by Total People and Asians by Field of Study, 2008–09

(total number of bachelor's degrees conferred and number and percent earned by Asians, by field of study, 2008–09)

		earned by Asians	
	total	number	share of total
Total bachelor's degrees	**1,601,368**	**112,510**	**7.0%**
Agriculture and natural resources	24,988	1,075	4.3
Architecture and related services	10,119	922	9.1
Area, ethnic, cultural, and gender studies	8,772	1,087	12.4
Biological and biomedical sciences	80,756	13,666	16.9
Business	347,985	25,493	7.3
Communications, journalism, and related programs	78,009	3,565	4.6
Communications technologies	5,100	308	6.0
Computer and information sciences	37,994	3,216	8.5
Construction trades	168	8	4.8
Education	101,708	1,974	1.9
Engineering	69,133	8,832	12.8
Engineering technologies	15,112	611	4.0
English language and literature/letters	55,462	2,805	5.1
Family and consumer sciences	21,905	1,108	5.1
Foreign languages, literatures, and linguistics	21,158	1,246	5.9
Health professions and related clinical sciences	120,488	8,237	6.8
Legal professions and studies	3,822	255	6.7
Liberal arts and sciences, general studies, and humanities	47,096	1,653	3.5
Library science	78	0	0.0
Mathematics and statistics	15,496	1,598	10.3
Mechanics and repair technologies	223	9	4.0
Military technologies	55	2	3.6
Multi/interdisciplinary studies	37,444	2,780	7.4
Parks, recreation, leisure, and fitness studies	31,667	1,210	3.8
Philosophy and religious studies	12,444	749	6.0
Physical sciences and science technologies	22,466	2,330	10.4
Precision production	29	2	6.9
Psychology	94,271	6,416	6.8
Public administration and social service professions	23,851	883	3.7
Security and protective services	41,800	1,268	3.0
Social sciences and history	168,500	13,202	7.8
Theology and religious vocations	8,940	219	2.4
Transportation and materials moving	5,189	185	3.6
Visual and performing arts	89,140	5,596	6.3

Source: National Center for Education Statistics, Digest of Education Statistics 2010, Table 297, Internet site http://nces.ed.gov/programs/digest/d10/; calculations by New Strategist

Table 2.15 Master's Degrees Earned by Total People and Asians by Field of Study, 2008–09

(total number of master's degrees conferred and number and percent earned by Asians, by field of study, 2008–09)

		earned by Asians	
	total	number	share of total
Total master's degrees	**656,784**	**39,944**	**6.1%**
Agriculture and natural resources	4,877	160	3.3
Architecture and related services	6,587	437	6.6
Area, ethnic, cultural, and gender studies	1,779	134	7.5
Biological and biomedical sciences	9,898	1,233	12.5
Business	168,375	14,327	8.5
Communications, journalism, and related programs	7,092	351	4.9
Communications technologies	475	32	6.7
Computer and information sciences	17,907	1,781	9.9
Education	178,564	4,919	2.8
Engineering	34,750	4,239	12.2
Engineering technologies	3,455	259	7.5
English language and literature/letters	9,261	363	3.9
Family and consumer sciences	2,453	93	3.8
Foreign languages, literatures, and linguistics	3,592	152	4.2
Health professions and related clinical sciences	62,620	4,717	7.5
Legal professions and studies	5,150	288	5.6
Liberal arts and sciences, general studies, and humanities	3,728	216	5.8
Library science	7,091	275	3.9
Mathematics and statistics	5,211	437	8.4
Military technologies	3	0	0.0
Multi/interdisciplinary studies	5,344	264	4.9
Parks, recreation, leisure, and fitness studies	4,822	136	2.8
Philosophy and religious studies	1,859	83	4.5
Physical sciences and science technologies	5,658	309	5.5
Precision production	10	0	0.0
Psychology	23,415	947	4.0
Public administration and social service professions	33,933	1,437	4.2
Security and protective services	6,128	200	3.3
Social sciences and history	19,240	933	4.8
Theology and religious vocations	7,541	304	4.0
Transportation and materials moving	1,048	34	3.2
Visual and performing arts	14,918	884	5.9

Source: National Center for Education Statistics, Digest of Education Statistics 2010, Table 300, Internet site http://nces.ed.gov/programs/digest/d10/; calculations by New Strategist

Table 2.16 Doctoral Degrees Earned by Total People and Asians by Field of Study, 2008–09

(total number of doctoral degrees conferred and number and percent earned by Asians, by field of study, 2008–09)

		earned by Asians	
	total	number	share of total
Total doctoral degrees	**67,716**	**3,875**	**5.7%**
Agriculture and natural resources	1,328	41	3.1
Architecture and related services	212	22	10.4
Area, ethnic, cultural, and gender studies	239	15	6.3
Biological and biomedical sciences	6,957	573	8.2
Business	2,123	129	6.1
Communications, journalism, and related programs	533	13	2.4
Communications technologies	2	0	0.0
Computer and information sciences	1,580	131	8.3
Education	9,028	301	3.3
Engineering	7,931	557	7.0
Engineering technologies	59	2	3.4
English language and literature/letters	1,271	59	4.6
Family and consumer sciences	333	15	4.5
Foreign languages, literatures, and linguistics	1,111	77	6.9
Health professions and related clinical sciences	12,112	699	5.8
Legal professions and studies	259	8	3.1
Liberal arts and sciences, general studies, and humanities	67	1	1.5
Library science	35	2	5.7
Mathematics and statistics	1,535	87	5.7
Multi/interdisciplinary studies	1,273	90	7.1
Parks, recreation, leisure, and fitness studies	285	7	2.5
Philosophy and religious studies	686	31	4.5
Physical sciences and science technologies	5,048	227	4.5
Psychology	5,477	322	5.9
Public administration and social service professions	812	37	4.6
Security and protective services	97	9	9.3
Social sciences and history	4,234	200	4.7
Theology and religious vocations	1,520	128	8.4
Visual and performing arts	1,569	92	5.9

Source: National Center for Education Statistics, Digest of Education Statistics 2010, Table 303, Internet site http://nces.ed.gov/programs/digest/d10/; calculations by New Strategist

Table 2.17 First-Professional Degrees Earned by Total People and Asians by Field of Study, 2008–09

(total number of first-professional degrees conferred and number and percent earned by Asians, by field of study, 2008–09)

		earned by Asians	
	total	number	share of total
Total first-professional degrees	**92,004**	**12,182**	**13.2%**
Dentistry (D.D.S. or D.M.D.)	4,918	991	20.2
Medicine (M.D.)	15,987	3,384	21.2
Optometry (O.D.)	1,338	297	22.2
Osteopathic medicine (D.O.)	3,665	670	18.3
Pharmacy (Pharm.D.)	11,291	2,524	22.4
Podiatry (Pod.D., D.P., or D.P.M.)	431	48	11.1
Veterinary medicine (D.V.M.)	2,377	92	3.9
Chiropractic (D.C. or D.C.M.)	2,512	154	6.1
Naturopathic medicine	78	9	11.5
Law (LL.B. or J.D.)	44,045	3,702	8.4
Theology (M.Div., M.H.L., B.D., or Ord.)	5,362	311	5.8

Source: National Center for Education Statistics, Digest of Education Statistics 2010, Table 306, Internet site http://nces.ed.gov/programs/digest/d10/; calculations by New Strategist

CHAPTER
3

Health

■ Sixty-six percent of Asians aged 18 or older rate their health highly compared with 60 percent of all adults. Asians are less likely than average to say their health is only fair or poor—10 versus 13 percent.

■ Only 12 percent of Asians aged 18 or older are current smokers, well below the 21 percent rate for all Americans.

■ The 53 percent majority of Asians have a healthy weight, a much greater share than the 35 percent of all Americans aged 18 or older whose weight is in the healthy range. Forty-two percent of Asians are overweight.

■ Of the 4.1 million births in the United States in 2009, only 6 percent were to Asian women. Among all births in California, Asians accounted for 14 percent of the total.

■ Of the nation's 15 million Asians, 67 percent have private health insurance. Twenty-three percent of Asians have government-provided health insurance, and 16 percent do not have health insurance.

■ Among all Americans, heart disease is the leading cause of death. Among Asians, cancer is number one.

Asians Are Healthier than Average

The percentage of Asians who rate their health as excellent or very good has declined, however.

Asian adults are more likely than the average American adult to rate their health as excellent or very good. Sixty-six percent of Asians aged 18 or older rate their health highly compared with 60 percent of all adults, according to the federal government's National Health Interview Survey. Asians are much less likely than average to say their health is only fair or poor—10 versus 13 percent.

Between 2000 and 2009, the percentage of Asians who rated their health as excellent or very good fell by 3 percentage points. During those same years, the proportion of Asians who rated their health as only fair or poor climbed 4 percentage points.

■ The growing number of people without health insurance may be affecting how healthy people feel.

Asians are more likely than the average American to rate their health highly

(percent of total people and Asians aged 18 or older who rate their health as excellent or very good, 2009)

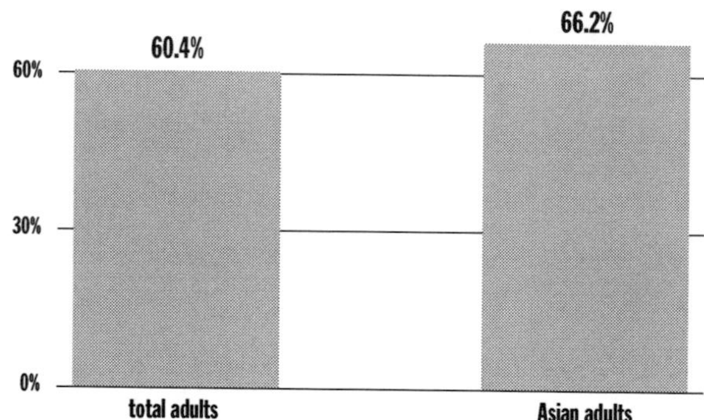

Table 3.1 Health Status of Total and Asian Adults, 2009

(percent distribution of total people and Asians aged 18 or older by self-reported health status, and index of Asian to total, 2009)

	total	Asian	index Asian to total
Total people	**100.0%**	**100.0%**	–
Excellent/very good	60.4	66.2	110
Good	26.6	23.5	88
Fair or poor	13.0	10.3	79

Note: Asians are those who identify themselves as being Asian alone. The index is calculated by dividing the Asian figure by the total figure and multiplying by 100. "–" means not applicable.
Source: National Center for Health Statistics, Summary Health Statistics for U.S. Adults: National Health Interview Survey, 2009, Vital and Health Statistics, Series 10, No. 249, 2010, Internet site http://www.cdc.gov/nchs/nhis.htm; calculations by New Strategist

Table 3.2 Asian Health Status, 2000 and 2009

(percent distribution of Asians aged 18 or older by self-reported health status, 2000 and 2009; percentage point change, 2000–09)

	2009	2000	percentage point change
Total Asians	**100.0%**	**100.0%**	–
Excellent/very good	66.2	69.6	–3.4
Good	23.5	24.4	–0.9
Fair or poor	10.3	6.0	4.3

Note: Asians are those who identify themselves as being Asian alone. "–" means not applicable.
Source: National Center for Health Statistics, Summary Health Statistics for U.S. Adults: National Health Interview Survey, 2009, Vital and Health Statistics, Series 10, No. 249, 2010, Internet site http://www.cdc.gov/nchs/nhis.htm; and Summary Health Statistics for the U.S. Adults: National Health Interview Survey, 2000, Series 10, No. 215, 2003, Internet site http://www.cdc.gov/nchs/nhis.htm; calculations by New Strategist

Many Asians Are Teetotalers

Few Asians smoke cigarettes.

Only 12 percent of Asians aged 18 or older are current smokers, well below the 21 percent rate for all Americans. Fully 74 percent of Asians have never smoked. Among all Americans, the proportion of people who have never smoked is a smaller 57 percent.

Asians are also less likely to drink alcohol than the average American. Only 33 percent of Asians are current regular drinkers, meaning they consume more than 12 drinks a year. Fully 42 percent of Asians are lifetime abstainers, meaning they have consumed fewer than 12 drinks in their lifetime. Among all Americans only 20 percent are lifetime abstainers and 51 percent described themselves as current regular drinkers.

■ The high level of educational attainment among Asians explains their much lower smoking rates.

Asians are much less likely to smoke than the average American

(percent of total people and Asians aged 18 or older who are current smokers, 2009)

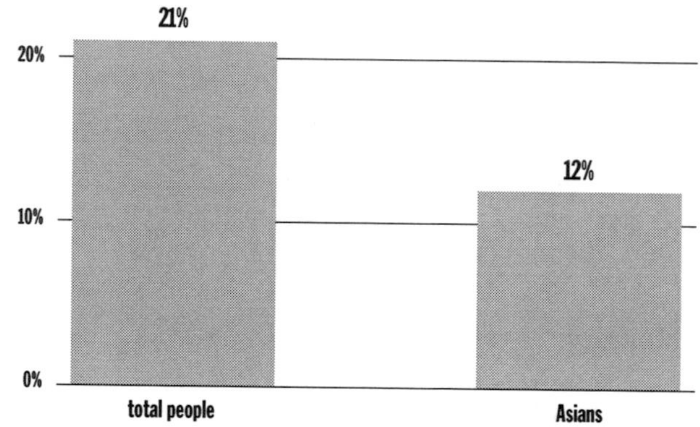

Table 3.3 Smoking Status of Total and Asian Adults, 2009

(number and percent distribution of total people and Asians aged 18 or older, by smoking status, 2009)

	total		Asians	
	number	percent distribution	number	percent distribution
Total people	**227,371**	**100.0%**	**10,763**	**100.0%**
All current smokers	46,641	20.5	1,287	12.0
Every-day smoker	36,434	16.0	924	8.6
Some-day smoker	10,206	4.5	363	3.4
Former smoker	49,878	21.9	1462	13.6
Nonsmoker	130,045	57.2	7,983	74.2

Note: Current smokers have smoked at least 100 cigarettes in lifetime and still smoke; every-day smokers are current smokers who smoke every day; some-day smokers are current smokers who smoke on some days; former smokers have smoked at least 100 cigarettes in lifetime but currently do not smoke; nonsmokers have smoked fewer than 100 cigarettes in lifestime. Numbers by smoking status may not add to total because "unknown" is not shown. Asians are those who identify themselves as being of the race alone.
Source: National Center for Health Statistics, Summary Health Statistics for U.S. Adults: National Health Interview Survey, 2009, Vital and Health Statistics, Series 10, No. 249, 2010, Internet site http://www.cdc.gov/nchs/nhis.htm; calculations by New Strategist

Table 3.4 Drinking Status of Total and Asian Adults, 2009

(number and percent distribution of total people and Asians aged 18 or older, by drinking status, 2009)

	total		Asians	
	number	percent distribution	number	percent distribution
Total people	**227,371**	**100.0%**	**10,763**	**100.0%**
Current regular drinker	116,236	51.1	3,594	33.4
Current infrequent drinker	28,945	12.7	1,376	12.8
Former drinker	33,567	13.9	1,162	8.4
Lifetime abstainer	44,661	19.6	4,522	42.0

Note: A lifetime abstainer had fewer than 12 drinks in lifetime; a former drinker had 12 or more drinks in lifetime, but no drinks in past year; a current drinker had 12 or more drinks in lifetime and had a drink in the past year; an infrequent drinker had fewer than 12 drinks in past year; a regular drinker had 12 or more drinks in past year. Numbers by drinking status may not add to total because "unknown" is not shown. Asians are those who identify themselves as being of the race alone.
Source: National Center for Health Statistics, Summary Health Statistics for U.S. Adults: National Health Interview Survey, 2009, Vital and Health Statistics, Series 10, No. 249, 2010, Internet site http://www.cdc.gov/nchs/nhis.htm; calculations by New Strategist

Few Asians Are Overweight

Asians are much less likely than the average American to be overweight.

The 53 percent majority of Asians have a healthy weight, a much greater share than the 35 percent of all Americans aged 18 or older whose weight is in the healthy range. Forty-two percent of Asians are overweight. Among all Americans, a much larger 63 percent are overweight.

Asians are much less likely than the average American to be obese. Among all Americans aged 18 or older, 28 percent are obese. Among Asians, the figure is just 9 percent.

■ As Asian immigrants adopt the American fast-food diet, their weight is likely to increase.

Most Asians are at a healthy weight

(percent of total people and Asians aged 18 or older who have a healthy weight, 2009)

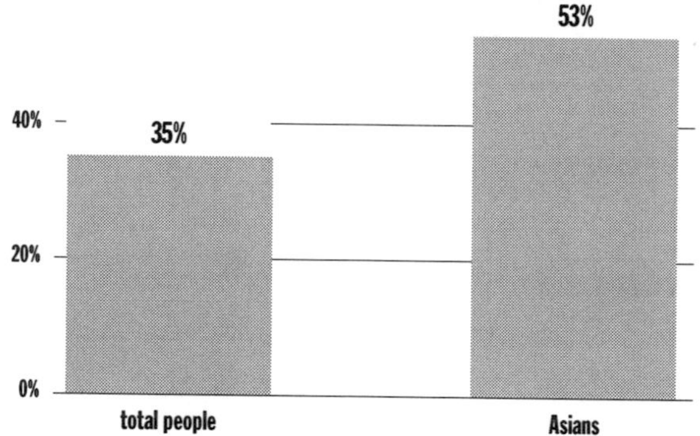

Table 3.5 Weight Status of Total and Asian Adults, 2009

(percent distribution of total people and Asians aged 18 or older by body weight status, and index of Asian to total, 2009)

	total	Asians	index Asian to total
Total people	**100.0%**	**100.0%**	–
Underweight	1.7	4.2	247
Healthy weight	35.1	53.4	152
Overweight, total	63.2	42.4	67
Obese	27.6	9.0	33

Note: Underweight is a body mass index (BMI) below 18.5; healthy weight is a BMI of 18.5 to 24.9; overweight is a BMI of 25.0 or higher; obese is a BMI of 30.0 or more. BMI is calculated by dividing weight in kilograms by height in meters squared. Data are based on self-reported heights and weights of a representative sample of the civilian noninstitutional population. Numbers may not add to total because "weight unknown" is not shown. Asians are those who identify themselves as being Asian alone. "–" means not applicable.
Source: National Center for Health Statistics, Summary Health Statistics for U.S. Adults: National Health Interview Survey, 2009, Vital and Health Statistics, Series 10, No. 249, 2010, Internet site http://www.cdc.gov/nchs/nhis.htm; calculations by New Strategist

Most Asians Births Are to Older Women

More than half of Asian births are to women aged 30 or older.

Of the 4.1 million births in the United States in 2009, only 6 percent were to Asian women. Among births to women aged 30 or older, however, a larger 9 percent were to Asians. Asians account for a larger share of births to older women because most Asian women postpone childbearing until age 30 or older. The 57 percent majority of Asian births are to women aged 30 or older.

Among the 250,935 births to Asians in 2009, nearly 30 percent occurred in California. Among all births in California, Asians accounted for 14 percent of the total.

■ Behind the older age of Asian mothers is their higher educational attainment, with most going to college before getting married and having children.

Most Asian women postpone childbearing

(percent distribution of births to Asians by age, 2009)

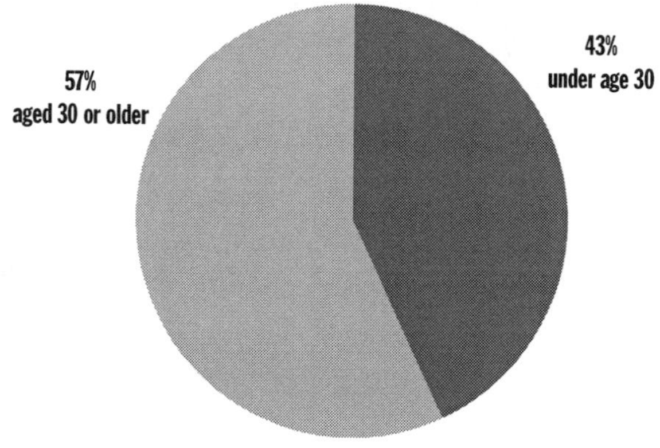

Table 3.6 Births to Total and Asian Women by Age, 2009

(total number of births, number and percent distribution of births to Asians, and Asian share of total, by age, 2009)

		Asian		
	total	number	percent distribution	share of total
Total births	**4,131,019**	**250,935**	**100.0%**	**6.1%**
Under age 15	5,030	76	0.0	1.5
Aged 15 to 19	409,840	7,041	2.8	1.7
Aged 20 to 24	1,006,055	29,395	11.7	2.9
Aged 25 to 29	1,166,904	70,496	28.1	6.0
Aged 30 to 34	955,300	85,280	34.0	8.9
Aged 35 to 39	474,143	48,078	19.2	10.1
Aged 40 to 44	105,813	9,854	3.9	9.3
Aged 45 to 54	7,934	714	0.3	9.0

Source: National Center for Health Statistics, Births: Preliminary Data for 2009, National Vital Statistics Reports, Vol. 59, No. 3, 2010, Internet site http://www.cdc.gov/nchs/births.htm; calculations by New Strategist

Table 3.7 Births to Asian Women by Age and Marital Status, 2008

(total number of births to Asians, number of births to unmarried Asians, and unmarried share of total, by age, 2008)

		unmarried	
	total	number	share of total
Births to Asians	**253,185**	**42,832**	**16.9%**
Under age 15	81	80	98.8
Aged 15 to 19	7,537	6,013	79.8
Aged 20 to 24	31,038	13,270	42.8
Aged 25 to 29	71,220	11,547	16.2
Aged 30 to 34	85,538	6,882	8.0
Aged 35 to 39	47,616	3,916	8.2
Aged 40 or older	10,155	1,124	11.1

Source: National Center for Health Statistics, Births: Final Data for 2008, National Vital Statistics Reports, Vol. 59, No. 1, 2010, Internet site http://www.cdc.gov/nchs/births.htm; calculations by New Strategist

Table 3.8 Births to Total and Asian Women by Birth Order, 2009

(total number of births, number and percent distribution of births to Asians, and Asian share of total, by birth order, 2009)

		Asian		
	total	number	percent distribution	share of total
Total births	**4,131,019**	**250,935**	**100.0%**	**6.1%**
First child	1,660,342	113,339	45.2	6.8
Second child	1,291,155	88,742	35.4	6.9
Third child	679,183	30,995	12.4	4.6
Fourth or later child	473,735	16,479	6.6	3.5

Note: Numbers do not add to total because "not stated" is not shown.
Source: National Center for Health Statistics, Births: Preliminary Data for 2009, National Vital Statistics Reports, Vol. 59, No. 3, 2010, Internet site http://www.cdc.gov/nchs/births.htm; calculations by New Strategist

Table 3.9 Births to Total and Asian Women by State, 2009

(total number of births, number and percent distribution of births to Asians, and Asian share of total, by state, 2009)

		Asian births		
	total	number	percent distribution	share of total
Total births	**4,131,019**	**250,935**	**100.0%**	**6.1%**
Alabama	62,476	989	0.4	1.6
Alaska	11,325	950	0.4	8.4
Arizona	92,816	3,442	1.4	3.7
Arkansas	39,853	669	0.3	1.7
California	527,011	71,457	28.5	13.6
Colorado	68,627	2,543	1.0	3.7
Connecticut	38,896	2,232	0.9	5.7
Delaware	11,562	517	0.2	4.5
District of Columbia	9,044	406	0.2	4.5
Florida	221,391	7,409	3.0	3.3
Georgia	141,375	5,976	2.4	4.2
Hawaii	18,888	12,562	5.0	66.5
Idaho	23,731	419	0.2	1.8
Illinois	171,255	9,616	3.8	5.6
Indiana	86,698	1,994	0.8	2.3
Iowa	39,700	1060	0.4	2.7
Kansas	41,396	1,366	0.5	3.3
Kentucky	57,558	1075	0.4	1.9
Louisiana	64,988	1,263	0.5	1.9
Maine	13,470	236	0.1	1.8
Maryland	75,061	5,388	2.1	7.2
Massachusetts	75,104	6,040	2.4	8.0
Michigan	117,293	4,091	1.6	3.5
Minnesota	70,648	5,313	2.1	7.5
Mississippi	42,905	479	0.2	1.1
Missouri	78,920	2,028	0.8	2.6
Montana	12,261	134	0.1	1.1
Nebraska	26,937	822	0.3	3.1
Nevada	37,627	3,146	1.3	8.4
New Hampshire	13,378	577	0.2	4.3
New Jersey	110,324	11,668	4.6	10.6
New Mexico	29,002	498	0.2	1.7
New York	248,110	23,274	9.3	9.4
North Carolina	126,846	4,107	1.6	3.2
North Dakota	9,001	159	0.1	1.8
Ohio	144,772	3,540	1.4	2.4
Oklahoma	54,574	1,365	0.5	2.5
Oregon	47,199	2,731	1.1	5.8
Pennsylvania	146,432	6,416	2.6	4.4

	total	Asian births number	percent distribution	share of total
Rhode Island	11,443	662	0.3%	5.8%
South Carolina	60,632	1,236	0.5	2.0
South Dakota	11,935	153	0.1	1.3
Tennessee	82,213	2,107	0.8	2.6
Texas	402,011	16,948	6.8	4.2
Utah	53,887	1,629	0.6	3.0
Vermont	6,109	111	0.0	1.8
Virginia	105,056	7,780	3.1	7.4
Washington	89,284	9,134	3.6	10.2
West Virginia	21,270	146	0.1	0.7
Wisconsin	70,840	2,969	1.2	4.2
Wyoming	7,884	102	0.0	1.3

Note: Asians include Pacific Islanders.
Source: National Center for Health Statistics, Births: Preliminary Data for 2009, National Vital Statistics Reports, Vol. 59, No. 3, 2010, Internet site http://www.cdc.gov/nchs/births.htm; calculations by New Strategist

Many Asians Are without Health Insurance

The percentage of Asians without health insurance peaks in the 18-to-24 age group.

Most Asians have employment-based health insurance coverage, but a minority has health insurance through their own employer. Of the nation's 15 million Asians, only 29 percent have health insurance through their own job. The rest depend on coverage provided by the employer of a spouse or parent.

Twenty-three percent of Asians have government-provided health insurance. Fourteen percent depend on Medicaid (the government's health insurance program for the poor), and 9 percent are on Medicare (the government's health insurance program for the elderly).

Sixteen percent of Asians do not have health insurance. In the 18-to-24 age group, the proportion is 29 percent.

■ The relatively high socioeconomic status of Asians insures that most do have health insurance, but a large percentage of Asians in every age group lack coverage.

Most Asians have private health insurance coverage

(percent of Asians by health insurance coverage status, 2009)

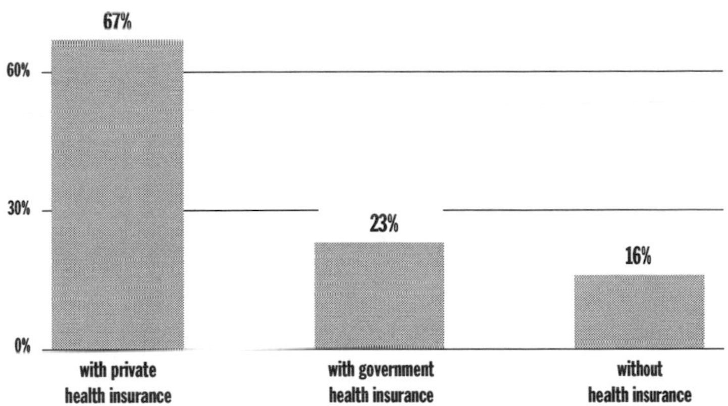

Table 3.10 Health Insurance Coverage of Total People and Asians by Age, 2009

(number of total people and Asians with and without health insurance coverage and Asian share of total, 2009; numbers in thousands)

	with health insurance			without health insurance		
	total	Asian	Asian share of total	total	Asian	Asian share of total
Total people	**253,606**	**12,778**	**5.0%**	**50,674**	**2,503**	**4.9%**
Under age 65	215,669	11,488	5.3	49,998	2,415	4.8
Under age 18	67,527	3,657	5.4	7,513	348	4.6
Aged 18 to 24	20,389	992	4.9	8,923	402	4.5
Aged 25 to 34	29,122	1,997	6.9	11,963	517	4.3
Aged 35 to 44	31,689	2,019	6.4	8,759	451	5.1
Aged 45 to 54	36,481	1,674	4.6	7,906	359	4.5
Aged 55 to 64	30,462	1,149	3.8	4,933	338	6.9
Aged 65 or older	37,937	1,290	3.4	676	88	13.0

Note: Asians are those who identify themselves as being of the race alone or as being of the race in combination with other races.

Source: Bureau of the Census, Health Insurance, Table HI01, Internet site http://www.census.gov/hhes/www/cpstables/032010/health/toc.htm; calculations by New Strategist

Table 3.11 Health Insurance Coverage of Asians by Age, 2009

(number and percent distribution of Asians by age and health insurance coverage status, 2009; numbers in thousands)

		with health insurance coverage during year			not covered at any time during the year
	total	total	private	government	
Total Asians	**15,281**	**12,778**	**10,302**	**3,530**	**2,503**
Under age 65	13,903	11,488	9,762	2,340	2,415
Under age 18	4,005	3,657	2,885	1,051	348
Aged 18 to 24	1,394	992	799	249	402
Aged 25 to 34	2,514	1,997	1,791	278	517
Aged 35 to 44	2,470	2,019	1,825	258	451
Aged 45 to 54	2,032	1,674	1,496	240	359
Aged 55 to 64	1,487	1,149	967	265	338
Aged 65 or older	1,378	1,290	540	1,190	88
PERCENT DISTRIBUTION BY COVERAGE STATUS					
Total Asians	**100.0%**	**83.6%**	**67.4%**	**23.1%**	**16.4%**
Under age 65	100.0	82.6	70.2	16.8	17.4
Under age 18	100.0	91.3	72.0	26.2	8.7
Aged 18 to 24	100.0	71.2	57.3	17.9	28.8
Aged 25 to 34	100.0	79.4	71.2	11.1	20.6
Aged 35 to 44	100.0	81.7	73.9	10.4	18.3
Aged 45 to 54	100.0	82.4	73.6	11.8	17.7
Aged 55 to 64	100.0	77.3	65.0	17.8	22.7
Aged 65 or older	100.0	93.6	39.2	86.4	6.4

Note: Asians are those who identify themselves as being of the race alone or as being of the race in combination with other races. Numbers do not add to total because some people have more than one type of health insurance.
Source: Bureau of the Census, Health Insurance, Table HI01, Internet site http://www.census.gov/hhes/www/cpstables/032010/health/toc.htm; calculations by New Strategist

Table 3.12 Asians with Private Health Insurance Coverage by Age, 2009

(number and percent distribution of Asians by age and private health insurance coverage status, 2009; numbers in thousands)

		with private health insurance			
			employment based		
	total	total	total	own	direct purchase
Total Asians	**15,281**	**10,302**	**9,050**	**4,410**	**1,390**
Under age 65	13,903	9,762	8,677	4,111	1,202
Under age 18	4,005	2,885	2,624	8	299
Aged 18 to 24	1,394	799	584	213	152
Aged 25 to 34	2,514	1,791	1,618	1,177	198
Aged 35 to 44	2,470	1,825	1,669	1,171	190
Aged 45 to 54	2,032	1,496	1,344	951	198
Aged 55 to 64	1,487	967	837	591	164
Aged 65 or older	1,378	540	373	299	188
PERCENT DISTRIBUTION BY COVERAGE STATUS					
Total Asians	**100.0%**	**67.4%**	**59.2%**	**28.9%**	**9.1%**
Under age 65	100.0	70.2	62.4	29.6	8.6
Under age 18	100.0	72.0	65.5	0.2	7.5
Aged 18 to 24	100.0	57.3	41.9	15.3	10.9
Aged 25 to 34	100.0	71.2	64.4	46.8	7.9
Aged 35 to 44	100.0	73.9	67.6	47.4	7.7
Aged 45 to 54	100.0	73.6	66.1	46.8	9.7
Aged 55 to 64	100.0	65.0	56.3	39.7	11.0
Aged 65 or older	100.0	39.2	27.1	21.7	13.6

Note: Asians are those who identify themselves as being of the race alone or as being of the race in combination with other races. Numbers do not add to total because some people have more than one type of health insurance.
Source: Bureau of the Census, Health Insurance, Table HI01, Internet site http://www.census.gov/hhes/www/cpstables/032010/health/toc.htm; calculations by New Strategist

Table 3.13 Asians with Government Health Insurance Coverage by Age, 2009

(number and percent distribution of Asians by age and government health insurance coverage status, 2009; numbers in thousands)

		with government health insurance			
	total	total	Medicaid	Medicare	military
Total Asians	**15,281**	**3,530**	**2,167**	**1,353**	**477**
Under age 65	13,903	2,340	1,846	182	401
Under age 18	4,005	1,051	933	20	122
Aged 18 to 24	1,394	249	202	5	46
Aged 25 to 34	2,514	278	222	13	49
Aged 35 to 44	2,470	258	200	24	52
Aged 45 to 54	2,032	240	163	38	56
Aged 55 to 64	1,487	265	126	81	76
Aged 65 or older	1,378	1,190	321	1,172	76
PERCENT DISTRIBUTION BY COVERAGE STATUS					
Total Asians	**100.0%**	**23.1%**	**14.2%**	**8.9%**	**3.1%**
Under age 65	100.0	16.8	13.3	1.3	2.9
Under age 18	100.0	26.2	23.3	0.5	3.0
Aged 18 to 24	100.0	17.9	14.5	0.4	3.3
Aged 25 to 34	100.0	11.1	8.8	0.5	1.9
Aged 35 to 44	100.0	10.4	8.1	1.0	2.1
Aged 45 to 54	100.0	11.8	8.0	1.9	2.8
Aged 55 to 64	100.0	17.8	8.5	5.4	5.1
Aged 65 or older	100.0	86.4	23.3	85.1	5.5

Note: Asians are those who identify themselves as being of the race alone or as being of the race in combination with other races. Numbers do not add to total because some people have more than one type of health insurance.
Source: Bureau of the Census, Health Insurance, Table HI01, Internet site http://www.census.gov/hhes/www/cpstables/032010/health/toc.htm; calculations by New Strategist

Hypertension Is the Most Common Condition among Asians

Lower back pain ranks second among Asians.

Because of their high levels of education, the Asian population is relatively healthy. The most common chronic condition is hypertension, experienced by 19 percent of Asians aged 18 or older. Lower back pain is second, followed by chronic joint symptoms and arthritis. Eight percent of Asian adults experience severe headaches.

A substantial 11 percent of Asian children have been diagnosed with asthma, but a smaller 8 percent still have asthma. Only 3 percent of Asian children have a learning disorder.

Asians are less likely than the average person to go to the doctor. One in four Asian adults has not been to a doctor or other health care professional in the past year compared with 19 percent of all Americans. Only 8 percent of Asians aged 18 or older have any difficulty in physical functioning. Asians account for fewer than 1 percent of cumulative AIDS cases through 2008.

■ Health status rises with educational attainment. Because Asians are highly educated, their health status is above average.

Four health conditions affect more than 10 percent of Asians

(percent of Asians aged 18 or older with selected health conditions, 2009)

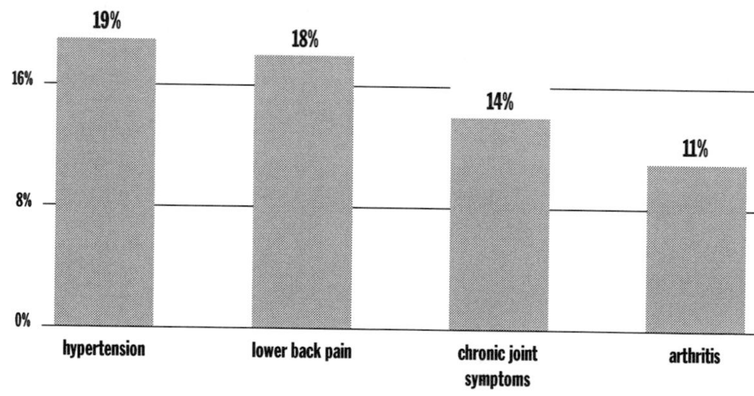

Table 3.14 Health Conditions among Total and Asian Adults, 2009

(number of total people and Asians aged 18 or older with selected health conditions, percent of Asians with condition, and Asian share of total with condition, 2009; numbers in thousands)

		Asians		
	total	number	percent with condition	share of total
Total people aged 18 or older	**227,371**	**10,763**	**100.0%**	**4.7%**
Selected circulatory diseases				
Heart disease, all types	26,845	579	6.3	2.2
Coronary	14,740	347	3.9	2.4
Hypertension	56,582	1,892	19.4	3.3
Stroke	6,011	106	1.3	1.8
Selected respiratory conditions				
Emphysema	4,895	59	0.6	1.2
Asthma, ever	29,734	968	9.2	3.3
Asthma, still	17,456	490	4.7	2.8
Hay fever	17,738	670	6.3	3.8
Sinusitis	29,305	694	6.4	2.4
Chronic bronchitis	9,908	184	1.8	1.9
Selected types of cancer				
Any cancer	18,648	286	3.1	1.5
Breast cancer	3,304	88	0.8	2.7
Cervical cancer	1,289	–	–	–
Prostate cancer	2,233	42	1.2	1.9
Other selected diseases and conditions				
Diabetes	20,490	779	8.2	3.8
Ulcers	17,665	527	5.0	3.0
Kidney disease	4,483	98	1.1	2.2
Liver disease	3,287	118	1.2	3.6
Arthritis	52,107	1,098	11.2	2.1
Chronic joint symptoms	64,929	1,462	14.3	2.3
Migraines or severe headaches	35,973	902	8.3	2.5
Pain in neck	34,954	935	8.5	2.7
Pain in lower back	64,810	1,879	17.8	2.9
Pain in face or jaw	11,501	303	2.8	2.6
Selected sensory problems				
Hearing	34,488	1,015	10.8	2.9
Vision	19,441	552	5.5	2.8
Absence of all natural teeth	17,271	467	5.0	2.7

Note: The conditions shown are those that have ever been diagnosed by a doctor, except as noted. Hay fever, sinusitis, and chronic bronchitis have been diagnosed in the past 12 months. Kidney and liver diseases have been diagnosed in the past 12 months and exclude kidney stones, bladder infections, and incontinence. Chronic joint symptoms are shown if respondent had pain, aching, or stiffness in or around a joint (excluding back and neck) and the condition began more than three months ago. Migraines, and pain in neck, lower back, face, or jaw are shown only if pain lasted a whole day or more. "–" means sample is too small to make a reliable estimate.

Source: National Center for Health Statistics, Summary Health Statistics for U.S. Adults: National Health Interview Survey, 2009, Vital and Health Statistics, Series 10, No. 249, 2010, Internet site http://www.cdc.gov/nchs/nhis.htm; calculations by New Strategist

Table 3.15 Health Conditions among Total and Asian Children, 2009

(number of total people and Asians under age 18 with selected health conditions, percent of Asians with condition, and Asian share of total, 2009; numbers in thousands)

		Asians		
	total	number	percent with condition	share of total
Total children	**73,996**	**3,023**	**100.0%**	**4.1%**
Asthma				
Ever had	10,196	347	11.3	3.4
Still have	7,111	232	7.6	3.3
Experienced in last 12 months				
Hay fever	7,198	236	7.6	3.3
Respiratory allergies	8,206	314	10.1	3.8
Food allergies	3,854	134	4.4	3.5
Skin allergies	8,913	410	13.4	4.6
Ever told had*				
Learning disability	5,059	78	3.0	1.5
Attention deficit hyperactivity disorder	5,288	21	0.8	0.4
Prescription medication taken regularly for at least three months	**9,873**	**163**	**5.3**	**1.7**

** Ever told by a school representative or health professional. Data exclude children under age 3.*
Source: National Center for Health Statistics, Summary Health Statistics for U.S. Children: National Health Interview Survey, 2009, Series 10, No. 247, 2010, Internet site http://www.cdc.gov/nchs/nhis.htm

Table 3.16 Health Care Visits by Total People and Asians, 2009

(total number of people and Asians aged 18 or older and percent distribution by number of visits to a doctor or other health care professional in past 12 months, and index of Asian to total, 2009; numbers in thousands)

	total	Asian	index, Asian to total
Total people 18 or older, number	**227,371**	**10,763**	–
Total people 18 or older, percent	**100.0%**	**100.0%**	–
No health care visits	**19.0**	**24.7**	**130**
One or more health care visits	**81.1**	**75.3**	**93**
One	16.6	21.2	128
Two to three	26.2	24.3	93
Four to nine	24.2	20.5	85
10 or more	14.1	9.3	66

Note: The index is calculated by dividing the percentage of Asians with the number of visits by the percentage of total people with the number of visits and multiplying by 100. "–" means not applicable.
Source: National Center for Health Statistics, Summary Health Statistics for U.S. Adults: National Health Interview Survey, 2009, Vital and Health Statistics, Series 10, No. 249, 2010, Internet site http://www.cdc.gov/nchs/nhis.htm; calculations by New Strategist

Table 3.17 Difficulties in Physical Functioning among Total and Asian Adults, 2009

(number of total people and Asians aged 18 or older, number with difficulties in physical functioning, percent of Asians with difficulty, and Asian share of total, by type of difficulty, 2009; numbers in thousands)

		Asian		
	total	number	percent with difficulty	share of total
Total people aged 18 or older	**227,371**	**10,763**	**100.0%**	**4.7%**
Total with any physical difficulty	35,600	825	7.7	2.3
Walk quarter of a mile	15,937	318	3.0	2.0
Climb 10 steps without resting	11,455	242	2.2	2.1
Stand for two hours	21,228	526	4.9	2.5
Sit for two hours	7,898	161	1.5	2.0
Stoop, bend, or kneel	20,651	400	3.7	1.9
Reach over head	5,415	156	1.4	2.9
Grasp or handle small objects	4,042	75	0.7	1.9
Lift or carry 10 pounds	9,538	293	2.7	3.1
Push or pull large objects	14,209	420	3.9	3.0

Note: Respondents were classified as having difficulties if they responded "very difficult" or "can't do at all."
Source: National Center for Health Statistics, Summary Health Statistics for U.S. Adults: National Health Interview Survey, 2009, Vital and Health Statistics, Series 10, No. 249, 2010, Internet site http://www.cdc.gov/nchs/nhis.htm; calculations by New Strategist

Table 3.18 Cumulative Number of AIDS Cases by Race and Hispanic Origin, through 2008

(cumulative number and percent distribution of AIDS cases by race and Hispanic origin, through 2008)

	number	percent distribution
Total cases	**1,073,128**	**100.0%**
American Indian	3,741	0.3
Asian	8,253	0.8
Black	452,916	42.2
Hispanic	180,061	16.8
Non-Hispanic white	419,905	39.1

Note: Numbers will not add to total because not all races are shown and Hispanics may be of any race.
Source: Centers for Disease Control and Prevention, HIV/AIDS, Internet site http://www.cdc.gov/hiv/surveillance/resources/reports/2008report/table2a.htm

Cancer Is the Leading Cause of Death among Asians

Heart disease ranks second.

Among all Americans, heart disease is the leading cause of death. Among Asians, cancer is number one, accounting for 27 percent of the total. Heart disease accounts for a smaller 23 percent of deaths among Asians. Heart disease is a less important cause of death among Asians in part because the average Asian is better educated, more affluent, and less likely to be overweight than the average American.

No other cause accounts for more than 10 percent of deaths among Asians. Cerebrovascular disease accounts for 8 percent of the total, accidents 5 percent, and diabetes 4 percent. Alzheimer's disease accounts for only 2 percent of deaths among Asians.

■ Many Asians are immigrants who have not yet adopted the fat-laden diet popular with native-born Americans, which limits their incidence of heart disease.

Cancer and heart disease are the two leading causes of death among Asians

(percent of deaths to Asians by selected causes, 2007)

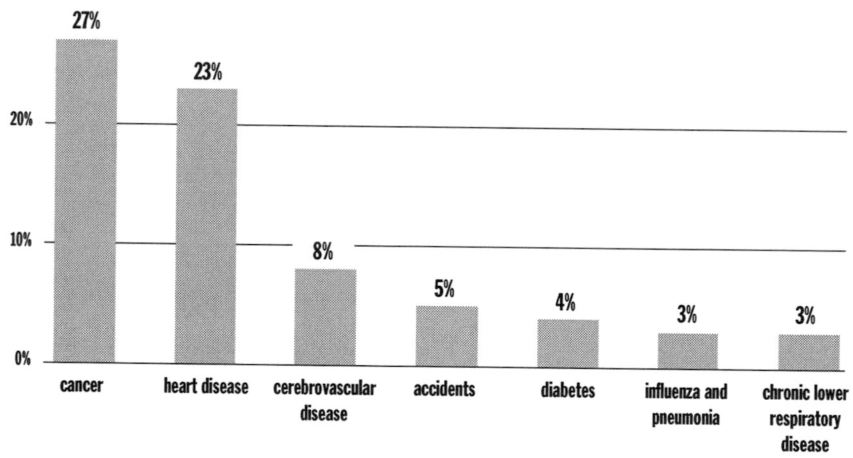

Table 3.19 Leading Causes of Death among Asians, 2007

(number and percent distribution of deaths to Asians accounted for by the 10 leading causes of death among Asians, 2007)

	number	percent distribution
Total deaths among Asians	**45,609**	**100.0%**
1. Malignant neoplasms (cancer) (2)	12,326	27.0
2. Diseases of the heart (1)	10,574	23.2
3. Cerebrovascular diseases (3)	3,586	7.9
4. Accidents (5)	2,194	4.8
5. Diabetes mellitus (7)	1,743	3.8
6. Influenza and pneumonia (8)	1,335	2.9
7. Chronic lower respiratory disease (4)	1,331	2.9
8. Suicide (11)	900	2.0
9. Nephritis, nephrotic syndrome, nephrosis (9)	893	2.0
10. Alzheimer's disease (6)	748	1.6
All other causes	9,979	21.9

Note: Number in parentheses shows rank for all Americans if the cause of death is among top 15.
Source: National Center for Health Statistics, Health United States, 2010, Internet site http://www.cdc.gov/nchs/hus.htm; calculations by New Strategist

CHAPTER

4

Housing

■ Fifty-nine percent of the nation's Asian householders owned their home in 2010, down from a peak of 61 percent in 2006.

■ Asian homeownership is 12 percent below average, but this is up from 22 percent below average in 2000.

■ The homeownership rate of Asian households is highest in the South, at 67 percent. Only 22 percent of Asian homeowners live in the South, however.

■ The West is home to 48 percent of Asian homeowners and 47 percent of Asian renters.

■ Among household types, Asian married couples are most likely to own their home. In 2009, Asian couples had a homeownership rate of 68 percent.

■ With a mobility rate of 13.9 percent, Asians are slightly more likely to move in a given year than is the average American. Fifteen percent of the movers are moving to the United States from abroad.

Most Asian Households Own Their Home

But their homeownership rate is below average.

Asian households are less likely than the average household to own a home. In 2010, 59 percent of Asian households owned their home versus 67 percent of all households.

The homeownership rate of Asians has fallen slightly since peaking in 2006, but it remains well above the 2000 level. In 2010, the homeownership rate of Asian households was 6.1 percentage points above the rate in 2000, but 1.9 percentage points below the Asian peak reached in 2006. Note: The overall homeownership rate peaked in 2004.

■ Asians are more likely to own a home than blacks or Hispanics because they are better educated and earn higher incomes.

The Asian homeownership rate has peaked

(percent of Asian households that own their home, 2000 to 2010)

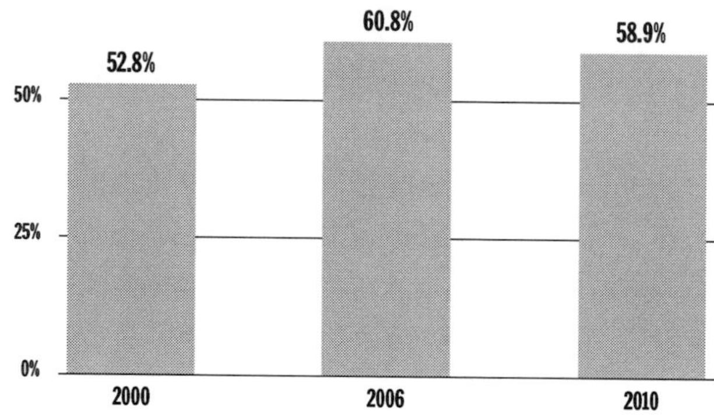

Table 4.1 Total and Asian Homeownership Rate, 2000 to 2010

(homeownership rate of total and Asian households and index of Asian to total, 2000 to 2010; percentage point change in homeownership rate, 2000 to 2010 and Asian peak year 2006 to 2010)

	homeownership rate		index,
	total	Asian	Asian to total
2010	66.9%	58.9%	88
2009	67.4	59.3	88
2008	67.8	59.5	88
2007	68.1	60.0	88
2006	68.8	60.8	88
2005	68.9	60.1	87
2004	69.0	59.8	87
2003	68.3	56.3	82
2002	67.9	54.7	81
2001	67.8	53.9	79
2000	67.4	52.8	78
Percentage point change			
2006 to 2010	–1.9	–1.9	–
2000 to 2010	–0.5	6.1	–

Note: Asians include only those who identify themselves as being of the race alone. The index is calculated by dividing the Asian homeownership rate by the total rate and multiplying by 100. "–" means not applicable.
Source: Bureau of the Census, Housing Vacancy Surveys, Internet site http://www.census.gov/hhes/www/housing/hvs/hvs.html; calculations by New Strategist

Asian Homeownership Is Highest in the South

Nearly half of Asian homeowners live in the West, however.

More than two out of three Asian households in the South own their home. Asian homeownership is a smaller 63 percent in the Midwest and West and an even lower 57 percent in the Northeast. Asians account for only 3 percent of homeowners nationally, but in the West they are a larger 8 percent of homeowners.

Nearly half of Asian homeowners and renters live in the West. Just 12 percent live in the Midwest.

■ Asian homeownership rates are below average in every region despite the fact that Asians have higher incomes than any other racial or ethnic group.

Few Asian homeowners live in the Midwest

(percent distribution of Asian homeowners by region, 2009)

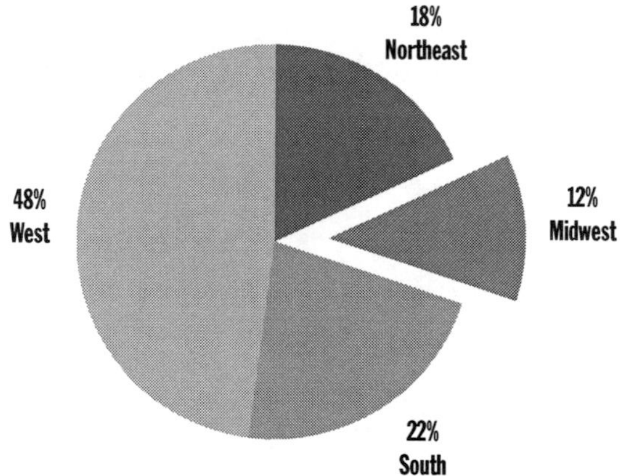

Table 4.2 Total and Asian Homeownership Rate by Region, 2009

(percent of total and Asian households owning a home by region, and index of Asian to total, 2009)

	homeownership rate		index,
	total	Asian	Asian to total
Total households	**68.4%**	**62.9%**	**92**
Northeast	65.4	57.1	87
Midwest	71.9	63.1	88
South	70.2	67.5	96
West	64.0	63.1	99

Note: Asians are those who identify themselves as being of the race alone. The index is calculated by dividing the Asian homeownership rate by the total rate and multiplying by 100.
Source: Bureau of the Census, American Housing Survey for the United States: 2009, Internet site http://www.census.gov/hhes/www/housing/ahs/ahs09/ahs09.html; calculations by New Strategist

Table 4.3 Total and Asian Homeowners by Region, 2009

(number of total homeowners, number and percent distribution of Asian homeowners, and Asian share of total, by region, 2009; numbers in thousands)

		Asian owners		
	total	number	percent distribution	share of total
Total homeowners	**76,428**	**2,516**	**100.0%**	**3.3%**
Northeast	13,378	444	17.6	3.3
Midwest	18,249	309	12.3	1.7
South	29,193	558	22.2	1.9
West	15,607	1,206	47.9	7.7

Note: Asians are those who identify themselves as being of the race alone.
Source: Bureau of the Census, American Housing Survey for the United States: 2009, Internet site http://www.census.gov/hhes/www/housing/ahs/ahs09/ahs09.html; calculations by New Strategist

Table 4.4 Total and Asian Renters by Region, 2009

(number of total renters, number and percent distribution of Asian renters, and Asian share of total, by region, 2009; numbers in thousands)

		Asian renters		
	total	number	percent distribution	share of total
Total renters	**35,378**	**1,487**	**100.0%**	**4.2%**
Northeast	7,073	333	22.4	4.7
Midwest	7,119	181	12.2	2.5
South	12,392	269	18.1	2.2
West	8,794	704	47.4	8.0

Note: Asians are those who identify themselves as being of the race alone.
Source: Bureau of the Census, American Housing Survey for the United States: 2009, Internet site http://www.census.gov/hhes/www/housing/ahs/ahs09/ahs09.html; calculations by New Strategist

Table 4.5 Asian Homeownership Status by Region, 2009

(number and percent distribution of Asian households by homeownership status and region, 2009; numbers in thousands)

	total	owners	renters
Total Asian households	**4,003**	**2,516**	**1,487**
Northeast	776	444	333
Midwest	490	309	181
South	827	558	269
West	1,910	1,206	704
PERCENT DISTRIBUTION BY HOMEOWNERSHIP STATUS			
Total Asian households	**100.0%**	**62.9%**	**37.1%**
Northeast	100.0	57.1	42.9
Midwest	100.0	63.1	36.9
South	100.0	67.5	32.5
West	100.0	63.1	36.9

Note: Asians are those who identify themselves as being of the race alone.
Source: Bureau of the Census, American Housing Survey for the United States: 2009, Internet site http://www.census.gov/hhes/www/housing/ahs/ahs09/ahs09.html; calculations by New Strategist

Most Asian Married Couples Are Homeowners

Most female- and male-headed family householders also own their home.

Among the 4.6 million Asian households in the United States in 2009, the 59 percent majority owned their home according to estimates from the Census Bureau's Current Population Survey. More than two-thirds of married couples own their home, as do the majority of male- and female-headed families. Asian married couples are less likely to own their home than the average married couple, but male- and female-headed families are more likely to be homeowners.

Among married couples who rent, Asians account for a disproportionate 9 percent of the total. Among married couples who own their home, Asians account for a smaller 4 percent.

■ The 68 percent homeownership rate of Asian married couples is well below the 82 percent rate of all married couples.

Asian homeownership is lowest among nonfamily households

(percent of Asian households that own their home, by household type, 2009)

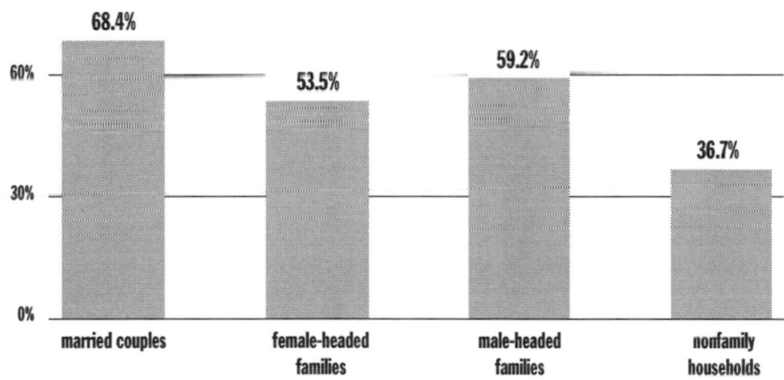

Table 4.6 Total and Asian Homeownership Rate by Household Type, 2009

(percent of total and Asian households owning a home by household type, and index of Asian to total, 2009)

	homeownership rate		index,
	total	Asian	Asian to total
Total households	**67.3%**	**59.0%**	**88**
Married couples	82.5	68.4	83
Female-headed families	47.8	53.5	112
Male-headed families	57.8	59.2	102
Nonfamily households	52.3	36.7	70

Note: Asians are those who identify themselves as being of the race alone. The index is calculated by dividing the Asian homeownership rate by the total rate and multiplying by 100.
Source: Bureau of the Census, Current Population Survey, Internet site http://www.census.gov/population/www/socdemo/race/api.html; calculations by New Strategist

Table 4.7 Total and Asian Homeowners by Household Type, 2009

(number of total homeowners, number and percent distribution of Asian homeowners and Asian share of total, by household type, 2009; numbers in thousands)

		Asian owners		
	total	number	percent distribution	share of total
Total homeowners	**78,825**	**2,700**	**100.0%**	**3.4%**
Married couples	48,799	1,933	71.6	4.0
Female-headed families	6,929	231	8.6	3.3
Male-headed families	3,038	138	5.1	4.5
Nonfamily households	20,059	397	14.7	2.0

Note: Asians are those who identify themselves as being of the race alone.
Source: Bureau of the Census, Current Population Survey, Internet site http://www.census.gov/population/www/socdemo/race/api.html; calculations by New Strategist

Table 4.8 Total and Asian Renters by Household Type, 2009

(number of total renters, number and percent distribution of Asian renters and Asian share of total, by household type, 2009; numbers in thousands)

		Asian renters		
	total	number	percent distribution	share of total
Total renters	**38,356**	**1,874**	**100.0%**	**4.9%**
Married couples	10,318	894	47.7	8.7
Female-headed families	7,551	201	10.7	2.7
Male-headed families	2,214	94	5.0	4.2
Nonfamily households	18,272	685	36.6	3.7

Note: Asians are those who identify themselves as being of the race alone.
Source: Bureau of the Census, Current Population Survey, Internet site http://www.census.gov/population/www/socdemo/race/api.html; calculations by New Strategist

Table 4.9 Asian Homeownership Status by Household Type, 2009

(number and percent distribution of Asian households by homeownership status and household type, 2009; numbers in thousands)

	total	owners	renters
Total Asian households	**4,573**	**2,700**	**1,874**
Married couples	2,827	1,933	894
Female-headed families	432	231	201
Male-headed families	233	138	94
Nonfamily households	1,082	397	685
PERCENT DISTRIBUTION BY HOMEOWNERSHIP STATUS			
Total Asian households	**100.0%**	**59.0%**	**41.0%**
Married couples	100.0	68.4	31.6
Female-headed families	100.0	53.5	46.5
Male-headed families	100.0	59.2	40.3
Nonfamily households	100.0	36.7	63.3

Note: Asians are those who identify themselves as being of the race alone.
Source: Bureau of the Census, Current Population Survey, Internet site http://www.census.gov/population/www/socdemo/race/api.html; calculations by New Strategist

Asian Mobility Is Slightly above Average

More than 2 million Asians moved between 2009 and 2010.

Asians are slightly more likely to move in a given year than is the average American. Between March 2009 and March 2010, 13.9 percent of Asians moved versus 12.5 percent of the total population aged 1 or older.

Among all movers in the U.S., most stay within the same county when they move. Among Asian movers, 62 percent remained within the county. Twelve percent of Asian movers crossed state lines, and a substantial 15 percent came from abroad.

■ Asian housing and mobility patterns differ somewhat from the averages because of many are highly educated immigrants moving for job-related reasons.

Few Asian movers cross county lines

(percent distribution of Asian movers by type of move, March 2009 to March 2010)

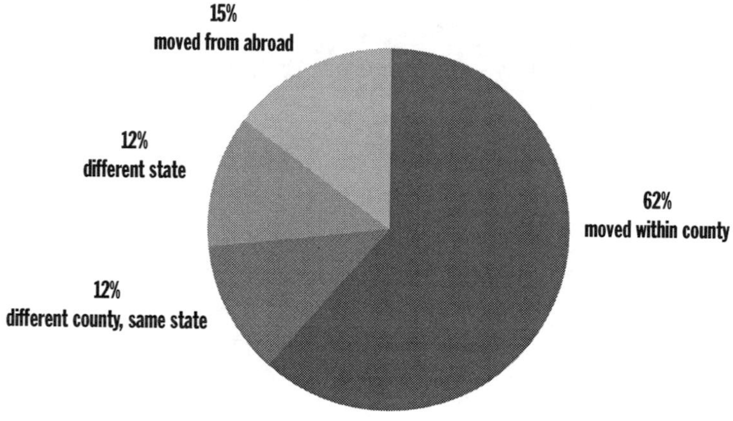

Table 4.10 Total and Asian Movers by Age, 2009–10

(number of total people and Asians aged 1 or older who moved and Asian share of total, percent of total people and Asians aged 1 or older moving, and index of Asian mobility rate to total, by age, March 2009 to March 2010; numbers in thousands)

	total	Asian	Asian share of total
NUMBER MOVING			
Total movers	**37,540**	**2,088**	**5.6%**
Aged 1 to 4	3,384	150	4.4
Aged 5 to 9	2,985	151	5.1
Aged 10 to 14	2,243	105	4.7
Aged 15 to 17	1,311	89	6.8
Aged 18 to 19	1,172	63	5.4
Aged 20 to 24	5,655	292	5.2
Aged 25 to 29	5,563	312	5.6
Aged 30 to 34	3,681	268	7.3
Aged 35 to 39	2,653	175	6.6
Aged 40 to 44	2,093	143	6.8
Aged 45 to 49	1,851	108	5.8
Aged 50 to 54	1,642	66	4.0
Aged 55 to 59	1,066	49	4.6
Aged 60 to 61	366	14	3.8
Aged 62 to 64	452	25	5.5
Aged 65 or older	1,422	80	5.6
	total	**Asian**	**index, Asian to total**
PERCENT MOVING			
Total movers	**12.5%**	**13.9%**	**111**
Aged 1 to 4	19.6	15.1	77
Aged 5 to 9	14.4	13.1	91
Aged 10 to 14	11.3	10.5	93
Aged 15 to 17	10.1	14.9	147
Aged 18 to 19	14.4	17.5	122
Aged 20 to 24	26.7	28.2	105
Aged 25 to 29	25.9	25.4	98
Aged 30 to 34	18.8	20.8	111
Aged 35 to 39	13.3	13.5	101
Aged 40 to 44	10.2	12.2	120
Aged 45 to 49	8.2	10.0	121
Aged 50 to 54	7.5	7.0	93
Aged 55 to 59	5.6	5.9	106
Aged 60 to 61	5.2	5.1	97
Aged 62 to 64	4.9	6.6	135
Aged 65 or older	3.7	5.8	157

Note: Asians are those who identify themselves as being of the race alone and those who identify themselves as being of the race in combination with other races. The index is calculated by dividing the Asian mobility rate by the total rate and multiplying by 100.

Source: Bureau of the Census, Geographic Mobility: 2009 to 2010, Detailed Tables, Internet site http://www.census.gov/hhes/migration/data/cps/cps2010.html; calculations by New Strategist

Table 4.11 Geographical Mobility of Asians by Age, 2009–10

(total number of Asians aged 1 or older, number who moved between March 2009 and March 2010, and percent distribution of movers by age and type of move; numbers in thousands)

		movers				
	total	total movers	same county	different county, same state	different state	from abroad
Total Asians	**15,021**	**2,088**	**1,289**	**245**	**250**	**304**
Aged 1 to 4	994	150	91	12	33	14
Aged 5 to 9	1,154	151	108	12	18	12
Aged 10 to 14	998	105	81	7	11	6
Aged 15 to 17	598	89	49	8	10	22
Aged 18 to 19	359	63	48	7	0	7
Aged 20 to 24	1,036	292	159	37	26	69
Aged 25 to 29	1,227	312	186	42	34	50
Aged 30 to 34	1,286	268	140	36	35	58
Aged 35 to 39	1,298	175	112	9	33	20
Aged 40 to 44	1,173	143	98	9	24	11
Aged 45 to 49	1,084	108	80	17	6	4
Aged 50 to 54	948	66	43	11	7	5
Aged 55 to 59	833	49	29	9	0	10
Aged 60 to 61	277	14	6	2	2	5
Aged 62 to 64	378	25	16	1	4	4
Aged 65 or older	1,379	80	42	25	6	7
PERCENT DISTRIBUTION OF MOVERS BY TYPE OF MOVE						
Total Asians	**–**	**100.0%**	**61.7%**	**11.7%**	**12.0%**	**14.6%**
Aged 1 to 4	–	100.0	60.7	8.0	22.0	9.3
Aged 5 to 9	–	100.0	71.5	7.9	11.9	7.9
Aged 10 to 14	–	100.0	77.1	6.7	10.5	5.7
Aged 15 to 17	–	100.0	55.1	9.0	11.2	24.7
Aged 18 to 19	–	100.0	76.2	11.1	0.0	11.1
Aged 20 to 24	–	100.0	54.5	12.7	8.9	23.6
Aged 25 to 29	–	100.0	59.6	13.5	10.9	16.0
Aged 30 to 34	–	100.0	52.2	13.4	13.1	21.6
Aged 35 to 39	–	100.0	64.0	5.1	18.9	11.4
Aged 40 to 44	–	100.0	68.5	6.3	16.8	7.7
Aged 45 to 49	–	100.0	74.1	15.7	5.6	3.7
Aged 50 to 54	–	100.0	65.2	16.7	10.6	7.6
Aged 55 to 59	–	100.0	59.2	18.4	0.0	20.4
Aged 60 to 61	–	100.0	42.9	14.3	14.3	35.7
Aged 62 to 64	–	100.0	64.0	4.0	16.0	16.0
Aged 65 or older	–	100.0	52.5	31.3	7.5	8.8

Note: Asians are those who identify themselves as being of the race alone and those who identify themselves as being of the race in combination with other races. "–" means not applicable.
Source: Bureau of the Census, Geographic Mobility: 2009 to 2010, Detailed Tables, Internet site http://www.census.gov/hhes/migration/data/cps/cps2010.html; calculations by New Strategist

CHAPTER

5

Income

■ Asians are the most affluent householders in the United States. Their $65,073 median household income in 2009 was 31 percent greater than the all-household median of $49,777.

■ Asian married couples rank among the nation's income elite. Their median household income was $83,453 in 2009.

■ Between 1990 and 2009, the incomes of Asian men and women increased substantially—up 20 percent among men and 37 percent among women, after adjusting for inflation. Between 2000 and 2009, however, the median income of Asian men fell 4 percent, while the median income of Asian women continued to grow.

■ Asian men who work full-time have a median income 7 percent higher than the median for all men with full-time jobs. The median income of Asian women who work full-time is 21 percent above the median for all women who work full-time.

■ Among Asian men aged 25 or older who work full-time, the 62 percent majority has a bachelor's degree and their median earnings stood at $72,352 in 2009.

■ Twelve percent of Asians had incomes below the poverty level in 2009, a rate that has varied only slightly since 1990.

Asians Have the Highest Household Incomes

But their household income fell between 2000 and 2009.

Asians are the most affluent householders in the United States. Their $65,073 median household income in 2009 was 31 percent greater than the all-household median of $49,777—and higher than that of any other racial or ethnic group. Between 1990 and 2009, the median income of Asian households increased by 6 percent, after adjusting for inflation, a rate that exceeded the 4 percent increase in the median income of all households.

The Great Recession has hurt Asian households. The median income of Asian households fell 6 percent between 2000 and 2009, after adjusting for inflation. This decline was greater than the 5 percent drop in the median income of all households during those years. Nevertheless, the median income of Asian households remains well above average.

■ Asian households have higher incomes than black, Hispanic, or non-Hispanic white households because Asians are much better educated and have more earners in the home.

The median income of Asian households is 31 percent above average

(median income of total and Asian households, 2009)

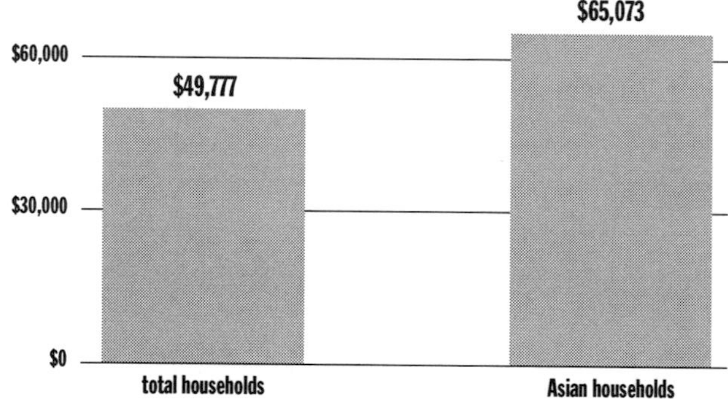

Table 5.1 Median Income of Total and Asian Households, 1990 to 2009

(median income of total and Asian households, and index of Asian to total, 1990 to 2009; percent change in income, 2000–09 and 1990–2009; in 2009 dollars)

	median income		
	total households	Asian households	index, Asian to total
2009	$49,777	$65,073	131
2008	50,112	65,318	130
2007	51,965	68,148	131
2006	51,278	67,979	133
2005	50,899	67,074	132
2004	50,343	65,236	130
2003	50,519	64,448	128
2002	50,563	62,338	123
2001	51,161	64,981	127
2000	52,301	69,448	133
1999	52,388	65,600	125
1998	51,100	61,288	120
1997	49,309	60,294	122
1996	48,315	58,911	122
1995	47,622	56,759	119
1994	46,175	57,937	125
1993	45,665	56,052	123
1992	45,888	56,621	123
1991	46,269	55,980	121
1990	47,637	61,170	128
Percent change			
2000 to 2009	–4.8%	–6.3%	–
1990 to 2009	4.5	6.4	–

Note: Beginning in 2002, data for Asians are for those who identify themselves as being of the race alone or being of the race in combination with other races. "–" means not applicable.
Source: Bureau of the Census, Historical Income Tables—Households, Internet site http://www.census.gov/hhes/www/income/histinc/h05.html; calculations by New Strategist

Asian Married Couples Have the Highest Incomes

More than 1 in 10 Asian couples have household incomes of $200,000 or more.

Asian married couples rank among the nation's income elite. Their median household income stood at a lofty $83,453 in 2009. Behind the high incomes of Asian households, and married couples in particular, are highly educated Asian men and women.

Median household income peaks at more than $100,000 for Asian married couples aged 35 to 44. This median is more than twice as high as the all-household median of $49,777.

Asian household income rises with education. The median income of Asian households headed by college graduates exceeded $90,000 in 2009. Most Asian householders with a graduate-level degree have household incomes of $100,000 or more.

■ Not only are Asian households headed by the highly educated, but they also have more earners than average, boosting incomes.

The median incomes of Asian households vary widely by household type

(median income of Asian households by household type, 2009)

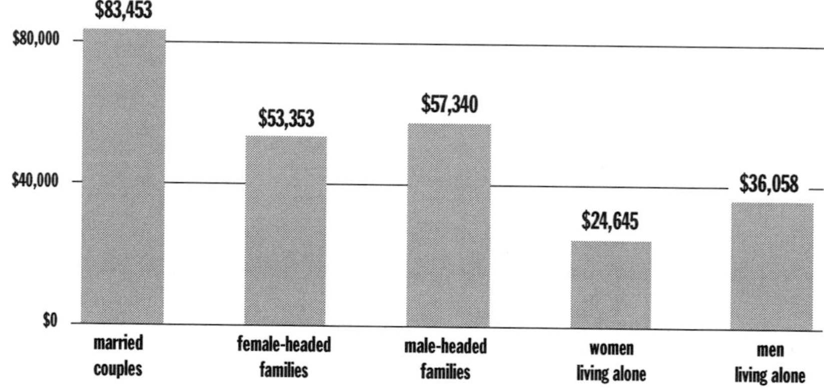

Table 5.2 Household Income by Household Type, 2009: Asian Households

(number and percent distribution of Asian households by household income and type of householder, 2009; households in thousands as of 2010)

		family households				nonfamily households				
							female householders		male householders	
	total	total	married couples	female hh, no spouse present	male hh, no spouse present	total	total	living alone	total	living alone
Asian households	**4,940**	**3,742**	**2,987**	**481**	**273**	**1,198**	**581**	**465**	**617**	**450**
Under $25,000	972	505	338	118	49	467	266	235	200	161
$25,000 to $49,999	968	686	512	107	69	281	124	104	157	121
$50,000 to $74,999	822	650	492	98	61	171	81	66	88	59
$75,000 to $99,999	588	474	379	68	28	115	38	25	77	57
$100,000 to $124,999	507	435	378	36	21	72	36	27	35	23
$125,000 to $149,999	318	293	257	20	16	26	7	4	19	12
$150,000 to $174,999	238	210	188	13	9	28	10	2	18	12
$175,000 to $199,999	145	133	122	9	1	12	4	2	8	1
$200,000 or more	381	354	320	13	22	26	14	2	12	5
Median income	$65,073	$76,089	$83,453	$53,353	$57,340	$35,259	$28,480	$24,645	$40,633	$36,058
Asian households	**100.0%**	**100.0%**	**100.0%**	**100.0%**	**100.0%**	**100.0%**	**100.0%**	**100.0%**	**100.0%**	**100.0%**
Under $25,000	19.7	13.5	11.3	24.5	17.9	39.0	45.8	50.5	32.4	35.8
$25,000 to $49,999	19.6	18.3	17.1	22.2	25.3	23.5	21.3	22.4	25.4	26.9
$50,000 to $74,999	16.6	17.4	16.5	20.4	22.3	14.3	13.9	14.2	14.3	13.1
$75,000 to $99,999	11.9	12.7	12.7	14.1	10.3	9.6	6.5	5.4	12.5	12.7
$100,000 to $124,999	10.3	11.6	12.7	7.5	7.7	6.0	6.2	5.8	5.7	5.1
$125,000 to $149,999	6.4	7.8	8.6	4.2	5.9	2.2	1.2	0.9	3.1	2.7
$150,000 to $174,999	4.8	5.6	6.3	2.7	3.3	2.3	1.7	0.4	2.9	2.7
$175,000 to $199,999	2.9	3.6	4.1	1.9	0.4	1.0	0.7	0.4	1.3	0.2
$200,000 or more	7.7	9.5	10.7	2.7	8.1	2.2	2.4	0.4	1.9	1.1

Note: Asians are those who identify themselves as being of the race alone and those who identify themselves as being of the race in combination with other races.
Source: Bureau of the Census, 2010 Current Population Survey, Internet site http://www.census.gov/hhes/www/cpstables/032010/hhinc/toc.htm; calculations by New Strategist

Table 5.3 Household Income by Age of Householder, 2009: Asian Households

(number and percent distribution of Asian households by household income and age of householder, 2009; households in thousands as of 2010)

	total	under 25	25 to 34	35 to 44	45 to 54	55 to 64	65 or older
Total Asian households	**4,940**	**292**	**1,057**	**1,180**	**1,020**	**709**	**682**
Under $25,000	972	105	196	139	142	113	278
$25,000 to $49,999	968	81	207	188	203	136	155
$50,000 to $74,999	822	50	208	203	166	113	82
$75,000 to $99,999	588	18	153	151	118	91	58
$100,000 to $124,999	507	20	108	151	110	79	40
$125,000 to $149,999	318	4	60	103	83	47	24
$150,000 to $174,999	238	4	51	60	59	50	16
$175,000 to $199,999	145	4	28	53	42	11	7
$200,000 or more	381	7	46	132	103	70	23
Median income	$65,073	$36,521	$63,066	$82,005	$75,335	$72,367	$31,926
Total Asian households	**100.0%**	**100.0%**	**100.0%**	**100.0%**	**100.0%**	**100.0%**	**100.0%**
Under $25,000	19.7	36.0	18.5	11.8	13.9	15.9	40.8
$25,000 to $49,999	19.6	27.7	19.6	15.9	19.9	19.2	22.7
$50,000 to $74,999	16.6	17.1	19.7	17.2	16.3	15.9	12.0
$75,000 to $99,999	11.9	6.2	14.5	12.8	11.6	12.8	8.5
$100,000 to $124,999	10.3	6.8	10.2	12.8	10.8	11.1	5.9
$125,000 to $149,999	6.4	1.4	5.7	8.7	8.1	6.6	3.5
$150,000 to $174,999	4.8	1.4	4.8	5.1	5.8	7.1	2.3
$175,000 to $199,999	2.9	1.4	2.6	4.5	4.1	1.6	1.0
$200,000 or more	7.7	2.4	4.4	11.2	10.1	9.9	3.4

Note: Asians are those who identify themselves as being of the race alone and those who identify themselves as being of the race in combination with other races.
Source: Bureau of the Census, 2010 Current Population Survey, Internet site http://www.census.gov/hhes/www/cpstables/032010/hhinc/toc.htm; calculations by New Strategist

Table 5.4 Median Household Income by Type of Household and Age of Householder, 2009: Asian Households

(median income of Asian households by household type and age of householder, and index of Asian median by type/age to $49,777 national median, 2009)

	total	under 25	25 to 34	35 to 44	45 to 54	55 to 64	65 or older
Total Asian households	**$65,073**	**$36,521**	**$63,066**	**$82,005**	**$75,335**	**$72,367**	**$31,926**
Married couples	83,453	–	74,124	100,763	95,441	82,448	45,385
Female householder, no spouse present	53,353	–	50,570	41,915	50,651	82,399	–
Male householder, no spouse present	57,340	–	–	–	–	–	–
Women living alone	24,645	–	47,599	–	–	–	14,345
Men living alone	36,058	–	35,051	56,800	–	–	–
INDEX							
Total Asian households	**131**	**73**	**127**	**165**	**151**	**145**	**64**
Married couples	168	–	149	202	192	166	91
Female householder, no spouse present	107	–	102	84	102	166	–
Male householder, no spouse present	115	–	–	–	–	–	–
Women living alone	50	–	96	–	–	–	29
Men living alone	72	–	70	114		–	–

Note: Asians are those who identify themselves as being of the race alone and those who identify themselves as being of the race in combination with other races. "–" means sample is too small to make a reliable estimate.
Source: Bureau of the Census, 2010 Current Population Survey, Internet site http://www.census.gov/hhes/www/cpstables/032010/hhinc/toc.htm; calculations by New Strategist

Table 5.5 Income of Asian Households by Educational Attainment of Householder, 2009

(number and percent distribution of Asian households headed by people aged 25 or older by household income and educational attainment of householder, 2009; households in thousands as of 2010)

							bachelor's degree or more				
	total	less than 9th grade	9th–12th grade, no diploma	high school graduate	some college, no degree	associate's degree	total	bachelor's degree	master's degree	professional degree	doctoral degree
Total Asian households	**4,648**	**197**	**174**	**802**	**450**	**357**	**2,668**	**1,600**	**709**	**145**	**214**
Under $25,000	867	104	74	213	126	47	301	221	55	13	13
$25,000 to $49,999	887	52	48	244	92	93	361	264	65	21	12
$50,000 to $74,999	772	25	17	145	80	75	429	292	93	19	26
$75,000 to $99,999	571	8	23	88	43	38	369	214	120	9	27
$100,000 to $124,999	486	4	6	48	41	49	336	204	86	11	33
$125,000 to $149,999	315	0	2	27	26	28	233	130	76	7	22
$150,000 to $174,999	235	2	2	8	15	12	194	100	66	12	18
$175,000 to $199,999	141	0	0	5	5	6	125	56	51	8	13
$200,000 or more	373	1	2	22	22	8	318	120	100	45	53
Median income	$67,164	$22,144	$30,695	$43,858	$51,868	$61,874	$90,854	$77,264	$104,719	$112,415	$116,635
Total Asian households	**100.0%**	**100.0%**	**100.0%**	**100.0%**	**100.0%**	**100.0%**	**100.0%**	**100.0%**	**100.0%**	**100.0%**	**100.0%**
Under $25,000	18.7	52.8	42.5	26.6	28.0	13.2	11.3	13.8	7.8	9.0	6.1
$25,000 to $49,999	19.1	26.4	27.6	30.4	20.4	26.1	13.5	16.5	9.2	14.5	5.6
$50,000 to $74,999	16.6	12.7	9.8	18.1	17.8	21.0	16.1	18.3	13.1	13.1	12.1
$75,000 to $99,999	12.3	4.1	13.2	11.0	9.6	10.6	13.8	13.4	16.9	6.2	12.6
$100,000 to $124,999	10.5	2.0	3.4	6.0	9.1	13.7	12.6	12.8	12.1	7.6	15.4
$125,000 to $149,999	6.8	0.0	1.1	3.4	5.8	7.8	8.7	8.1	10.7	4.8	10.3
$150,000 to $174,999	5.1	1.0	1.1	1.0	3.3	3.4	7.3	6.3	9.3	8.3	8.4
$175,000 to $199,999	3.0	0.0	0.0	0.6	1.1	1.7	4.7	3.5	7.2	5.5	6.1
$200,000 or more	8.0	0.5	1.1	2.7	4.9	2.2	11.9	7.5	14.1	31.0	24.8

Note: Asians are those who identify themselves as being of the race alone or the race in combination with other races.
Source: Bureau of the Census, 2010 Current Population Survey, Internet site http://www.census.gov/hhes/www/cpstables/032010/hhinc/toc.htm; calculations by New Strategist

Table 5.6 Income of Asian Households by Region, 2009

(number and percent distribution of Asian households by household income and region, 2009; households in thousands as of 2010)

	total	Northeast	Midwest	South	West
Total Asian households	**4,940**	**1,076**	**558**	**1,059**	**2,248**
Under $25,000	972	269	115	178	411
$25,000 to $49,999	968	198	88	225	458
$50,000 to $74,999	822	181	113	168	360
$75,000 to $99,999	588	120	59	130	278
$100,000 to $124,999	507	89	57	122	239
$125,000 to $149,999	318	60	46	53	160
$150,000 to $174,999	238	48	26	51	115
$175,000 to $199,999	145	39	21	37	47
$200,000 or more	381	75	34	92	180
Median income	$65,073	$58,226	$65,583	$69,313	$65,997
Total Asian households	**100.0%**	**100.0%**	**100.0%**	**100.0%**	**100.0%**
Under $25,000	19.7	25.0	20.6	16.8	18.3
$25,000 to $49,999	19.6	18.4	15.8	21.2	20.4
$50,000 to $74,999	16.6	16.8	20.3	15.9	16.0
$75,000 to $99,999	11.9	11.2	10.6	12.3	12.4
$100,000 to $124,999	10.3	8.3	10.2	11.5	10.6
$125,000 to $149,999	6.4	5.6	8.2	5.0	7.1
$150,000 to $174,999	4.8	4.5	4.7	4.8	5.1
$175,000 to $199,999	2.9	3.6	3.8	3.5	2.1
$200,000 or more	7.7	7.0	6.1	8.7	8.0

Note: Asians are those who identify themselves as being of the race alone or the race in combination with other races.
Source: Bureau of the Census, 2010 Current Population Survey, Internet site http://www.census.gov/hhes/www/cpstables/032010/hhinc/toc.htm; calculations by New Strategist

The Incomes of Asian Women Are Growing

Asian men have lost ground since 2000.

The median incomes of Asian men and women have increased substantially since 1990, up 20 percent for men and 37 percent for women, after adjusting for inflation. The median income of Asian men stood at $36,886 in 2009, a bit higher than the median income of the average man. Between 2000 and 2009, the median income of Asian men fell 4 percent, after adjusting for inflation—a smaller decrease than the 9 percent loss for all men.

The median income of Asian women stood at $24,170 in 2009, fully 15 percent greater than the median income of the average woman. The incomes of Asian women have been growing faster than average for years, and this trend has not let up. Between 2000 and 2009, the median income of Asian women climbed 12 percent versus a 5 percent gain for the average woman during those years.

■ The educational level of Asian men and women guarantees that their incomes will remain well above average in the years to come.

Asians have above-average incomes

(median income of total people and Asians, by sex, 2009)

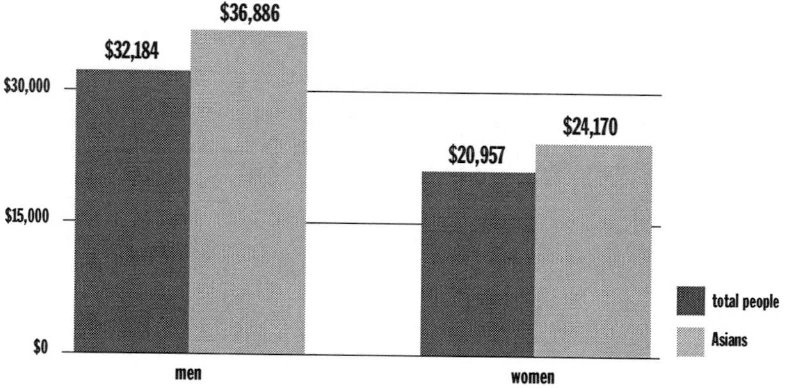

Table 5.7 Median Income of Total and Asian Men, 1990 to 2009

(median income of total and Asian men aged 15 or older with income, and index of Asian to total, 1990 to 2009; percent change in income for selected years; in 2009 dollars)

	median income		
	total men	Asian men	index, Asian to total
2009	$32,184	$36,886	115
2008	33,035	36,067	109
2007	34,341	37,996	111
2006	34,324	39,473	115
2005	34,362	36,297	106
2004	34,652	36,867	106
2003	34,907	37,013	106
2002	34,860	36,769	105
2001	35,257	37,674	107
2000	35,303	38,404	109
1999	35,134	35,887	102
1998	34,814	33,017	95
1997	33,595	33,373	99
1996	32,445	31,819	98
1995	31,531	30,972	98
1994	31,085	32,759	105
1993	30,845	31,633	103
1992	30,639	29,792	97
1991	31,437	30,145	96
1990	32,284	30,854	96
Percent change			
2000 to 2009	–8.8%	–4.0%	–
1990 to 2009	–0.3	19.5	–

Note: Beginning in 2002, data for Asians are for those who identify themselves as being of the race alone or the race in combination with other races. The Asian/total indexes are calculated by dividing the median income of Asian men by the median income of total men and multiplying by 100. "–" means not applicable.
Source: Bureau of the Census, Current Population Surveys, Internet site http://www.census.gov/hhes/www/income/data/historical/people/index.html; calculations by New Strategist

Table 5.8 Median Income of Total and Asian Women, 1990 to 2009

(median income of total and Asian women aged 15 or older with income, and index of Asian to total, 1990 to 2009; percent change in income for selected years; in 2009 dollars)

	median income		
	total women	Asian women	index, Asian to total
2009	$20,957	$24,170	115
2008	20,788	22,928	110
2007	21,643	24,926	115
2006	21,291	23,491	110
2005	20,410	23,757	116
2004	20,062	23,410	117
2003	20,128	20,851	104
2002	20,045	21,339	106
2001	20,129	22,444	112
2000	20,007	21,618	108
1999	19,701	21,623	110
1998	18,963	20,012	106
1997	18,259	19,071	104
1996	17,445	19,921	114
1995	16,952	17,975	106
1994	16,410	17,692	108
1993	16,146	18,074	112
1992	16,048	17,781	111
1991	16,089	16,934	105
1990	16,020	17,637	110
Percent change			
2000 to 2009	4.7%	11.8%	–
1990 to 2009	30.8	37.0	–

Note: Beginning in 2002, data for Asians are for those who identify themselves as being of the race alone or being of the race in combination with other races. The Asian/total indexes are calculated by dividing the median income of Asian women by the median income of total women and multiplying by 100. "–" means not applicable.
Source: Bureau of the Census, Current Population Surveys, Internet site http://www.census.gov/hhes/www/income/data/historical/people/index.html; calculations by New Strategist

Median Income of Asian Men Peaks in 35-to-44 Age Group

Nearly one in four Asian men aged 35 to 44 has an income of $100,000 or more.

The median income of Asian men peaks at $57,473 in the 35-to-44 age group. Among those in the age group who work full-time, median income was a lofty $70,312.

The median income of Asian women also peaks in the 35-to-44 age group. At $32,119, this is well below the median income of their male counterparts. Among Asian women who work full-time, median income tops $48,000 in the broad 25-to-44 age group.

Asian men who work full-time have a median income 7 percent above the median for all men with full-time jobs. The median income of Asian women who work full-time is 21 percent higher than the average for all women. Among Asians who work full-time, women earn 85 percent as much as men.

■ Asian incomes are above average because their educational attainment is far higher than any other racial or ethnic group.

The incomes of Asian men have been growing faster than average for years

(percent change in median income of total and Asian men working full-time, 1990 to 2009; in 2009 dollars)

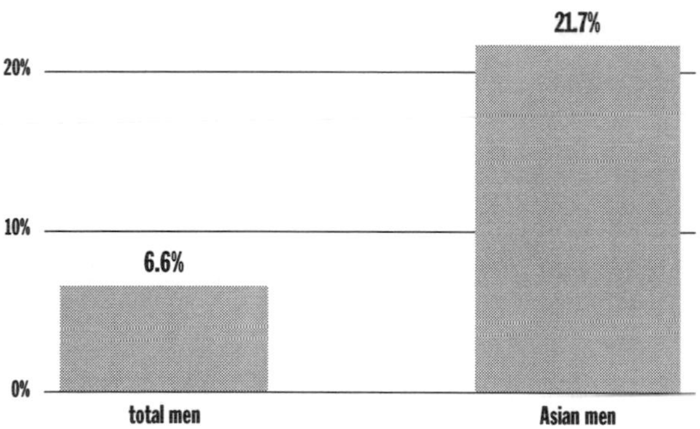

Table 5.9 Income of Asian Men by Age, 2009

(number and percent distribution of Asian men aged 15 or older by income and age, 2009; median income of men with income and of men working full-time, year-round; percent working full-time, year-round; men in thousands as of 2010)

	total	15 to 24	25 to 34	35 to 44	45 to 54	55 to 64	65 or older
Total Asian men	**5,614**	**1,009**	**1,215**	**1,169**	**965**	**680**	**576**
Without income	786	464	108	58	48	60	48
With income	4,828	545	1,107	1,111	917	620	528
Under $10,000	719	310	128	62	61	45	110
$10,000 to $19,999	672	90	148	103	110	81	138
$20,000 to $29,999	592	65	145	93	97	116	73
$30,000 to $39,999	562	35	153	111	130	80	52
$40,000 to $49,999	410	15	100	94	107	59	34
$50,000 to $59,999	350	6	107	102	66	43	28
$60,000 to $69,999	255	8	74	74	49	38	12
$70,000 to $79,999	245	4	76	75	38	32	23
$80,000 to $89,999	160	3	42	52	40	13	11
$90,000 to $99,999	159	4	24	68	35	26	2
$100,000 or more	701	5	109	275	183	87	44
Median income of men with income	$36,886	$7,742	$37,382	$57,473	$44,314	$36,937	$21,652
Median income of full-time workers	52,849	25,463	50,879	70,312	51,914	50,511	59,998
Percent working full-time	54.3%	14.8%	63.0%	75.5%	75.8%	60.9%	18.2%
PERCENT DISTRIBUTION							
Total Asian men	**100.0%**	**100.0%**	**100.0%**	**100.0%**	**100.0%**	**100.0%**	**100.0%**
Without income	14.0	46.0	8.9	5.0	5.0	8.8	8.3
With income	86.0	54.0	91.1	95.0	95.0	91.2	91.7
Under $10,000	12.8	30.7	10.5	5.3	6.3	6.6	19.1
$10,000 to $19,999	12.0	8.9	12.2	8.8	11.4	11.9	24.0
$20,000 to $29,999	10.5	6.4	11.9	8.0	10.1	17.1	12.7
$30,000 to $39,999	10.0	3.5	12.6	9.5	13.5	11.8	9.0
$40,000 to $49,999	7.3	1.5	8.2	8.0	11.1	8.7	5.9
$50,000 to $59,999	6.2	0.6	8.8	8.7	6.8	6.3	4.9
$60,000 to $69,999	4.5	0.8	6.1	6.3	5.1	5.6	2.1
$70,000 to $79,999	4.4	0.4	6.3	6.4	3.9	4.7	4.0
$80,000 to $89,999	2.9	0.3	3.5	4.4	4.1	1.9	1.9
$90,000 to $99,999	2.8	0.4	2.0	5.8	3.6	3.8	0.3
$100,000 or more	12.5	0.5	9.0	23.5	19.0	12.8	7.6

Note: Asians are those who identify themselves as being of the race alone and those who identify themselves as being of the race in combination with other races.
Source: Bureau of the Census, 2010 Current Population Survey, Internet site http://www.census.gov/hhes/www/cpstables/032010/perinc/toc.htm; calculations by New Strategist

Table 5.10 Income of Asian Women by Age, 2009

(number and percent distribution of Asian women aged 15 or older by income and age, 2009; median income of women with income and of women working full-time, year-round; percent working full-time, year-round; women in thousands as of 2010)

	total	15 to 24	25 to 34	35 to 44	45 to 54	55 to 64	65 or older
Total Asian women	**6,260**	**983**	**1,299**	**1,301**	**1,068**	**807**	**802**
Without income	1,337	461	267	221	124	131	131
With income	4,923	522	1,032	1,080	944	676	671
Under $10,000	1,315	309	202	209	161	154	280
$10,000 to $19,999	831	88	157	112	148	128	196
$20,000 to $29,999	703	68	143	177	146	94	75
$30,000 to $39,999	495	32	107	118	113	92	33
$40,000 to $49,999	376	18	113	88	86	55	16
$50,000 to $59,999	286	1	93	78	53	35	25
$60,000 to $69,999	209	6	41	67	49	26	19
$70,000 to $79,999	174	0	58	46	41	26	2
$80,000 to $89,999	113	0	35	30	35	9	6
$90,000 to $99,999	103	0	26	43	20	11	4
$100,000 or more	316	0	54	113	92	44	13
Median income of women with income	$24,170	$7,368	$30,670	$32,119	$30,761	$25,616	$11,757
Median income of full-time workers	45,020	23,190	48,278	48,569	41,678	38,603	–
Percent working full-time	36.9%	9.6%	44.6%	49.7%	54.1%	43.7%	7.4%
PERCENT DISTRIBUTION							
Total Asian women	**100.0%**	**100.0%**	**100.0%**	**100.0%**	**100.0%**	**100.0%**	**100.0%**
Without income	21.4	46.9	20.6	17.0	11.6	16.2	16.3
With income	78.6	53.1	79.4	83.0	88.4	83.8	83.7
Under $10,000	21.0	31.4	15.6	16.1	15.1	19.1	34.9
$10,000 to $19,999	13.3	9.0	12.1	8.6	13.9	15.9	24.4
$20,000 to $29,999	11.2	6.9	11.0	13.6	13.7	11.6	9.4
$30,000 to $39,999	7.9	3.3	8.2	9.1	10.6	11.4	4.1
$40,000 to $49,999	6.0	1.8	8.7	6.8	8.1	6.8	2.0
$50,000 to $59,999	4.6	0.1	7.2	6.0	5.0	4.3	3.1
$60,000 to $69,999	3.3	0.6	3.2	5.1	4.6	3.2	2.4
$70,000 to $79,999	2.8	0.0	4.5	3.5	3.8	3.2	0.2
$80,000 to $89,999	1.8	0.0	2.7	2.3	3.3	1.1	0.7
$90,000 to $99,999	1.6	0.0	2.0	3.3	1.9	1.4	0.5
$100,000 or more	5.0	0.0	4.2	8.7	8.6	5.5	1.6

Note: Asians are those who identify themselves as being of the race alone and those who identify themselves as being of the race in combination with other races. "–" means sample is too small to make a reliable estimate.
Source: Bureau of the Census, 2010 Current Population Survey, Internet site http://www.census.gov/hhes/www/cpstables/032010/perinc/toc.htm; calculations by New Strategist

Table 5.11 Median Income of Total and Asian Men Who Work Full-Time, 1990 to 2009

(median income of total and Asian men who work full-time, year-round, and index of Asian to total, 1990 to 2009; percent change in income for selected years; in 2009 dollars)

	median income of full-time workers		
	total men	Asian men	index, Asian to total
2009	$49,164	$52,849	107
2008	47,598	51,415	108
2007	47,818	52,760	110
2006	47,828	55,076	115
2005	46,352	53,903	116
2004	47,315	52,848	112
2003	48,402	53,439	110
2002	48,296	50,610	105
2001	48,626	51,727	106
2000	48,441	51,479	106
1999	48,209	49,446	103
1998	47,640	46,801	98
1997	46,968	47,027	100
1996	45,655	48,717	107
1995	44,999	44,785	100
1994	45,242	46,499	103
1993	45,426	45,733	101
1992	46,182	46,315	100
1991	46,583	47,894	103
1990	46,103	43,429	94
Percent change			
2000 to 2009	1.5%	2.7%	–
1990 to 2009	6.6	21.7	–

Note: Beginning in 2002, data for Asians are for those who identify themselves as being of the race alone or the race in combination with other races. The Asian/total indexes are calculated by dividing the median income of Asian men by the median income of total men and multiplying by 100. "–" means not applicable.
Source: Bureau of the Census, Current Population Surveys, Internet site http://www.census.gov/hhes/www/income/data/historical/people/index.html; calculations by New Strategist

Table 5.12 Median Income of Total and Asian Women Who Work Full-Time, 1990 to 2009

(median income of total and Asian women who work full-time, year-round, and index of Asian to total, 1990 to 2009; percent change in income for selected years; in 2009 dollars)

	median income of full-time workers		
	total women	Asian women	index, Asian to total
2009	$37,234	$45,020	121
2008	36,549	43,892	120
2007	37,414	42,677	114
2006	37,222	42,874	115
2005	36,539	40,386	111
2004	36,469	41,456	114
2003	36,915	40,185	109
2002	36,925	38,190	103
2001	36,855	37,902	103
2000	36,274	38,519	106
1999	35,228	38,916	110
1998	35,291	36,720	104
1997	34,683	38,791	112
1996	33,943	35,819	106
1995	33,229	35,644	107
1994	33,296	35,773	107
1993	32,843	36,600	111
1992	33,092	36,158	109
1991	32,629	33,165	102
1990	32,758	35,051	107
Percent change			
2000 to 2009	2.6%	16.9%	–
1990 to 2009	13.7	28.4	–

Note: Beginning in 2002, data for Asians are for those who identify themselves as being of the race alone or the race in combination with other races. The Asian/total indexes are calculated by dividing the median income of Asian women by the median income of total women and multiplying by 100. "–" means not applicable.
Source: Bureau of the Census, Current Population Surveys, Internet site http://www.census.gov/hhes/www/income/data/historical/people/index.html; calculations by New Strategist

Table 5.13 Median Income of Asians Who Work Full-Time by Sex, 1990 to 2009

(median income of Asians working full-time, year-round, by sex, and Asian women's income as a percent of Asian men's income, 1990 to 2009; percent change in income for selected years; in 2009 dollars)

	median income of full-time workers		women's income as a percent of men's income
	Asian men	Asian women	
2009	$52,849	$45,020	85.2%
2008	51,415	43,892	85.4
2007	52,760	42,677	80.9
2006	55,076	42,874	77.8
2005	53,903	40,386	74.9
2004	52,848	41,456	78.4
2003	53,439	40,185	75.2
2002	50,610	38,190	75.5
2001	51,727	37,902	73.3
2000	51,479	38,519	74.8
1999	49,446	38,916	78.7
1998	46,801	36,720	78.5
1997	47,027	38,791	82.5
1996	48,717	35,819	73.5
1995	44,785	35,644	79.6
1994	46,499	35,773	76.9
1993	45,733	36,600	80.0
1992	46,315	36,158	78.1
1991	47,894	33,165	69.2
1990	43,429	35,051	80.7
Percent change			
2000 to 2009	2.7%	16.9%	–
1990 to 2009	21.7	28.4	–

Note: Beginning in 2002, data for Asians are for those who identify themselves as being of the race alone or the race in combination with other races. "–" means not applicable.
Source: Bureau of the Census, Current Population Surveys, Internet site http://www.census.gov/hhes/www/income/data/historical/people/index.html; calculations by New Strategist

Asian Earnings Rise with Education

Most Asians with full-time jobs have a bachelor's degree.

Asian household incomes and earnings are well above average because most Asians are college educated. Among Asian men aged 25 or older who work full-time, the 62 percent majority has at least a bachelor's degree. Their median earnings stood at $72,352 in 2009. Asian woman are almost as well educated, with 57 percent of full-time workers aged 25 or older having a bachelor's degree. Their median earnings were $60,547 in 2009.

Less-educated Asian men and women have much lower earnings. Asian men who went no further than high school earned only $32,189 in 2009. Asian women who went no further than high school earned just $27,411.

■ Two out of three Asian men with a professional degree earn $100,000 or more.

Asian men with a bachelor's degree earn more than twice as much as high school graduates

(median earnings of Asian men aged 25 or older who work full-time, by educational attainment, 2009)

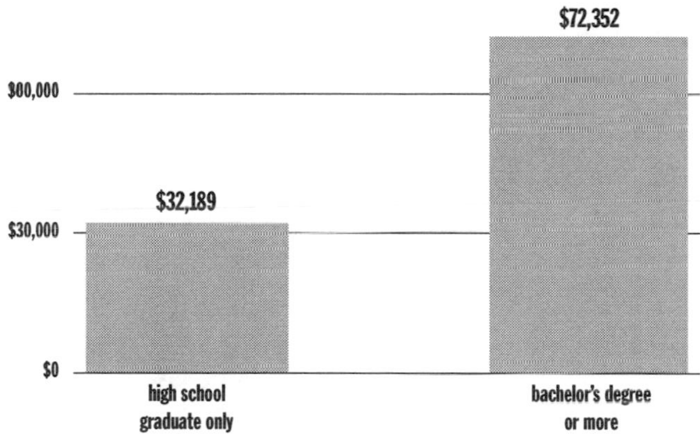

Table 5.14 Earnings of Asian Men Who Work Full-Time by Education, 2009

(number and percent distribution of Asian men aged 25 or older working full-time, year-round by earnings and educational attainment, and median earnings of those with earnings, 2009; men in thousands as of 2010)

							bachelor's degree or more				
	total	less than 9th grade	9th–12th grade, no diploma	high school graduate	some college, no degree	associate's degree	total	bachelor's degree	master's degree	professional degree	doctoral degree
Asian men working full-time	**2,898**	**52**	**102**	**481**	**273**	**188**	**1,803**	**969**	**527**	**127**	**181**
Under $10,000	45	1	3	15	3	4	18	12	4	0	2
$10,000 to $19,999	193	17	29	68	21	7	52	36	10	0	7
$20,000 to $29,999	310	15	37	113	45	25	74	64	7	3	2
$30,000 to $39,999	411	4	10	104	50	42	198	159	29	4	7
$40,000 to $49,999	318	9	14	64	46	30	154	111	23	11	11
$50,000 to $59,999	303	4	0	42	49	33	177	97	52	12	18
$60,000 to $69,999	227	0	4	30	32	10	152	106	34	5	8
$70,000 to $79,999	195	0	3	12	8	7	162	83	67	2	10
$80,000 to $89,999	125	0	0	7	5	4	110	54	41	4	9
$90,000 to $99,999	141	0	0	9	2	7	123	51	50	2	19
$100,000 or more	630	0	0	17	9	19	585	199	212	84	90
Median earnings	$52,394	–	$23,860	$32,189	$41,604	$45,199	$72,352	$60,300	$89,698	$144,883	$99,282
Asian men working full-time	**100.0%**	**100.0%**	**100.0%**	**100.0%**	**100.0%**	**100.0%**	**100.0%**	**100.0%**	**100.0%**	**100.0%**	**100.0%**
Under $10,000	1.6	1.9	2.9	3.1	1.1	2.1	1.0	1.2	0.8	0.0	1.1
$10,000 to $19,999	6.7	32.7	28.4	14.1	7.7	3.7	2.9	3.7	1.9	0.0	3.9
$20,000 to $29,999	10.7	28.8	36.3	23.5	16.5	13.3	4.1	6.6	1.3	2.4	1.1
$30,000 to $39,999	14.2	7.7	9.8	21.6	18.3	22.3	11.0	16.4	5.5	3.1	3.9
$40,000 to $49,999	11.0	17.3	13.7	13.3	16.8	16.0	8.5	11.5	4.4	8.7	6.1
$50,000 to $59,999	10.5	7.7	0.0	8.7	17.9	17.6	9.8	10.0	9.9	9.4	9.9
$60,000 to $69,999	7.8	0.0	3.9	6.2	11.7	5.3	8.4	10.9	6.5	3.9	4.4
$70,000 to $79,999	6.7	0.0	2.9	2.5	2.9	3.7	9.0	8.6	12.7	1.6	5.5
$80,000 to $89,999	4.3	0.0	0.0	1.5	1.8	2.1	6.1	5.6	7.8	3.1	5.0
$90,000 to $99,999	4.9	0.0	0.0	1.9	0.7	3.7	6.8	5.3	9.5	1.6	10.5
$100,000 or more	21.7	0.0	0.0	3.5	3.3	10.1	32.4	20.5	40.2	66.1	49.7

Note: Asians are those who identify themselves as being of the race alone and those who identify themselves as being of the race in combination with other races. "–" means sample is too small to make a reliable estimate.
Source: Bureau of the Census, 2010 Current Population Survey, Internet site http://www.census.gov/hhes/www/cpstables/032010/perinc/toc.htm; calculations by New Strategist

Table 5.15 Earnings of Asian Women Who Work Full-Time by Education, 2009

(number and percent distribution of Asian women aged 25 or older working full-time, year-round by earnings and educational attainment, and median earnings of those with earnings, 2009; women in thousands as of 2010)

							bachelor's degree or more				
	total	less than 9th grade	9th–12th grade, no diploma	high school graduate	some college, no degree	associate's degree	total	bachelor's degree	master's degree	professional degree	doctoral degree
Asian women working full-time	**2,209**	**86**	**64**	**425**	**189**	**183**	**1,263**	**807**	**322**	**62**	**72**
Under $10,000	47	9	3	15	10	0	11	11	0	0	0
$10,000 to $19,999	211	35	10	93	18	11	46	44	1	2	0
$20,000 to $29,999	361	23	33	126	45	30	104	88	10	2	4
$30,000 to $39,999	337	13	7	90	41	51	135	113	21	0	2
$40,000 to $49,999	283	6	6	46	26	30	171	123	34	8	6
$50,000 to $59,999	230	0	0	22	29	27	151	110	29	2	9
$60,000 to $69,999	158	0	1	11	9	13	124	66	42	6	10
$70,000 to $79,999	145	0	2	5	9	9	120	57	51	6	5
$80,000 to $89,999	90	0	0	5	0	7	77	44	22	7	6
$90,000 to $99,999	86	0	0	2	0	2	83	49	22	2	9
$100,000 or more	257	0	0	13	3	1	240	103	88	28	21
Median earnings	$45,087	$20,071	–	$27,411	$35,383	$39,288	$60,547	$51,135	$72,149	–	–
Asian women working full-time	**100.0%**	**100.0%**	**100.0%**	**100.0%**	**100.0%**	**100.0%**	**100.0%**	**100.0%**	**100.0%**	**100.0%**	**100.0%**
Under $10,000	2.1	10.5	4.7	3.5	5.3	0.0	0.9	1.4	0.0	0.0	0.0
$10,000 to $19,999	9.6	40.7	15.6	21.9	9.5	6.0	3.6	5.5	0.3	3.2	0.0
$20,000 to $29,999	16.3	26.7	51.6	29.6	23.8	16.4	8.2	10.9	3.1	3.2	5.6
$30,000 to $39,999	15.3	15.1	10.9	21.2	21.7	27.9	10.7	14.0	6.5	0.0	2.8
$40,000 to $49,999	12.8	7.0	9.4	10.8	13.8	16.4	13.5	15.2	10.6	12.9	8.3
$50,000 to $59,999	10.4	0.0	0.0	5.2	15.3	14.8	12.0	13.6	9.0	3.2	12.5
$60,000 to $69,999	7.2	0.0	1.6	2.6	4.8	7.1	9.8	8.2	13.0	9.7	13.9
$70,000 to $79,999	6.6	0.0	3.1	1.2	4.8	4.9	9.5	7.1	15.8	9.7	6.9
$80,000 to $89,999	4.1	0.0	0.0	1.2	0.0	3.8	6.1	5.5	6.8	11.3	8.3
$90,000 to $99,999	3.9	0.0	0.0	0.5	0.0	1.1	6.6	6.1	6.8	3.2	12.5
$100,000 or more	11.6	0.0	0.0	3.1	1.6	0.5	19.0	12.8	27.3	45.2	29.2

Note: Asians are those who identify themselves as being of the race alone and those who identify themselves as being of the race in combination with other races. "–" means sample is too small to make a reliable estimate.
Source: Bureau of the Census, 2010 Current Population Survey, Internet site http://www.census.gov/hhes/www/cpstables/032010/perinc/toc.htm; calculations by New Strategist

Few Asians Are Poor

Asians account for just 4 percent of the nation's poor.

In 2009, 12.4 percent of Asians lived below the poverty level, a rate that has varied only slightly since 1990. The Asian poverty rate peaks at 23.8 percent among those aged 18 to 24. Many of these young adults are students, and their incomes will rise after they earn their degree and embark on a career. The Asian poverty rate bottoms out at 7.1 percent among those aged 55 to 59.

Among Asian married couples, 8.0 percent are poor. The poverty rate is highest, at 23.4 percent, among Asian female-headed families with children.

■ The high level of educational attainment among Asians boosts their incomes and keeps them out of poverty.

The poverty rate of Asians is below average

(percent of total people and Asians below poverty level, 2009)

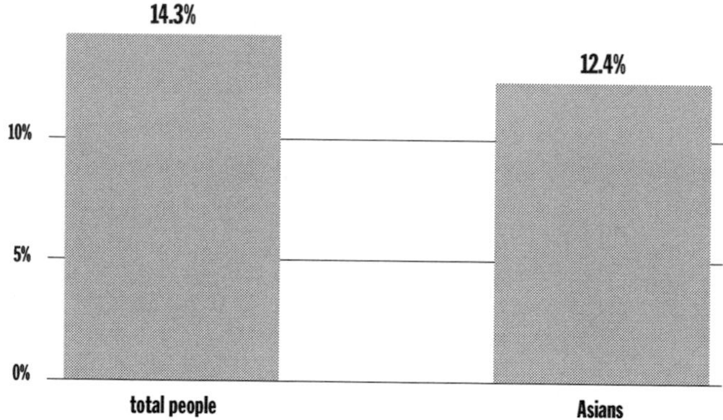

Table 5.16 Total People and Asians below Poverty Level, 1990 to 2009

(number and percent of total people and Asians below poverty level, and Asian share of poor, 1990 to 2009; people in thousands as of the following year)

	total people in poverty		Asians in poverty		Asian share
	number	percent	number	percent	of total
2009	43,569	14.3%	1,901	12.4%	4.4%
2008	39,829	13.2	1,686	11.6	4.2
2007	37,276	12.5	1,467	10.2	3.9
2006	36,460	12.3	1,447	10.1	4.0
2005	36,950	12.6	1,501	10.9	4.1
2004	37,040	12.7	1,295	9.7	3.5
2003	35,861	12.5	1,527	11.8	4.3
2002	34,570	12.1	1,243	10.0	3.6
2001	32,907	11.7	1,275	10.2	3.9
2000	31,581	11.3	1,258	9.9	4.0
1999	32,791	11.9	1,285	10.7	3.9
1998	34,476	12.7	1,360	12.5	3.9
1997	35,574	13.3	1,468	14.0	4.1
1996	36,529	13.7	1,454	14.5	4.0
1995	36,425	13.8	1,411	14.6	3.9
1994	38,059	14.5	974	14.6	2.6
1993	39,265	15.1	1,134	15.3	2.9
1992	38,014	14.8	985	12.7	2.6
1991	35,708	14.2	996	13.8	2.8
1990	33,585	13.5	858	12.2	2.6

Note: Beginning in 2002, data for Asians are for those who identify themselves as being of the race alone or as being of the race in combination with other races.
Source: Bureau of the Census, Current Population Surveys, Internet site http://www.census.gov/hhes/www/poverty/data/historical/index.html; calculations by New Strategist

Table 5.17 Total People and Asians below Poverty Level by Age, 2009

(number and percent of total people and Asians below poverty level by age, and Asian share of total, 2009; numbers in thousands)

	total		Asian		
	number	percent	number	percent	share of total
Total people in poverty	**43,569**	**14.3%**	**1,901**	**12.4%**	**4.4%**
Under age 18	15,451	20.7	531	13.3	3.4
Under age 5	5,211	24.5	164	13.1	3.1
Aged 5 to 17	10,241	19.2	367	13.4	3.6
Aged 18 to 64	24,684	12.9	1,154	11.7	4.7
Aged 18 to 24	6,071	20.7	332	23.8	5.5
Aged 25 to 34	6,123	14.9	281	11.2	4.6
Aged 35 to 44	4,756	11.8	222	9.0	4.7
Aged 45 to 54	4,421	10.0	180	8.8	4.1
Aged 55 to 59	1,792	9.3	60	7.1	3.3
Aged 60 to 64	1,520	9.4	79	12.0	5.2
Aged 65 or older	3,433	8.9	216	15.7	6.3
Aged 65 to 74	1,675	8.0	104	13.7	6.2
Aged 75 or older	1,758	10.0	112	18.1	6.4

Note: Asians are those who identify themselves as being of the race alone or in combination with other races.
Source: Bureau of the Census, 2010 Current Population Survey, Internet site http://www.census.gov/hhes/www/cpstables/032010/pov/toc.htm; calculations by New Strategist

Table 5.18 Asians below Poverty Level by Age and Sex, 2009

(number and percent of Asians below poverty level by age and sex, and female share of poor, 2009; numbers in thousands)

	total	males		females		
		number	percent	number	percent	share of poor
Total Asians in poverty	**1,901**	**897**	**12.2%**	**1,004**	**12.7%**	**52.8%**
Under age 18	531	254	12.6	277	14.0	52.2
Under age 5	164	81	12.7	84	13.6	51.2
Aged 5 to 17	367	174	12.6	193	14.1	52.6
Aged 18 to 64	1,154	549	11.5	605	11.8	52.4
Aged 18 to 24	332	170	23.4	162	24.4	48.8
Aged 25 to 34	281	146	12.0	136	10.5	48.4
Aged 35 to 44	222	95	8.1	127	9.8	57.2
Aged 45 to 54	180	85	8.8	95	8.9	52.8
Aged 55 to 59	60	21	5.5	39	8.6	65.0
Aged 60 to 64	79	33	11.1	46	12.8	58.2
Aged 65 or older	216	93	16.2	122	15.3	56.5
Aged 65 to 74	104	47	13.6	57	13.8	54.8
Aged 75 or older	112	46	20.1	65	16.8	58.0

Note: Asians are those who identify themselves as being of the race alone or in combination with other races.
Source: Bureau of the Census, 2010 Current Population Survey, Internet site http://www.census.gov/hhes/www/cpstables/032010/pov/toc.htm; calculations by New Strategist

Table 5.19 Number and Percent of Asian Families below Poverty Level by Family Type, 2002 to 2009

(number and percent of Asian families below poverty level by family type, 2002 to 2009; families in thousands as of the following year)

	total Asian families in poverty		married couples		female householder, no spouse present		male householder, no spouse present	
	number	percent	number	percent	number	percent	number	percent
2009	359	9.6%	239	8.0%	87	18.0%	34	12.3%
2008	356	9.8	254	8.7	76	16.5	26	10.1
2007	281	8.1	187	6.8	77	17.0	17	7.0
2006	272	7.8	183	6.4	61	15.6	27	11.4
2005	306	9.1	201	7.5	83	20.0	22	8.8
2004	243	7.4	150	5.7	54	14.0	39	14.8
2003	320	10.0	203	7.9	89	23.5	28	11.8
2002	218	7.4	137	5.9	51	14.3	30	12.6

Note: Asians are those who identify themselves as being of the race alone or the race in combination with other races.
Source: Bureau of the Census, Current Population Surveys, Internet site http://www.census.gov/hhes/www/poverty/data/historical/index.html; calculations by New Strategist

Table 5.20 Number and Percent of Asian Families with Children below Poverty Level by Family Type, 2002 to 2009

(number and percent of Asian families with related children under age 18 below poverty level by family type, 2002 to 2009; families in thousands as of the following year)

	total Asian families with children in poverty		married couples		female householder, no spouse present		male householder, no spouse present	
	number	percent	number	percent	number	percent	number	percent
2009	238	11.5%	153	9.0%	64	23.4%	21	20.7%
2008	204	10.5	141	8.8	52	21.4	11	12.5
2007	178	9.6	109	7.1	65	27.8	4	5.1
2006	178	9.5	116	7.3	46	23.8	16	19.2
2005	189	10.4	121	8.1	54	24.3	14	15.5
2004	154	8.4	97	6.3	43	19.5	15	15.4
2003	199	10.9	121	8.0	66	28.2	12	15.2
2002	151	9.2	94	6.9	39	21.0	18	21.1

Note: Asians are those who identify themselves as being of the race alone or the race in combination with other races.
Source: Bureau of the Census, Current Population Surveys, Internet site http://www.census.gov/hhes/www/poverty/data/historical/index.html; calculations by New Strategist

CHAPTER

6

Labor Force

■ In 2010, Asians accounted for 4.7 percent of the labor force. Seventy-three percent of Asian men and 57 percent of Asian women are in the labor force.

■ Asians are less likely to be unemployed than the average worker. In 2010, the Asian unemployment rate was 7.5 percent, substantially lower than the 9.6 percent rate among all workers.

■ Asians account for a large share of some occupations. They are 28 percent of medical scientists and computer software engineers. Sixteen percent of physicians and 15 percent of pharmacists are Asian.

■ Asians are the most highly educated workers. The 57 percent majority of Asian workers has a bachelor's degree.

■ Asian households have more workers than average. There are 1.50 workers in Asian households compared with 1.32 workers in the average household.

■ The Asian labor force is projected to grow 30 percent between 2008 and 2018, faster than the 8 percent growth projected for the overall labor force.

The Asian Population Is a Small Share of Workers

The labor force participation rate peaks among Asian men aged 45 to 49.

Seven million Asians aged 16 or older were in the civilian labor force in 2010, but they account for fewer than 5 percent of the nation's workers. Seventy-three percent of Asian men and 57 percent of Asian women are in the labor force.

The labor force participation rate of Asians is well below average among men and women under age 25. College enrollment is behind the low rates. Most Asians have a college degree, and many postpone getting a job until they earn a bachelor's degree. Asian men aged 45 or older are more likely to be in the labor force than the average man.

■ Unemployment among Asians is higher than it was a few years ago, but well below average in most age groups.

Unemployment rate among Asians is lower than average

(unemployment rate of total people and Asians in the civilian labor force, 2010)

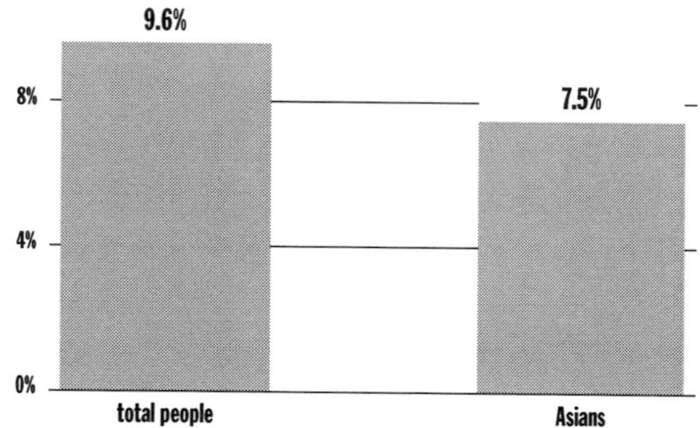

Table 6.1 Total and Asian Labor Force by Sex and Age, 2010

(number of total people and Asians aged 16 or older in the civilian labor force, and Asian share of total, by sex and age, 2010; numbers in thousands)

	total	Asian	Asian share of total
Total in labor force	**153,889**	**7,248**	**4.7%**
Aged 16 to 19	5,905	143	2.4
Aged 20 to 24	15,028	503	3.3
Aged 25 to 34	33,615	1,740	5.2
Aged 35 to 44	33,366	1,987	6.0
Aged 45 to 54	35,960	1,642	4.6
Aged 55 to 64	23,297	990	4.2
Aged 65 or older	6,718	243	3.6
Men in labor force	**81,985**	**3,893**	**4.7**
Aged 16 to 19	2,991	73	2.4
Aged 20 to 24	7,864	265	3.4
Aged 25 to 34	18,352	946	5.2
Aged 35 to 44	18,119	1,074	5.9
Aged 45 to 54	18,856	858	4.6
Aged 55 to 64	12,103	529	4.4
Aged 65 or older	3,701	149	4.0
Women in labor force	**71,904**	**3,355**	**4.7**
Aged 16 to 19	2,914	70	2.4
Aged 20 to 24	7,164	238	3.3
Aged 25 to 34	15,263	794	5.2
Aged 35 to 44	15,247	913	6.0
Aged 45 to 54	17,104	784	4.6
Aged 55 to 64	11,194	461	4.1
Aged 65 or older	3,017	94	3.1

Note: The civilian labor force equals the number of employed plus the number of unemployed.
Source: Bureau of Labor Statistics, Current Population Survey, Internet site http://www.bls.gov/cps/tables.htm#empstat

Table 6.2 Labor Force Participation Rate of Total People and Asians by Sex and Age, 2010

(percent of total people and Asians aged 16 or older in the civilian labor force, and index of Asian to total, by sex and age, 2010)

	total	Asian	index, Asian to total
Total people	**64.7%**	**64.7%**	**100**
Aged 16 to 19	34.9	22.0	63
Aged 20 to 24	71.4	53.6	75
Aged 25 to 34	82.2	75.2	91
Aged 35 to 44	83.2	81.8	98
Aged 45 to 54	81.2	83.2	102
Aged 55 to 64	64.9	67.2	104
Aged 65 or older	17.4	17.1	98
Men	**71.2**	**73.2**	**103**
Aged 16 to 19	34.9	22.1	63
Aged 20 to 24	74.5	56.3	76
Aged 25 to 34	89.7	85.3	95
Aged 35 to 44	91.5	91.4	100
Aged 45 to 54	86.8	91.3	105
Aged 55 to 64	70.0	78.2	112
Aged 65 or older	22.1	24.3	110
Women	**58.6**	**57.0**	**97**
Aged 16 to 19	35.0	22.0	63
Aged 20 to 24	68.3	50.9	74
Aged 25 to 34	74.7	65.8	88
Aged 35 to 44	75.2	72.7	97
Aged 45 to 54	75.7	75.8	100
Aged 55 to 64	60.2	57.9	96
Aged 65 or older	13.8	11.7	85

Note: The civilian labor force equals the number of employed plus the number of unemployed. The index is calculated by dividing the Asian rate by the total rate and multiplying by 100.
Source: Bureau of Labor Statistics, Current Population Survey, Internet site http://www.bls.gov/cps/tables.htm#empstat

Table 6.3 Labor Force Participation Rate of Asians by Detailed Age and Sex, 2010

(percent of Asians aged 16 or older in the civilian labor force, by age and sex, 2010)

	total	men	women
Total Asians	**64.7%**	**73.2%**	**57.0%**
Aged 16 to 19	22.0	22.1	22.0
Aged 16 to 17	11.1	9.7	12.4
Aged 18 to 19	34.0	34.4	33.5
Aged 20 to 24	53.6	56.3	50.9
Aged 25 to 34	75.2	85.3	65.8
Aged 25 to 29	72.8	80.5	65.7
Aged 30 to 34	77.4	89.8	66.0
Aged 35 to 44	81.8	91.4	72.7
Aged 35 to 39	81.1	91.1	71.4
Aged 40 to 44	82.6	91.8	74.2
Aged 45 to 54	83.2	91.3	75.8
Aged 45 to 49	84.2	93.6	75.7
Aged 50 to 54	82.0	88.7	75.9
Aged 55 to 64	67.2	78.2	57.9
Aged 55 to 59	75.3	87.4	65.0
Aged 60 to 64	57.3	66.8	49.3
Aged 65 or older	17.1	24.2	11.7
Aged 65 to 69	31.6	42.9	21.4
Aged 70 to 74	17.5	22.1	13.8
Aged 75 or older	6.1	8.9	4.4

Note: The civilian labor force equals the number of employed plus the number of unemployed.
Source: Bureau of Labor Statistics, 2010 Current Population Survey, Internet site http://www.bls.gov/cps/tables.htm#empstat

Table 6.4 Employment Status of Asians by Sex and Age, 2010

(number and percent of Asians aged 16 or older in the civilian labor force by sex, age, and employment status, 2010; numbers in thousands)

	civilian noninstitutional population	civilian labor force				
					unemployed	
		total	percent of population	employed	number	percent of labor force
Total Asians	**11,199**	**7,248**	**64.7%**	**6,705**	**543**	**7.5%**
Aged 16 to 19	649	143	22.0	108	35	24.8
Aged 20 to 24	940	504	53.6	442	62	12.3
Aged 25 to 34	2,314	1,740	75.2	1,620	120	6.9
Aged 35 to 44	2,430	1,987	81.8	1,869	118	6.0
Aged 45 to 54	1,975	1,642	83.2	1,530	112	6.8
Aged 55 to 64	1,472	990	67.2	916	74	7.5
Aged 65 or older	1,419	243	17.1	221	22	8.9
Total Asian men	**5,315**	**3,893**	**73.2**	**3,588**	**305**	**7.8**
Aged 16 to 19	331	73	22.1	54	19	25.8
Aged 20 to 24	472	265	56.3	228	38	14.2
Aged 25 to 34	1,108	946	85.3	887	58	6.2
Aged 35 to 44	1,174	1,074	91.4	1,005	69	6.5
Aged 45 to 54	940	858	91.3	794	64	7.5
Aged 55 to 64	676	529	78.2	487	42	7.9
Aged 65 or older	614	149	24.3	133	15	7.5
Total Asian women	**5,884**	**3,355**	**57.0**	**3,117**	**238**	**7.1**
Aged 16 to 19	318	70	22.0	53	17	23.7
Aged 20 to 24	468	238	50.9	214	24	10.2
Aged 25 to 34	1,206	794	65.8	732	62	7.8
Aged 35 to 44	1,255	913	72.7	864	49	5.4
Aged 45 to 54	1,035	784	75.8	737	48	6.1
Aged 55 to 64	796	461	57.9	429	33	7.1
Aged 65 or older	806	94	11.7	88	6	6.4

Note: The civilian labor force equals the number of employed plus the number of unemployed. The civilian population equals the number in the labor force plus the number not in the labor force.
Source: Bureau of Labor Statistics, Current Population Survey, Internet site http://www.bls.gov/cps/tables.htm#empstat

Table 6.5 Unemployment Rate of Total People and Asians by Sex and Age, 2010

(unemployment rate of the total and Asian civilian labor force and index of Asian to total, by sex and age, 2010)

	total	Asian	index, Asian to total
Total unemployment rate	**9.6%**	**7.5%**	**78**
Aged 16 to 19	25.9	24.8	96
Aged 20 to 24	15.5	12.3	79
Aged 25 to 34	10.1	6.9	68
Aged 35 to 44	8.1	6.0	74
Aged 45 to 54	7.7	6.8	89
Aged 55 to 64	7.1	7.5	105
Aged 65 or older	6.7	8.9	133
Men's unemployment rate	**10.5**	**7.8**	**74**
Aged 16 to 19	28.8	25.8	90
Aged 20 to 24	17.8	14.2	80
Aged 25 to 34	10.9	6.2	57
Aged 35 to 44	8.5	6.5	77
Aged 45 to 54	8.6	7.5	87
Aged 55 to 64	8.0	7.9	99
Aged 65 or older	7.1	7.5	106
Women's unemployment rate	**8.6**	**7.1**	**82**
Aged 16 to 19	22.8	23.7	104
Aged 20 to 24	13.0	10.2	78
Aged 25 to 34	9.1	7.8	86
Aged 35 to 44	7.7	5.4	70
Aged 45 to 54	6.8	6.1	91
Aged 55 to 64	6.2	7.1	114
Aged 65 or older	6.2	6.4	103

Note: The civilian labor force equals the number of employed plus the number of unemployed. The unemployment rate is calculated by dividing the number of unemployed by the civilian labor force. The index is calculated by dividing the Asian rate by the total rate and multiplying by 100.
Source: Bureau of Labor Statistics, Current Population Survey, Internet site http://www.bls.gov/cps/tables.htm#empstat

Asians Account for a Large Share of Professional Workers

Few administrative support workers are Asian.

Asians account for only 4.8 percent of the nation's workers, but they are a much larger share of workers in a variety of professional occupations. Asians account for 28 percent of medical scientists and computer software engineers. Sixteen percent of physicians and 15 percent of pharmacists are Asian.

Asians account for 51 percent of workers in the occupation labeled "miscellaneous personal appearance workers." This occupation includes employees in establishments such as nail salons.

Asians account for few workers in blue-collar occupations. They are only 1 to 2 percent of construction laborers, electricians, roofers, and bus drivers.

■ Asians are the most highly educated workers in the nation, which accounts for their disproportionate representation in professional occupations.

The largest share of Asians work in professional occupations

(percent distribution of employed Asians aged 16 or older by major occupational groups, 2010)

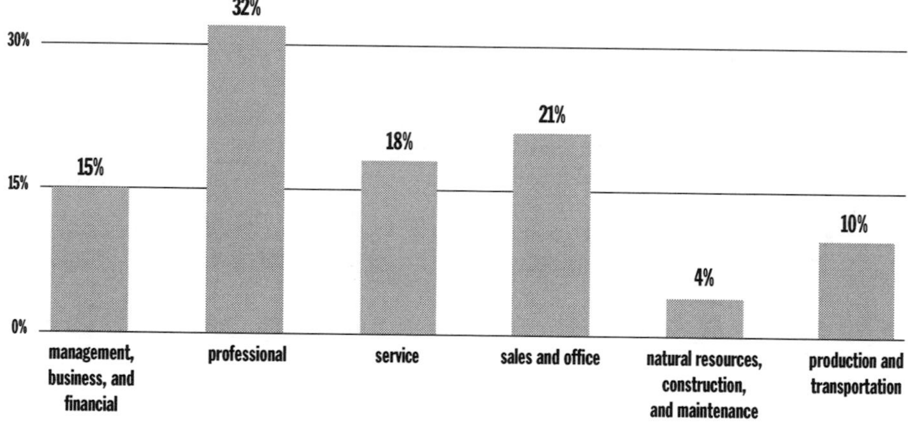

Table 6.6 Total and Asian Workers by Occupation, 2010

(total number of employed persons aged 16 or older in the civilian labor force, number and percent distribution of employed Asians, and Asian share of total, by occupation, 2010; numbers in thousands)

		Asian		
	total	number	percent distribution	share of total
TOTAL EMPLOYED	139,064	6,705	100.0%	4.8%
Management, professional and related occupations	**51,743**	**3,149**	**47.0**	**6.1**
Management, business and financial operations	20,938	999	14.9	4.8
Management	15,001	662	9.9	4.4
Business and financial operations	5,937	336	5.0	5.7
Professional and related occupations	30,805	2,150	32.1	7.0
Computer and mathematical	3,531	568	8.5	16.1
Architecture and engineering	2,619	236	3.5	9.0
Life, physical, and social science	1,409	152	2.3	10.8
Community and social services	2,337	77	1.1	3.3
Legal	1,716	58	0.9	3.4
Education, training, and library	8,628	330	4.9	3.8
Art, design, entertainment, sports, and media	2,759	117	1.7	4.2
Health care practitioner and technical occupations	7,805	612	9.1	7.8
Service occupations	**24,634**	**1,205**	**18.0**	**4.9**
Health care support	3,332	137	2.0	4.1
Protective service	3,289	79	1.2	2.4
Food preparation and serving related	7,660	431	6.4	5.6
Building and grounds cleaning and maintenance	5,328	166	2.5	3.1
Personal care and service	5,024	392	5.8	7.8
Sales and office occupations	**33,433**	**1,416**	**21.1**	**4.2**
Sales and related	15,386	766	11.4	5.0
Office and administrative support	18,047	649	9.7	3.6
Natural resources, construction, maintenance occupations	**13,073**	**261**	**3.9**	**2.0**
Farming, fishing, and forestry	987	19	0.3	1.9
Construction and extraction	7,175	102	1.5	1.4
Installation, maintenance, and repair	4,911	140	2.1	2.9
Production, transportation, material-moving occupations	**16,180**	**674**	**10.1**	**4.2**
Production	7,998	441	6.6	5.5
Transportation and material moving	8,182	232	3.5	2.8

Source: Bureau of Labor Statistics, Current Population Survey, Internet site http://www.bls.gov/cps/tables.htm#empstat; calculations by New Strategist

Table 6.7 Asian Workers by Detailed Occupation, 2010

(total number of employed workers aged 16 or older and percent Asian, by detailed occupation, 2010; numbers in thousands)

	total	percent Asian
TOTAL EMPLOYED	**139,064**	**4.8%**
Management, professional and related occupations	**51,743**	**6.1**
Management, business and financial operations occupations	20,938	4.8
Management occupations	15,001	4.4
Chief executives	1,505	3.2
General and operations managers	1,007	3.3
Advertising and promotions managers	78	2.3
Marketing and sales managers	959	5.0
Public relations managers	85	4.8
Administrative services managers	104	5.5
Computer and information systems managers	537	9.0
Financial managers	1,141	6.9
Human resources managers	268	3.0
Industrial production managers	254	4.4
Purchasing managers	203	2.8
Transportation, storage, and distribution managers	278	2.8
Farm, ranch, and other agricultural managers	237	0.8
Farmers and ranchers	713	0.7
Construction managers	1,083	2.0
Education administrators	830	2.0
Engineering managers	113	13.3
Food service managers	960	10.8
Lodging managers	143	11.3
Medical and health services managers	549	3.2
Property, real estate, and community association managers	604	2.6
Social and community service managers	326	1.6
Managers, all other	2,898	4.8
Business and financial operations occupations	5,937	5.7
Wholesale and retail buyers, except farm products	180	2.2
Purchasing agents, except wholesale, retail, and farm products	235	3.2
Claims adjusters, appraisers, examiners, and investigators	282	3.3
Compliance officers, except agriculture, construction, health and safety, and transportation	188	2.2
Cost estimators	115	0.6
Human resources, training, and labor relations specialists	824	2.6
Logisticians	68	8.7
Management analysts	658	7.6
Meeting and convention planners	63	3.0
Other business operations specialists	243	4.4
Accountants and auditors	1,646	9.1
Appraisers and assessors of real estate	79	1.8
Financial analysts	97	6.9
Personal financial advisors	369	4.9
Insurance underwriters	125	4.2
Loan counselors and officers	363	4.6
Tax examiners, collectors, and revenue agents	71	3.5
Tax preparers	106	6.1
Financial specialists, all other	84	5.3

	total	percent Asian
Professional and related occupations	30,805	7.0%
Computer and mathematical occupations	3,531	16.1
Computer scientists and systems analysts	784	14.9
Computer programmers	470	12.4
Computer software engineers	1,026	28.0
Computer support specialists	388	7.9
Database administrators	101	11.8
Network and computer systems administrators	229	9.4
Network systems and data communications analysts	366	7.4
Operations research analysts	107	5.8
Architecture and engineering occupations	2,619	9.0
Architects, except naval	184	1.9
Aerospace engineers	126	3.7
Chemical engineers	63	11.5
Civil engineers	318	8.9
Computer hardware engineers	70	26.7
Electrical and electronics engineers	307	16.7
Industrial engineers, including health and safety	159	10.2
Mechanical engineers	293	11.0
Engineers, all other	334	12.5
Drafters	143	4.1
Engineering technicians, except drafters	374	4.6
Surveying and mapping technicians	61	0.3
Life, physical, and social science occupations	1,409	10.8
Biological scientists	113	9.8
Medical scientists	143	28.4
Chemists and materials scientists	103	18.2
Environmental scientists and geoscientists	108	3.0
Physical scientists, all other	144	21.1
Market and survey researchers	150	7.7
Psychologists	179	3.3
Chemical technicians	62	8.4
Other life, physical, and social science technicians	162	6.9
Community and social services occupations	2,337	3.3
Counselors	702	3.8
Social workers	771	3.3
Miscellaneous community and social service specialists	297	1.7
Clergy	429	2.9
Directors, religious activities and education	53	4.3
Religious workers, all other	84	6.2
Legal occupations	1,716	3.4
Lawyers	1,040	3.4
Judges, magistrates, and other judicial workers	71	3.9
Paralegals and legal assistants	345	2.4
Miscellaneous legal support workers	259	4.4
Education, training, and library occupations	8,628	3.8
Postsecondary teachers	1,300	11.0
Preschool and kindergarten teachers	712	2.7
Elementary and middle school teachers	2,813	2.4
Secondary school teachers	1,221	1.6
Special education teachers	387	2.0
Other teachers and instructors	806	4.8
Archivists, curators, and museum technicians	50	0.6
Librarians	216	1.7

	total	percent Asian
Teacher assistants	966	2.9%
Other education, training, and library workers	114	1.7
Arts, design, entertainment, sports, and media occupations	2,759	4.3
Artists and related workers	195	3.6
Designers	793	5.2
Producers and directors	152	5.5
Athletes, coaches, umpires, and related workers	260	4.1
Musicians, singers, and related workers	182	2.1
Announcers	52	2.0
News analysts, reporters, and correspondents	81	6.0
Public relations specialists	148	2.6
Editors	162	5.0
Technical writers	56	3.8
Writers and authors	199	2.3
Miscellaneous media and communication workers	83	10.6
Broadcast and sound engineering technicians and radio operators	102	4.1
Photographers	161	3.3
Television, video, and motion picture camera operators and editors	54	4.0
Health care practitioner and technical occupations	7,805	7.8
Chiropractors	57	5.3
Dentists	175	13.7
Dietitians and nutritionists	105	9.1
Pharmacists	255	15.1
Physicians and surgeons	872	15.7
Physician assistants	99	5.8
Registered nurses	2,843	7.5
Occupational therapists	109	2.6
Physical therapists	187	7.6
Respiratory therapists	131	4.8
Speech-language pathologists	132	0.7
Therapists, all other	138	4.0
Veterinarians	73	1.8
Clinical laboratory technologists and technicians	342	10.3
Dental hygienists	141	5.9
Diagnostic related technologists and technicians	349	4.8
Emergency medical technicians and paramedics	179	0.9
Health diagnosing and treating practitioner support technicians	505	6.8
Licensed practical and licensed vocational nurses	573	3.8
Medical records and health information technicians	118	6.5
Opticians, dispensing	55	4.5
Miscellaneous health technologists and technicians	167	6.5
Other health care practitioners and technical occupations	70	3.0
Service occupations	**24,634**	**4.9**
Health care support occupations	3,332	4.1
Nursing, psychiatric, and home health aides	1,928	4.0
Physical therapist assistants and aides	86	6.6
Massage therapists	162	4.9
Dental assistants	296	5.6
Medical assistants and other health care support occupations	850	3.5
Protective service occupations	3,289	2.4
First-line supervisors/managers of police and detectives	103	2.5
Supervisors, protective service workers, all other	105	2.3
Fire fighters	301	0.5
Bailiffs, correctional officers, and jailers	465	1.2

	total	percent Asian
Detectives and criminal investigators	159	3.7%
Police and sheriff's patrol officers	714	2.7
Private detectives and investigators	89	3.2
Security guards and gaming surveillance officers	993	3.4
Crossing guards	59	1.8
Lifeguards and other protective service workers	166	2.2
Food preparation and serving related occupations	7,660	5.6
Chefs and head cooks	337	16.5
First-line supervisors/managers of food preparation and serving workers	551	3.0
Cooks	1,951	5.0
Food preparation workers	717	5.3
Bartenders	393	2.1
Combined food preparation and serving workers, including fast food	294	4.6
Counter attendants, cafeteria, food concession, and coffee shop	269	5.7
Waiters and waitresses	2,067	6.1
Food servers, nonrestaurant	174	6.5
Dining room and cafeteria attendants and bartender helpers	371	7.0
Dishwashers	246	4.2
Hosts and hostesses, restaurant, lounge, and coffee shop	284	4.0
Building and grounds cleaning and maintenance occupations	5,328	3.1
First-line supervisors/managers of housekeeping and janitorial workers	234	2.8
First-line supervisors/managers of landscaping, lawn service, and grounds keeping workers	229	1.1
Janitors and building cleaners	2,186	3.2
Maids and housekeeping cleaners	1,407	5.0
Pest control workers	76	1.7
Grounds maintenance workers	1,195	1.3
Personal care and service occupations	5,024	7.8
First-line supervisors/managers of gaming workers	136	8.3
First-line supervisors/managers of personal service workers	185	14.5
Nonfarm animal caretakers	169	2.0
Gaming services workers	121	29.6
Ushers, lobby attendants, and ticket takers	51	7.9
Miscellaneous entertainment attendants and related workers	173	3.1
Barbers	96	1.2
Hairdressers, hairstylists, and cosmetologists	770	4.7
Miscellaneous personal appearance workers	273	51.4
Baggage porters, bellhops, and concierges	77	6.9
Transportation attendants	110	4.9
Child care workers	1,247	3.4
Personal and home care aides	973	6.4
Recreation and fitness workers	379	1.8
Residential advisors	60	2.0
Personal care and service workers, all other	91	3.6
Sales and office occupations	**33,433**	**4.2**
Sales and related occupations	15,386	5.0
First-line supervisors/managers of retail sales workers	3,132	5.4
First-line supervisors/managers of nonretail sales workers	1,131	5.6
Cashiers	3,109	6.8
Counter and rental clerks	150	6.9
Parts salespersons	129	0.5
Retail salespersons	3,286	4.1
Advertising sales agents	214	2.7
Insurance sales agents	513	3.2

	total	percent Asian
Securities, commodities, and financial services sales agents	308	8.0%
Travel agents	76	6.5
Sales representatives, services, all other	524	4.9
Sales representatives, wholesale and manufacturing	1,284	3.3
Models, demonstrators, and product promoters	61	2.7
Real estate brokers and sales agents	854	3.8
Telemarketers	118	1.2
Door-to-door sales workers, news and street vendors, related workers	203	3.6
Sales and related workers, all other	268	4.1
Office and administrative support occupations	18,047	3.6
First-line supervisors/managers of office and administrative support workers	1,507	3.8
Bill and account collectors	216	2.9
Billing and posting clerks and machine operators	472	4.1
Bookkeeping, accounting, and auditing clerks	1,297	3.4
Payroll and timekeeping clerks	167	1.9
Tellers	453	5.2
Court, municipal, and license clerks	95	3.1
Customer service representatives	1,896	3.9
Eligibility interviewers, government programs	89	6.2
File clerks	334	3.9
Hotel, motel, and resort desk clerks	129	4.4
Interviewers, except eligibility and loan	210	5.8
Library assistants, clerical	115	3.2
Loan interviewers and clerks	127	4.7
Order clerks	117	6.4
Receptionists and information clerks	1,281	3.3
Reservation and transportation ticket agents and travel clerks	100	3.9
Information and record clerks, all other	116	2.8
Couriers and messengers	270	2.4
Dispatchers	293	1.6
Postal service clerks	124	8.3
Postal service mail carriers	321	6.6
Postal service mail sorters, processors, processing machine operators	76	16.2
Production, planning, and expediting clerks	259	3.4
Shipping, receiving, and traffic clerks	558	3.6
Stock clerks and order fillers	1,456	3.4
Weighers, measurers, checkers, and samplers, recordkeeping	70	3.1
Secretaries and administrative assistants	3,082	1.9
Computer operators	122	9.1
Data entry keyers	338	4.2
Word processors and typists	144	2.5
Insurance claims and policy processing clerks	231	2.3
Mail clerks and mail machine operators, except postal service	94	3.5
Office clerks, general	994	5.2
Office and administrative support workers, all other	501	3.2
Natural resources, construction, and maintenance occupations	**13,073**	**2.0**
Farming, fishing, and forestry occupations	987	1.9
Graders and sorters, agricultural products	103	7.3
Miscellaneous agricultural workers	691	1.3
Logging workers	63	0.7
Construction and extraction occupations	7,175	1.4
First-line supervisors/managers of construction trades, extraction workers	659	1.0
Brickmasons, blockmasons, and stonemasons	162	0.8

	total	percent Asian
Carpenters	1,242	1.4%
Carpet, floor, and tile installers and finishers	209	3.3
Cement masons, concrete finishers, and terrazzo workers	88	–
Construction laborers	1,267	2.2
Operating engineers and other construction equipment operators	363	1.1
Drywall installers, ceiling tile installers, and tapers	171	0.3
Electricians	691	1.6
Painters, construction and maintenance	578	1.3
Pipelayers, plumbers, pipefitters, and steamfitters	526	1.3
Roofers	214	1.3
Sheet metal workers	108	0.4
Structural iron and steel workers	59	–
Helpers, construction trades	60	0.2
Construction and building inspectors	104	2.3
Highway maintenance workers	110	2.6
Mining machine operators	60	–
Other extraction workers	55	–
Installation, maintenance, and repair occupations	4,911	2.9
First-line supervisors/managers of mechanics, installers, repairers	381	1.9
Computer, automated teller, and office machine repairers	305	8.0
Radio and telecommunications equipment installers and repairers	166	6.2
Electronic home entertainment equipment installers and repairers	52	6.0
Security and fire alarm systems installers	60	1.9
Aircraft mechanics and service technicians	136	7.1
Automotive body and related repairers	168	0.8
Automotive service technicians and mechanics	802	3.5
Bus and truck mechanics and diesel engine specialists	339	1.6
Heavy vehicle and mobile equipment service technicians and mechanics	235	1.1
Small-engine mechanics	57	2.7
Misc. vehicle and mobile equipment mechanics, installers, and repairers	99	0.7
Heating, air conditioning, and refrigeration mechanics and installers	392	2.2
Home appliance repairers	53	6.1
Industrial and refractory machinery mechanics	447	2.2
Maintenance and repair workers, general	347	2.7
Electrical power-line installers and repairers	124	0.7
Telecommunications line installers and repairers	163	1.6
Precision instrument and equipment repairers	73	0.5
Other installation, maintenance, and repair workers	197	1.4
Production, transportation, and material-moving occupations	**16,180**	**4.2**
Production occupations	7,998	5.5
First-line supervisors/managers of production and operating workers	702	5.5
Electrical, electronics, and electromechanical assemblers	151	22.6
Miscellaneous assemblers and fabricators	805	6.1
Bakers	206	5.8
Butchers and other meat, poultry, and fish processing workers	331	10.4
Food batchmakers	107	2.6
Computer control programmers and operators	56	2.1
Cutting, punching, press machine setters, operators, tenders, metal, plastic	78	2.6
Grinding, lapping, polishing, and buffing machine tool setters, operators, and tenders, metal and plastic	54	1.5
Machinists	408	5.5
Molders and molding machine setters, operators, and tenders, metal and plastic	55	1.9
Tool and die makers	68	1.0

	total	percent Asian
Welding, soldering, and brazing workers	479	3.6%
Metalworkers and plastic workers, all other	337	7.2
Job printers	50	4.4
Printing machine operators	162	1.8
Laundry and dry-cleaning workers	195	9.3
Pressers, textile, garment, and related materials	59	9.2
Sewing machine operators	170	10.8
Tailors, dressmakers, and sewers	76	20.9
Cabinetmakers and bench carpenters	62	2.8
Stationary engineers and boiler operators	91	5.3
Water and liquid waste treatment plant and system operators	77	3.4
Chemical processing machine setters, operators, and tenders	58	2.7
Crushing, grinding, polishing, mixing, and blending workers	90	2.2
Cutting workers	67	3.0
Inspectors, testers, sorters, samplers, and weighers	669	5.3
Medical, dental, and ophthalmic laboratory technicians	92	7.8
Packaging and filling machine operators and tenders	255	4.1
Painting workers	139	0.5
Production workers, all other	921	4.2
Transportation and material-moving occupations	8,182	2.8
Supervisors, transportation and material-moving workers	263	3.0
Aircraft pilots and flight engineers	110	1.0
Bus drivers	600	2.2
Driver/sales workers and truck drivers	3,028	1.5
Taxi drivers and chauffeurs	390	13.0
Motor vehicle operators, all other	54	2.7
Locomotive engineers and operators	57	2.4
Railroad conductors and yardmasters	58	1.2
Parking lot attendants	75	12.8
Service station attendants	77	4.0
Crane and tower operators	50	0.4
Dredge, excavating, and loading machine operators	51	0.1
Industrial truck and tractor operators	499	1.2
Cleaners of vehicles and equipment	333	3.7
Laborers and freight, stock, and material movers, hand	1,700	3.0
Packers and packagers, hand	403	4.2
Refuse and recyclable material collectors	88	0.2
Material-moving workers, all other	59	2.7

Note: "–" means sample is too small to make a reliable estimate.
Source: Bureau of Labor Statistics, 2010 Current Population Survey, Internet site http://www.bls.gov/cps/tables.htm#empstat

Table 6.8 Asian Workers by Industry, 2010

(total number of employed people aged 16 or older in the civilian labor force; number and percent distribution of employed Asians, and Asian share of total, by industry, 2010; numbers in thousands)

		Asian		
	total	number	percent distribution	share of total
Total employed	**139,064**	**6,705**	**100.0%**	**4.8%**
Agriculture, forestry, fishing, hunting	2,206	25	0.4	1.1
Mining	731	8	0.1	1.1
Construction	9,077	156	2.3	1.7
Manufacturing	14,081	806	12.0	5.7
Wholesale/retail trade	19,739	911	13.6	4.6
Transportation and utilities	7,134	269	4.0	3.8
Information	3,149	174	2.6	5.5
Financial activities	9,350	500	7.5	5.3
Professional and business services	15,253	864	12.9	5.7
Educational and health services	32,062	1,538	22.9	4.8
Leisure and hospitality	12,530	798	11.9	6.4
Other services	6,769	423	6.3	6.2
Public administration	6,983	233	3.5	3.3

Source: Bureau of Labor Statistics, 2010 Current Population Survey, Internet site http://www.bls.gov/cps/tables.htm#empstat; calculations by New Strategist

Most Asian Workers Have a College Degree

Asians are less likely than the average worker to have lengthy job tenure.

Asians are the most highly educated of the nation's workers. The 57 percent majority of Asian workers aged 25 or older has a college degree compared with 35 percent of all workers. Asians account for 8 percent of the nation's college-educated work force.

Asians are less likely than the average worker to have held their current job for 10 or more years. Among all workers, 29 percent have been on the current job for at least 10 years. Among Asians, the proportion is a smaller 21 percent. Behind the shorter job tenure of Asians is the fact the Asian workers are younger, on average, than the typical American worker.

Most employed Asians have full-time jobs. Among men, 83 percent work full-time. Among women, the figure is 71 percent.

■ Among Asians who work part-time, 20 percent of the men and 18 percent of the women would rather have a full-time job.

Few Asian workers are high school dropouts

(percent distribution of employed Asians by educational attainment, 2010)

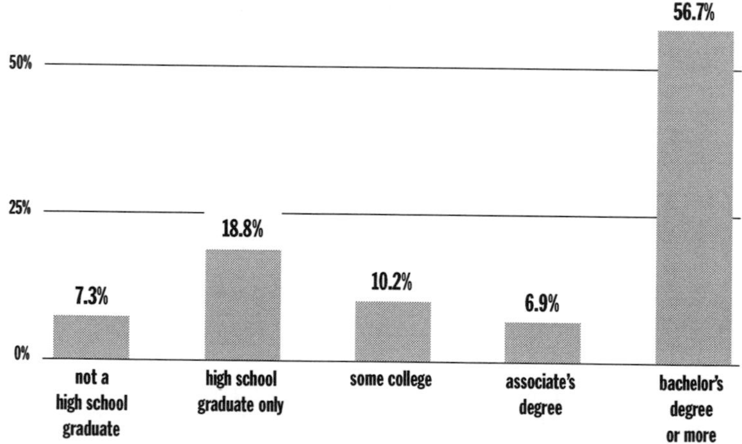

Table 6.9 Asian Labor Force by Educational Attainment, 2010

(number of total people and Asians aged 25 or older in the civilian labor force, Asian labor force participation rate, distribution of Asians in labor force, and Asian share of total labor force, by educational attainment, 2010; numbers in thousands)

		Asian labor force			
	total labor force	number	participation rate	percent distribution	share of total
Total aged 25 or older	**132,954**	**6,601**	**68.7%**	**100.0%**	**5.0%**
Not a high school graduate	11,880	485	44.1	7.3	4.1
High school graduate only	38,236	1,244	62.8	18.8	3.3
Some college	22,958	675	69.8	10.2	2.9
Associate's degree	13,882	454	71.8	6.9	3.3
Bachelor's degree or more	45,998	3,743	75.9	56.7	8.1

Source: Bureau of Labor Statistics, 2010 Current Population Survey, Internet site http://www.bls.gov/cps/tables.htm#empstat; calculations by New Strategist

Table 6.10 Total and Asian Workers by Job Tenure, 2010

(number of total and Asian employed wage and salary workers aged 16 or older, percent distribution by tenure with current employer, and index of Asian to total, 2010; numbers in thousands)

	total	Asian	index Asian to total
Total workers, number	**121,931**	**5,598**	–
Total workers, percent	**100.0%**	**100.0%**	**100**
12 months or less	19.0	18.1	95
13 to 23 months	7.0	7.0	100
Two years	5.8	6.8	117
Three to four years	18.9	22.1	117
Five to nine years	20.5	25.4	124
10 to 14 years	12.2	11.8	97
15 to 19 years	6.1	3.3	54
20 or more years	10.5	5.5	52

Note: The index is calculated by dividing the Asian figure by the total figure and multiplying by 100. "–" means not applicable.
Source: Bureau of Labor Statistics, Employee Tenure, Internet site http://www.bls.gov/news.release/tenure.toc.htm; calculations by New Strategist

Table 6.11 Asian Full-Time and Part-Time Workers by Age and Sex, 2010

(number and percent distribution of employed Asians aged 16 or older by age, sex, and full- and part-time employment status, 2010; numbers in thousands)

	men			women		
	total	full-time	part-time	total	full-time	part-time
Total employed Asians	**3,513**	**2,903**	**610**	**3,037**	**2,154**	**883**
Aged 16 to 19	54	15	39	54	9	45
Aged 20 to 24	226	129	97	211	111	100
Aged 25 to 54	2,632	2,277	355	2,268	1,694	574
Aged 55 or older	603	484	119	504	340	164
PERCENT DISTRIBUTION BY EMPLOYMENT STATUS						
Total employed Asians	**100.0%**	**82.6%**	**17.4%**	**100.0%**	**70.9%**	**29.1%**
Aged 16 to 19	100.0	27.8	72.2	100.0	16.7	83.3
Aged 20 to 24	100.0	57.1	42.9	100.0	52.6	47.4
Aged 25 to 54	100.0	86.5	13.5	100.0	74.7	25.3
Aged 55 or older	100.0	80.3	19.7	100.0	67.5	32.5
PERCENT DISTRIBUTION BY AGE						
Total employed Asians	**100.0%**	**100.0%**	**100.0%**	**100.0%**	**100.0%**	**100.0%**
Aged 16 to 19	1.5	0.5	6.4	1.8	0.4	5.1
Aged 20 to 24	6.4	4.4	15.9	6.9	5.2	11.3
Aged 25 to 54	74.9	78.4	58.2	74.7	78.6	65.0
Aged 55 or older	17.2	16.7	19.5	16.6	15.8	18.6

Source: Bureau of Labor Statistics, 2010 Current Population Survey, Internet site http://www.bls.gov/cps/tables.htm#empstat; calculations by New Strategist

Table 6.12 Asian Part-Time Workers by Age, Sex, and Reason, 2010

(total number of Asians aged 16 or older who work part-time, and number and percent working part-time for economic reasons, by sex and age, 2010; numbers in thousands)

		working part-time for economic reasons	
	total	number	share of total
Asian men working part-time	**610**	**122**	**20.0%**
Aged 16 to 19	39	3	7.7
Aged 20 to 24	97	13	13.4
Aged 25 to 54	355	83	23.4
Aged 55 or older	119	23	19.3
Asian women working part-time	**883**	**159**	**18.0**
Aged 16 to 19	45	3	6.7
Aged 20 to 24	100	17	17.0
Aged 25 to 54	574	110	19.2
Aged 55 or older	164	29	17.7

Note: Part-time work is less than 35 hours per week. Part-time workers exclude those who worked less than 35 hours in the previous week because of vacation, holidays, child care problems, weather issues, and other temporary, noneconomic reasons. "Economic reasons" means a worker's hours have been reduced or workers cannot find full-time employment.
Source: Bureau of Labor Statistics, 2010 Current Population Survey, Internet site http://www.bls.gov/cps/tables.htm#empstat; calculations by New Strategist

Asian Households Have More Earners

Among Asian couples, most are dual earners.

The average Asian household has 1.50 earners, more than the 1.32 earners in the typical American household. Only 36 percent of Asian households have one earner, while 49 percent have two or more.

Fifty-six percent of Asian couples are dual earners, slightly above the 54 percent average for all married couples. Twenty-six percent of Asian husbands are the couple's sole provider, however, compared with only 22 percent of husbands nationally.

■ Neither husband nor wife works in 13 percent of Asian couples, including 66 percent of those aged 65 or older.

Among Asian households, nearly half have two or more earners

(percent distribution of Asian households by number of earners, 2010)

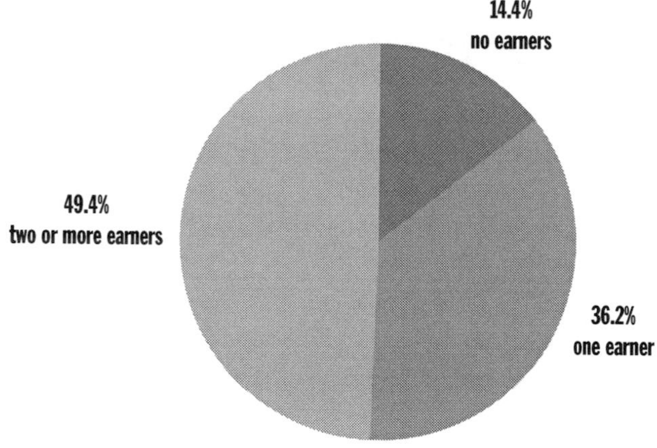

Table 6.13 Asian Households by Number of Earners, 2010

(number of total households, number and percent distribution of Asian households and Asian share of total, by number of earners per household, 2010; numbers in thousands)

		Asian		
	total	number	percent distribution	share of total
Total households	**117,538**	**4,940**	**100.0%**	**4.2%**
No earners	26,172	712	14.4	2.7
One earner	43,712	1,790	36.2	4.1
Two or more earners	47,654	2,438	49.4	5.1
Two earners	38,302	1,909	38.6	5.0
Three earners	7,023	380	7.7	5.4
Four or more earners	2,330	149	3.0	6.4
Average number of earners per household	1.32	1.50	–	–

Note: Asians are those who identify themselves as being of the race alone or as being of the race in combination with other races. "–" means not applicable.
Source: Bureau of the Census, 2010 Current Population Survey, Internet site http://www.census.gov/hhes/www/cpstables/032010/hhinc/toc.htm; calculations by New Strategist

Table 6.14 Labor Force Status of Asian Married Couples, 2010

(number and percent distribution of Asian married-couple family groups aged 20 or older by age of householder and labor force status of husband and wife, 2010; numbers in thousands)

		husband and/or wife in labor force			neither husband nor wife in labor force
	total	husband and wife	husband only	wife only	
Total Asian couples	**3,306**	**1,838**	**864**	**189**	**415**
Under age 25	47	22	22	2	3
Aged 25 to 29	211	126	73	5	5
Aged 30 to 34	390	231	130	15	15
Aged 35 to 39	456	284	161	9	2
Aged 40 to 44	447	283	129	21	14
Aged 45 to 54	780	556	173	33	19
Aged 55 to 64	554	296	119	61	77
Aged 65 or older	420	44	55	43	279
Total Asian couples	**100.0%**	**55.6%**	**26.1%**	**5.7%**	**12.6%**
Under age 25	100.0	46.8	46.8	4.3	6.4
Aged 25 to 29	100.0	59.7	34.6	2.4	2.4
Aged 30 to 34	100.0	59.2	33.3	3.8	3.8
Aged 35 to 39	100.0	62.3	35.3	2.0	0.4
Aged 40 to 44	100.0	63.3	28.9	4.7	3.1
Aged 45 to 54	100.0	71.3	22.2	4.2	2.4
Aged 55 to 64	100.0	53.4	21.5	11.0	13.9
Aged 65 or older	100.0	10.5	13.1	10.2	66.4

Note: Asians are those who identify themselves as being of the race alone or as being of the race in combination with other races.

Source: Bureau of the Census, America's Families and Living Arrangements: 2010, Internet site http://www.census.gov/population/www/socdemo/hh-fam/cps2010.html; calculations by New Strategist

Few Asians Are in Unions

Only 3 percent of Asian workers earn minimum wage or less.

Of the 4.4 million workers who earned at or below minimum wage in 2010, only 140,000 were Asian. Just 4.3 percent of Asian men and 5.3 percent of Asian women are minimum wage workers.

Asian workers are slightly less likely to be represented by a union than the average worker—12.1 versus 13.1 percent. Median weekly earnings for Asians are higher than average whether or not they belong to a union. Among Asian workers, those represented by a union earned a median of $918 a week in 2010 compared with $842 earned by those without union representation.

Among Asian workers, 67 percent drive alone on their commute to work. This is less than the 76 percent of all workers who drive to work alone. Ten percent of Asians use public transportation to get to work, twice the 5 percent of all workers who use mass transit for the commute. Asians account for 10 percent of all mass transit users.

■ Asian workers are highly educated. Consequently, few must take jobs that pay only minimum wage.

Asian workers earn more than average whether they are in a union or not

(median weekly earnings of total and Asian full-time wage and salary workers by union representation status, 2010)

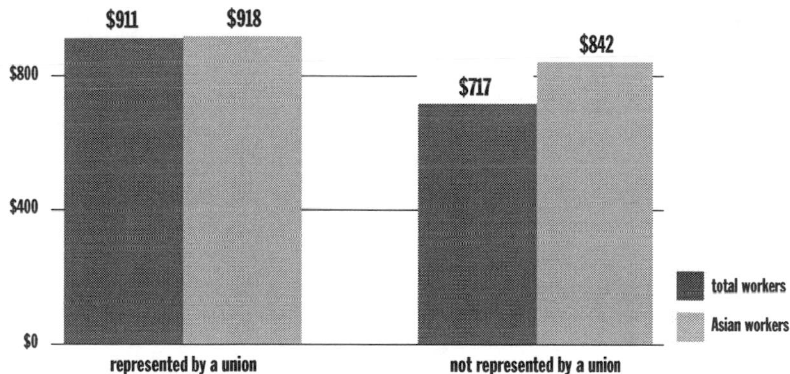

Table 6.15 Asian Minimum Wage Workers, 2010

(number and percent distribution of total and Asian wage and salary workers aged 16 or older paid hourly rates and those paid at or below minimum wage, by sex, 2010; numbers in thousands)

	total paid hourly rates	paid at or below minimum wage
Total workers 16 or older	**72,902**	**4,360**
Asian workers aged 16 or older	2,920	140
Asian men	1,406	60
Asian women	1,513	80
PERCENT DISTRIBUTION BY RACE/SEX		
Total workers aged 16 or older	**100.0%**	**100.0%**
Asian workers aged 16 or older	4.0	3.2
Asian men	1.9	1.4
Asian women	2.1	1.8
PERCENT DISTRIBUTION BY WAGE STATUS		
Total workers aged 16 or older	**100.0%**	**6.0%**
Asian workers aged 16 or older	100.0	4.8
Asian men	100.0	4.3
Asian women	100.0	5.3

Source: Bureau of Labor Statistics, 2010 Current Population Survey, Internet site http://www.bls.gov/cps/tables.htm#empstat; calculations by New Strategist

Table 6.16 Union Representation of Total and Asian Workers, 2010

(number of total and Asian employed wage and salary workers aged 16 or older, number and percent represented by unions, and median weekly earnings of those working full-time by union representation status, 2010; number in thousands)

	total	Asians
Total employed	**124,073**	**5,900**
Number represented by unions	16,290	713
Percent represented by unions	13.1%	12.1%
Median weekly earnings of full-time workers	**$747**	**$855**
Workers represented by unions	911	918
Workers not represented by unions	717	842

Note: Workers represented by unions are either members of a labor union or similar employee association or workers who report no union affiliation but whose jobs are covered by a union or an employee association contract.
Source: Bureau of Labor Statistics, 2010 Current Population Survey, Internet site http://www.bls.gov/cps/tables.htm#empstat; calculations by New Strategist

Table 6.17 Journey to Work by Asians, 2009

(number and percent distribution of total and Asian workers aged 16 or older by principal means of transportation to work, 2009; numbers in thousands)

		Asians		
	total	number	percent distribution	share of total
Total workers	**138,592**	**6,635**	**100.0%**	**4.8%**
Drove car, truck, or van alone	105,476	4,459	67.2	4.2
Carpooled in car, truck, or van	13,917	886	13.4	6.4
Took public transportation (incl. taxis)	6,922	690	10.4	10.0
Walked	3,966	259	3.9	6.5
Traveled by other means	2,393	105	1.6	4.4
Worked at home	5,918	236	3.6	4.0

Source: Bureau of the Census, 2009 American Community Survey, Internet site http://factfinder.census.gov/servlet/DatasetMainPageServlet?_program=ACS&_submenuld=&_lang=en&_ts=; calculations by New Strategist

The Asian Labor Force Will Grow Rapidly

Asians will account for only 6 percent of the labor force in 2018, however.

The Asian labor force will grow by a substantial 30 percent by 2018, while the total labor force will increase by a much smaller 8 percent. Despite the rapid increase in the Asian labor force, Asian workers will account for a small share of total workers for years to come. Labor force participation rates are projected to decline among Asian men and women between 2008 and 2018.

Asians will account for a larger share of workers entering than exiting the labor force during the next decade. Between 2008 and 2018, Asians will account for 7.5 percent of labor force entrants and for a smaller 5.0 percent of those exiting the labor force. Consequently, the Asian share of the labor force will rise from 4.7 to 5.6 percent during those years.

■ The rapid growth of the Asian labor force has not attracted as much attention as the growth of the Hispanic labor force because Asian workers are still few in number.

The Asian labor force is growing much faster than average

(percent change in total and Asian workers aged 16 or older, 2008–18)

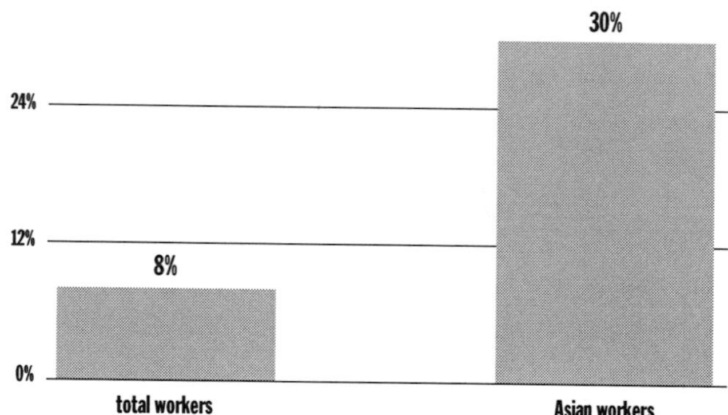

Table 6.18 Asian Labor Force Projections, 2008 and 2018

(projected number and percent of total people and Asians aged 16 or older in the civilian labor force by sex, 2008 and 2018; percent change in number and percentage point change in rate, 2008–18; numbers in thousands)

	2008	2018	percent change
NUMBER			
Total labor force	**154,287**	**166,911**	**8.2%**
Asian labor force	7,202	9,345	29.8
Total men in labor force	**82,520**	**88,682**	**7.5**
Asian men in labor force	3,852	4,895	27.1
Total women in labor force	**71,767**	**78,229**	**9.0**
Asian women in labor force	3,350	4,450	32.8

	2008	2018	percentage point change
PARTICIPATION RATE			
Total people	**66.0%**	**64.5%**	**–1.5**
Total Asians	67.0	65.0	–2.0
Total men	**73.0**	**70.6**	**–2.4**
Asian men	75.3	73.8	–1.5
Total women	**59.5**	**58.7**	**–0.8**
Asian women	59.4	57.4	–2.0

Note: Asians include only those who identified their race as Asian alone.
Source: Bureau of Labor Statistics, Labor Force Projections to 2018: Older Workers Staying More Active, Monthly Labor Review, November 2009, Internet site http://www.bls.gov/opub/mlr/2009/11/home.htm; calculations by New Strategist

Table 6.19 Asian Labor Force Entrants and Leavers, 2008 to 2018

(projected number and percent distribution of total people and Asians aged 16 or older in the civilian labor force in 2008 and 2018, and number and percent distribution of entrants, leavers, and stayers, 2008–18; numbers in thousands)

	2008 labor force	2008–18 entrants	2008–18 leavers	2008–18 stayers	2018 labor force
NUMBER					
Total labor force	**154,287**	**37,632**	**25,008**	**129,279**	**166,911**
Asian labor force	7,202	2,837	694	6,508	9,345
PERCENT DISTRIBUTION					
Total labor force	**100.0%**	**100.0%**	**100.0%**	**100.0%**	**100.0%**
Asian labor force	4.7	7.5	2.8	5.0	5.6

Note: Asians are those who identify their race as Asian alone.
Source: Bureau of Labor Statistics, Labor Force Projections to 2018: Older Workers Staying More Active, Monthly Labor Review, November 2009, Internet site http://www.bls.gov/opub/mlr/2009/11/home.htm; calculations by New Strategist

CHAPTER

7

Living Arrangements

■ Asian households are much more likely to be headed by married couples than is the average household—60 versus 50 percent.

■ The average Asian household includes 2.95 people, significantly larger than the 2.59 people in the average American household. Only 8 percent of Asians live alone.

■ Thirty-eight percent of Asian households include children under age 18, and just over 50 percent—the majority—include children of any age.

■ Most Asian adults are married. Only 8 to 11 percent of Asian men and women have ever divorced.

Married Couples Dominate Asian Households

Female-headed families are a small share of Asian households.

Asians headed 5 million of the nation's 118 million households in 2010, 4 percent of the total. Asian households are much more likely to be headed by married couples than is the average household—60 versus 50 percent, according to the Census Bureau's 2010 Current Population Survey.

Asian householders are slightly younger than average. Consequently, they account for a larger share of younger than older householders. They account for 5 to 6 percent of householders under age 45, but for only 2 percent of those aged 75 or older.

Female-headed families head only 10 percent of Asian households. Married couples dominate Asian households with householders ranging in age from 30 to 74. Even in the oldest age group, married couples account for a substantial 45 percent of households. Asian men and women are less likely than average to live alone in old age.

■ Because many Asians are immigrants from countries with traditional family values, married couples are more common in Asian households than in the average household.

Few Asian households are female-headed families

(percent distribution of Asian households by household type, 2010)

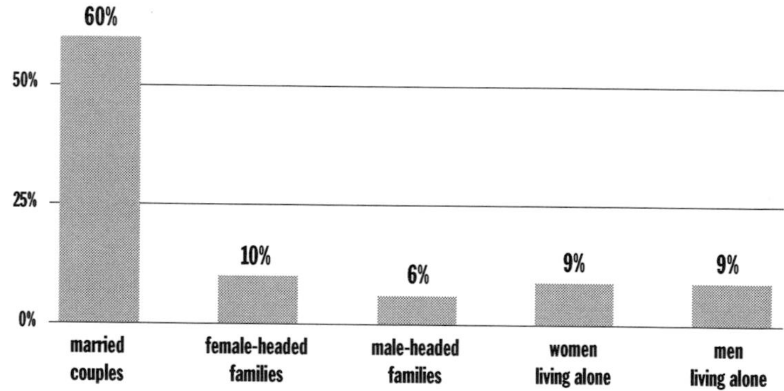

Table 7.1 Total and Asian Households by Age of Householder, 2010

(number and percent distribution of total and Asian households, and Asian share of total, by age of householder, 2010; numbers in thousands)

	total		Asian		
	number	percent distribution	number	percent distribution	share of total
Total households	**117,538**	**100.0%**	**4,940**	**100.0%**	**4.2%**
Under age 25	6,233	5.3	292	5.9	4.7
Aged 25 to 29	9,446	8.0	475	9.6	5.0
Aged 30 to 34	9,811	8.3	581	11.8	5.9
Aged 35 to 39	10,551	9.0	631	12.8	6.0
Aged 40 to 44	10,968	9.3	549	11.1	5.0
Aged 45 to 49	12,449	10.6	540	10.9	4.3
Aged 50 to 54	12,423	10.6	480	9.7	3.9
Aged 55 to 64	20,387	17.3	709	14.4	3.5
Aged 65 to 74	13,164	11.2	383	7.8	2.9
Aged 75 or older	12,106	10.3	299	6.1	2.5
Avg. age of householder	50.2	–	46.0	–	–

Note: Asians are those who identify themselves as being of the race alone or as being of the race in combination with other races. "–" means not applicable.
Source: Bureau of the Census, Current Population Survey Annual Social and Economic Supplement, Internet site http://www.census.gov/hhes/www/income/dinctabs.html; calculations by New Strategist

Table 7.2 Total and Asian Households by Household Type, 2010

(number and percent distribution of total and Asian households, and Asian share of total, by type, 2010; numbers in thousands)

	total		Asian		
	number	percent distribution	number	percent distribution	share of total
TOTAL HOUSEHOLDS	**117,538**	**100.0%**	**4,940**	**100.0%**	**4.2%**
Family households	**78,833**	**67.1**	**3,742**	**75.7**	**4.7**
Married couples	58,410	49.7	2,987	60.5	5.1
With own children under age 18	24,575	20.9	1,622	32.8	6.6
Female householders, no spouse present	14,843	12.6	481	9.7	3.2
With own children under age 18	8,419	7.2	205	4.1	2.4
Male householders, no spouse present	5,580	4.7	273	5.5	4.9
With own children under age 18	2,224	1.9	62	1.3	2.8
Nonfamily households	**38,705**	**32.9**	**1,198**	**24.3**	**3.1**
Female householders	20,442	17.4	581	11.8	2.8
Living alone	17,428	14.8	465	9.4	2.7
Male householders	18,263	15.5	617	12.5	3.4
Living alone	13,971	11.9	450	9.1	3.2

Note: Asians are those who identify themselves as being of the race alone or as being of the race in combination with other races.

Source: Bureau of the Census, Current Population Survey Annual Social and Economic Supplement, Internet site http://www.census.gov/hhes/www/income/dinctabs.html; calculations by New Strategist

Table 7.3 Asian Households by Age of Householder and Household Type, 2010

(number and percent distribution of Asian households by age of householder and household type, 2010; numbers in thousands)

		family households			nonfamily households			
					female-headed		male-headed	
	total	married couples	female hh, no spouse present	male hh, no spouse present	total	living alone	total	living alone
Total Asian households	**4,940**	**2,987**	**481**	**273**	**581**	**465**	**617**	**450**
Under age 25	292	33	44	72	68	26	75	20
Aged 25 to 29	475	182	50	44	68	45	130	89
Aged 30 to 34	581	365	39	29	54	39	94	67
Aged 35 to 39	631	432	55	34	44	42	67	60
Aged 40 to 44	549	407	56	8	30	27	49	34
Aged 45 to 49	540	370	63	22	42	33	42	35
Aged 50 to 54	480	344	37	29	36	33	34	26
Aged 55 to 64	709	493	79	15	67	53	55	51
Aged 65 to 74	383	227	28	17	68	64	43	41
Aged 75 or older	299	135	29	3	103	103	29	27
PERCENT DISTRIBUTION BY AGE								
Total Asian households	**100.0%**	**100.0%**	**100.0%**	**100.0%**	**100.0%**	**100.0%**	**100.0%**	**100.0%**
Under age 25	5.9	1.1	9.1	26.4	11.7	5.6	12.2	4.4
Aged 25 to 29	9.6	6.1	10.4	16.1	11.7	9.7	21.1	19.8
Aged 30 to 34	11.8	12.2	8.1	10.6	9.3	8.4	15.2	14.9
Aged 35 to 39	12.8	14.5	11.4	12.5	7.6	9.0	10.9	13.3
Aged 40 to 44	11.1	13.6	11.6	2.9	5.2	5.8	7.9	7.6
Aged 45 to 49	10.9	12.4	13.1	8.1	7.2	7.1	6.8	7.8
Aged 50 to 54	9.7	11.5	7.7	10.6	6.2	7.1	5.5	5.8
Aged 55 to 64	14.4	16.5	16.4	5.5	11.5	11.4	8.9	11.3
Aged 65 to 74	7.8	7.6	5.8	6.2	11.7	13.8	7.0	9.1
Aged 75 or older	6.1	4.5	6.0	1.1	17.7	22.2	4.7	6.0
PERCENT DISTRIBUTION BY HOUSEHOLD TYPE								
Total Asian households	**100.0%**	**60.5%**	**9.7%**	**5.5%**	**11.8%**	**9.4%**	**12.5%**	**9.1%**
Under age 25	100.0	11.3	15.1	24.7	23.3	8.9	25.7	6.8
Aged 25 to 29	100.0	38.3	10.5	9.3	14.3	9.5	27.4	18.7
Aged 30 to 34	100.0	62.8	6.7	5.0	9.3	6.7	16.2	11.5
Aged 35 to 39	100.0	68.5	8.7	5.4	7.0	6.7	10.6	9.5
Aged 40 to 44	100.0	74.1	10.2	1.5	5.5	4.9	8.9	6.2
Aged 45 to 49	100.0	68.5	11.7	4.1	7.8	6.1	7.8	6.5
Aged 50 to 54	100.0	71.7	7.7	6.0	7.5	6.9	7.1	5.4
Aged 55 to 64	100.0	69.5	11.1	2.1	9.4	7.5	7.8	7.2
Aged 65 to 74	100.0	59.3	7.3	4.4	17.8	16.7	11.2	10.7
Aged 75 or older	100.0	45.2	9.7	1.0	34.4	34.4	9.7	9.0

Note: Asians are those who identify themselves as being of the race alone or the race in combination with other races.
Source: Bureau of the Census, Current Population Survey Annual Social and Economic Supplement, Internet site http://www.census.gov/hhes/www/income/dinctabs.html; calculations by New Strategist

Asian Households Are Larger than Average

Even in old age, few Asians live alone.

The average Asian household includes 2.95 people, significantly larger than the 2.59 people in the average American household. Among households with seven or more people, Asians head a disproportionately large 8 percent. Among single-person households, Asians head just 3 percent.

Only 8 percent of Asians live alone. The proportion rises to 21 percent among those aged 75 or older. In the oldest age group, Asian women are more likely than Asian men to live alone—27 versus 12 percent.

■ Asian households are larger than average because they are more likely to include children.

Asians account for a disproportionate share of large households

(Asian share of total households by household size, 2010)

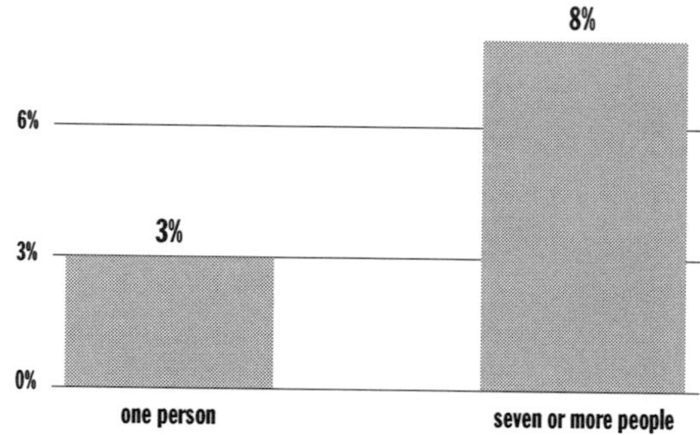

Table 7.4 Total and Asian Households by Size, 2010

(number and percent distribution of total and Asian households, and Asian share of total, by size, 2010; numbers in thousands)

	total		Asian		
	number	percent distribution	number	percent distribution	share of total
Total households	**117,538**	**100.0%**	**4,940**	**100.0%**	**4.2%**
One person	31,399	26.7	915	18.5	2.9
Two people	39,487	33.6	1,330	26.9	3.4
Three people	18,638	15.9	987	20.0	5.3
Four people	16,122	13.7	988	20.0	6.1
Five people	7,367	6.3	422	8.5	5.7
Six people	2,784	2.4	164	3.3	5.9
Seven or more people	1,740	1.5	132	2.7	7.6
Average number of people per household	2.59	–	2.95	–	–

Note: Asians are those who identify themselves as being of the race alone or the race in combination with other races. "–" means not applicable.
Source: Bureau of the Census, Current Population Survey Annual Social and Economic Supplement, Internet site http://www.census.gov/hhes/www/income/dinctabs.html; calculations by New Strategist

Table 7.5 Asians Who Live Alone by Sex and Age, 2010

(total number of Asians aged 15 or older, number and percent who live alone, and percent distribution of Asians living alone, by sex and age, 2010; numbers in thousands)

		living alone		
	total	number	percent distribution	share of total
Total Asians	**11,874**	**915**	**100.0%**	**7.7%**
Under age 25	1,993	46	5.0	2.3
Aged 25 to 34	2,514	240	26.2	9.5
Aged 35 to 44	2,470	163	17.8	6.6
Aged 45 to 54	2,032	127	13.9	6.3
Aged 55 to 64	1,487	104	11.4	7.0
Aged 65 to 74	761	105	11.5	13.8
Aged 75 or older	618	130	14.2	21.0
Asian men	**5,614**	**450**	**100.0**	**8.0**
Under age 25	1,009	20	4.4	2.0
Aged 25 to 34	1,215	156	34.7	12.8
Aged 35 to 44	1,169	94	20.9	8.0
Aged 45 to 54	965	61	13.6	6.3
Aged 55 to 64	680	51	11.3	7.5
Aged 65 to 74	345	41	9.1	11.9
Aged 75 or older	231	27	6.0	11.7
Asian women	**6,260**	**465**	**100.0**	**7.4**
Under age 25	983	26	5.6	2.6
Aged 25 to 34	1,299	84	18.1	6.5
Aged 35 to 44	1,301	69	14.8	5.3
Aged 45 to 54	1,068	66	14.2	6.2
Aged 55 to 64	807	53	11.4	6.6
Aged 65 to 74	415	64	13.8	15.4
Aged 75 or older	387	103	22.2	26.6

Note: Asians are those who identify themselves as being of the race alone or in combination with other races.
Source: Bureau of the Census, 2010 Current Population Survey Annual Social and Economic Supplement, Internet site http://www.census.gov/hhes/www/income/data/incpovhlth/2009/dtables.html; calculations by New Strategist

Asian Households Are Likely to include Children

Most Asian children live with both parents.

Thirty-eight percent of Asian households include children under age 18, significantly greater than the 30 percent share among all U.S. households. Just over 50 percent of Asian households—the majority—include children of any age. This compares with a smaller 40 percent of all households that include children of any age. Most Asian married couples in all but the oldest age group have children (of any age) living under their roof.

Asian children under age 18 are much more likely than the average American child to live with married parents. Eighty-three percent of Asian children live with married parents. Among all children, the figure is a smaller 66 percent.

■ The Great Recession has likely boosted the percentage of Asian households that include adult children.

Most Asian householders have children in their home

(percent of total and Asian households with children under age 18 and children of any age in the household, 2010)

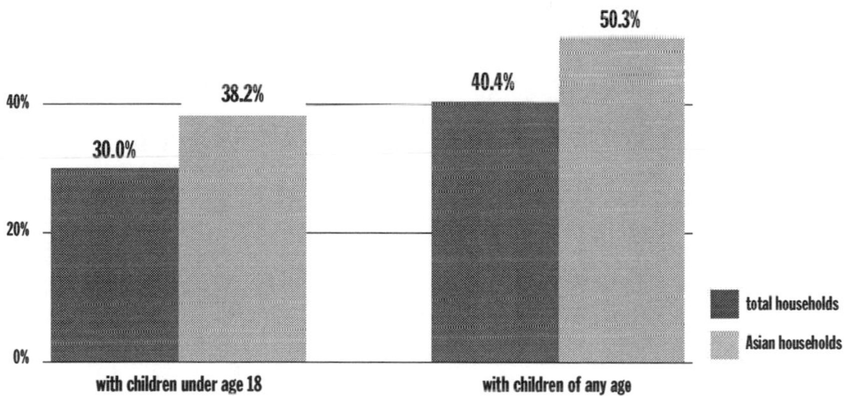

Table 7.6 Total and Asian Households with Children under Age 18 by Age of Householder, 2010

(number of total and Asian households, number and percent with own children under age 18, and number and percent distribution of total and Asian households with children under age 18 by age of householder and Asian share of total, 2010; numbers in thousands)

	total		Asian		
	number	percent distribution	number	percent distribution	share of total
Total households	**117,538**	**100.0%**	**4,940**	**100.0%**	**4.2%**
Households with children under 18	35,218	30.0	1,889	38.2	5.4
Total households with children under 18	**35,218**	**100.0**	**1,889**	**100.0**	**5.4**
Under age 25	1,746	5.0	33	1.7	1.9
Aged 25 to 29	4,046	11.5	127	6.7	3.1
Aged 30 to 34	5,813	16.5	293	15.5	5.0
Aged 35 to 39	7,115	20.2	415	22.0	5.8
Aged 40 to 44	6,557	18.6	402	21.3	6.1
Aged 45 to 49	5,527	15.7	333	17.6	6.0
Aged 50 to 54	2,826	8.0	190	10.1	6.7
Aged 55 to 64	1,347	3.8	77	4.1	5.7
Aged 65 or older	241	0.7	20	1.1	8.3

Note: Asians are those who identify themselves as being of the race alone or the race in combination with other races.
Source: Bureau of the Census, America's Families and Living Arrangements: 2010, Current Population Survey Annual Social and Economic Supplement, Internet site http://www.census.gov/population/www/socdemo/hh-fam/cps2010.html; calculations by New Strategist

Table 7.7 Total and Asian Households with Children of Any Age by Age of Householder, 2010

(number of total and Asian households, number and percent with own children of any age, and number and percent distribution of total and Asian households with children of any age by age of householder and Asian share of total, 2010; numbers in thousands)

	total		Asian		
	number	percent distribution	number	percent distribution	share of total
Total households	**117,538**	**100.0%**	**4,940**	**100.0%**	**4.2%**
Households with children of any age	47,463	40.4	2,483	50.3	5.2
Households with children of any age	**47,463**	**100.0**	**2,483**	**100.0**	**5.2**
Under age 25	1,779	3.7	35	1.4	2.0
Aged 25 to 29	4,059	8.6	127	5.1	3.1
Aged 30 to 34	5,868	12.4	299	12.0	5.1
Aged 35 to 39	7,299	15.4	423	17.0	5.8
Aged 40 to 44	7,297	15.4	421	17.0	5.8
Aged 45 to 49	7,306	15.4	393	15.8	5.4
Aged 50 to 54	5,457	11.5	298	12.0	5.5
Aged 55 to 64	5,170	10.9	325	13.1	6.3
Aged 65 or older	3,228	6.8	163	6.6	5.0

Note: Asians are those who identify themselves as being of the race alone or the race in combination with other races.
Source: Bureau of the Census, America's Families and Living Arrangements: 2010, Current Population Survey Annual Social and Economic Supplement, Internet site http://www.census.gov/population/www/socdemo/hh-fam/cps2010.html; calculations by New Strategist

Table 7.8 Total and Asian Households with Children by Type of Household, 2010

(number and percent distribution of total and Asian households with own children under age 18 or of any age, and Asian share of total, by type of household, 2010; numbers in thousands)

	total		Asian		
	number	percent distribution	number	percent distribution	share of total
Total households with own children under 18	**35,218**	**100.0%**	**1,889**	**100.0%**	**5.4%**
Married couples	24,575	69.8	1,622	85.9	6.6
Female-headed families	8,419	23.9	205	10.9	2.4
Male-headed families	2,224	6.3	62	3.3	2.8
Total households with own children of any age	**47,463**	**100.0**	**2,483**	**100.0**	**5.2**
Married couples	31,514	66.4	2,051	82.6	6.5
Female-headed families	12,624	26.6	344	13.9	2.7
Male-headed families	3,325	7.0	88	3.5	2.6

Note: Asians are those who identify themselves as being of the race alone or as being of the race in combination with other races.

Source: Bureau of the Census, America's Families and Living Arrangements: 2010, Current Population Survey Annual Social and Economic Supplement, Internet site http://www.census.gov/population/www/socdemo/hh-fam/cps2010.html; calculations by New Strategist

Table 7.9 Asian Households by Age of Householder, Type of Household, and Presence of Children under Age 18, 2010

(number and percent distribution of Asian households by age of householder, type of household, and presence of own children under age 18, and average age of householder, 2010; numbers in thousands)

	total		married couples		female-headed families		male-headed families	
	total	with children <18	total	with children <18	total	with children <18	total	with children <18
Total Asian households	**4,940**	**1,889**	**2,987**	**1,622**	**481**	**205**	**273**	**62**
Under age 25	292	33	32	22	44	6	72	3
Aged 25 to 29	475	127	182	105	50	18	44	4
Aged 30 to 34	581	293	365	267	39	20	29	5
Aged 35 to 39	631	415	432	352	55	46	34	17
Aged 40 to 44	549	402	407	350	56	45	8	7
Aged 45 to 49	540	333	370	281	63	45	22	7
Aged 50 to 54	480	190	344	159	37	18	29	12
Aged 55 to 64	709	77	493	68	79	6	15	2
Aged 65 or older	682	20	362	17	57	0	20	2
Average age of householder	46.0	40.9	47.8	41.1	46.4	39.5	36.9	40.3
PERCENT OF HOUSEHOLDS WITH CHILDREN BY TYPE								
Total Asian households	**100.0%**	**38.2%**	**100.0%**	**54.3%**	**100.0%**	**42.6%**	**100.0%**	**22.7%**
Under age 25	100.0	11.3	100.0	68.8	100.0	13.6	100.0	4.2
Aged 25 to 29	100.0	26.7	100.0	57.7	100.0	36.0	100.0	9.1
Aged 30 to 34	100.0	50.4	100.0	73.2	100.0	51.3	100.0	17.2
Aged 35 to 39	100.0	65.8	100.0	81.5	100.0	83.6	100.0	50.0
Aged 40 to 44	100.0	73.2	100.0	86.0	100.0	80.4	100.0	87.5
Aged 45 to 49	100.0	61.7	100.0	75.9	100.0	71.4	100.0	31.8
Aged 50 to 54	100.0	39.6	100.0	46.2	100.0	48.6	100.0	41.4
Aged 55 to 64	100.0	10.9	100.0	13.8	100.0	7.6	100.0	13.3
Aged 65 or older	100.0	2.9	100.0	4.7	100.0	0.0	100.0	10.0

Note: Asians are those who identify themselves as being of the race alone or the race in combination with other races.
Source: Bureau of the Census, America's Families and Living Arrangements: 2010, Current Population Survey Annual Social and Economic Supplement, Internet site http://www.census.gov/population/www/socdemo/hh-fam/cps2010.html; calculations by New Strategist

Table 7.10 Asian Households by Age of Householder, Type of Household, and Presence of Children of Any Age, 2010

(number and percent distribution of Asian households by age of householder, type of household, and presence of own children of any age, and average age of householder, 2010; numbers in thousands)

	total		married couples		female-headed families		male-headed families	
	total	with children of any age	total	with children of any age	total	with children of any age	total	with children of any age
Total Asian households	**4,940**	**2,483**	**2,987**	**2,051**	**481**	**344**	**273**	**88**
Under age 25	292	35	32	24	44	6	72	3
Aged 25 to 29	475	127	182	105	50	18	44	4
Aged 30 to 34	581	299	365	267	39	26	29	5
Aged 35 to 39	631	423	432	357	55	49	34	18
Aged 40 to 44	549	421	407	363	56	51	8	7
Aged 45 to 49	540	393	370	326	63	59	22	9
Aged 50 to 54	480	298	344	251	37	30	29	17
Aged 55 to 64	709	325	493	258	79	57	15	10
Aged 65 or older	682	163	362	100	57	47	20	16
Average age of householder	46.0	45.5	47.8	44.8	46.4	49.0	36.9	46.6
PERCENT OF HOUSEHOLDS WITH CHILDREN BY TYPE								
Total Asian households	**100.0%**	**50.3%**	**100.0%**	**68.7%**	**100.0%**	**71.5%**	**100.0%**	**32.2%**
Under age 25	100.0	12.0	100.0	75.0	100.0	13.6	100.0	4.2
Aged 25 to 29	100.0	26.7	100.0	57.7	100.0	36.0	100.0	9.1
Aged 30 to 34	100.0	51.5	100.0	73.2	100.0	66.7	100.0	17.2
Aged 35 to 39	100.0	67.0	100.0	82.6	100.0	89.1	100.0	52.9
Aged 40 to 44	100.0	76.7	100.0	89.2	100.0	91.1	100.0	87.5
Aged 45 to 49	100.0	72.8	100.0	88.1	100.0	93.7	100.0	40.9
Aged 50 to 54	100.0	62.1	100.0	73.0	100.0	81.1	100.0	58.6
Aged 55 to 64	100.0	45.8	100.0	52.3	100.0	72.2	100.0	66.7
Aged 65 or older	100.0	23.9	100.0	27.6	100.0	82.5	100.0	80.0

Note: Asians are those who identify themselves as being of the race alone or the race in combination with other races.
Source: Bureau of the Census, America's Families and Living Arrangements: 2010, Current Population Survey Annual Social and Economic Supplement, Internet site http://www.census.gov/population/www/socdemo/hh-fam/cps2010.html; calculations by New Strategist

Table 7.11 Living Arrangements of Total and Asian Children, 2010

(number and percent distribution of total and Asian children under age 18 by living arrangement, and Asian share of total, 2010; numbers in thousands)

	total		Asian		
	number	percent distribution	number	percent distribution	share of total
TOTAL CHILDREN	**74,718**	**100.0%**	**3,984**	**100.0%**	**5.3%**
Living with two parents	**51,823**	**69.4**	**3,372**	**84.6**	**6.5**
Married parents	49,106	65.7	3,314	83.2	6.7
Unmarried parents	2,717	3.6	58	1.5	2.1
Biological mother and father	46,438	62.2	3,171	79.6	6.8
Married parents	44,099	59.0	3,123	78.4	7.1
Biological mother and stepfather	3,252	4.4	68	1.7	2.1
Biological father and stepmother	955	1.3	29	0.7	3.0
Biological mother and adoptive father	167	0.2	3	0.1	1.8
Biological father and adoptive mother	33	0.0	–	–	–
Adoptive mother and father	768	1.0	93	2.3	12.1
Other	210	0.3	7	0.2	3.3
Living with one parent	**19,857**	**26.6**	**535**	**13.4**	**2.7**
Mother only	17,285	23.1	441	11.1	2.6
Father only	2,572	3.4	94	2.4	3.7
Living with no parents	**3,038**	**4.1**	**77**	**1.9**	**2.5**
Grandparents	1,655	2.2	24	0.6	1.5
Other	1,383	1.9	53	1.3	3.8
At least one biological parent	**70,236**	**94.0**	**3,776**	**94.8**	**5.4**
At least one stepparent	**4,615**	**6.2**	**113**	**2.8**	**2.4**
At least one adoptive parent	**1,258**	**1.7**	**120**	**3.0**	**9.5**

Note: Asians are those who identify themselves as being of the race alone and those who identify themselves as being of the race in combination with other races. "–" means sample is too small to make a reliable estimate.
Source: Bureau of the Census, Current Population Survey Annual Social and Economic Supplement, America's Families and Living Arrangements: 2010, detailed tables, Internet site http://www.census.gov/population/www/socdemo/hh-fam/cps2010 .html; calculations by New Strategist

Table 7.12 Living Arrangements of Total and Asian Adults, 2010

(number and percent distribution of total people and Asians aged 15 or older and Asian share of total, by relationship to householder, 2010; numbers in thousands)

	total		Asian		
	number	percent distribution	number	percent distribution	share of total
Total people	**242,168**	**100.0**	**11,874**	**100.0**	**4.9**
Householder	78,867	32.6	3,742	31.5	4.7
Spouse of householder	58,428	24.1	3,171	26.7	5.4
Child of householder	36,605	15.1	1,738	14.6	4.7
Other relative of householder	14,476	6.0	1,369	11.5	9.5
Nonrelatives	53,791	22.2	1,855	15.6	3.4

Note: Asians are those who identify themselves as being of the race alone or as being of the race in combination with other races.

Source: Bureau of the Census, Current Population Survey Annual Social and Economic Supplement, Internet site http://www.census.gov/hhes/www/income/dinctabs.html; calculations by New Strategist

Table 7.13 Living Arrangements of Asians by Sex, 2010

(number and percent distribution of Asian men and women aged 15 or older by relationship to householder, 2010; numbers in thousands)

	men		women	
	number	percent distribution	number	percent distribution
Total Asians	**5,614**	**100.0%**	**6,260**	**100.0%**
Householder	2,249	40.1	1,493	23.8
Spouse of householder	923	16.4	2,247	35.9
Child of householder	925	16.5	813	13.0
Other relative of householder	556	9.9	813	13.0
Nonrelatives	961	17.1	894	14.3

Note: Asians are those who identify themselves as being of the race alone or as being of the race in combination with other races.

Source: Bureau of the Census, Current Population Survey Annual Social and Economic Supplement, Internet site http://www.census.gov/hhes/www/income/dinctabs.html; calculations by New Strategist

Most Asian Men and Women Are Married

Few have ever divorced.

The majority of Asian men and women aged 18 or older are married. Among Asian men, the percentage who are married and living with their spouse rises rapidly from just 24 percent in the 25-to-29 age group to 62 percent in the 30-to-34 age group. Among Asian women, the married-and-living-with-spouse share rises 50 percent in the 25-to-29 age group.

Only 8 to 11 percent of Asian men and women have ever divorced, according to a Census Bureau study. The percentage ever divorced rises to a peak of 19 percent among Asian women aged 40 to 49. The majority of Asian men aged 30 or older have been married only once and are still married. Among Asian women, most have married once and are still married from ages 30 to 69. The figure falls below 50 percent among Asian women aged 70 or older because many have become widows.

■ Divorce rates among Asians may rise as Asian immigrants become assimilated into the American culture.

Asians are more likely to marry once and stay married

(percent distribution of Asians aged 15 or older by marital history and sex, 2009)

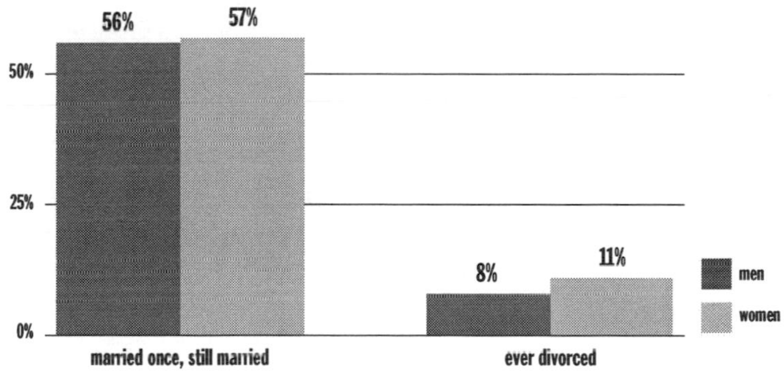

Table 7.14 Total and Asian Marital Status, 2010

(number and percent distribution of total people and Asians aged 15 or older, and Asian share of total, by marital status, 2010; numbers in thousands)

	total		Asians		
	number	percent distribution	number	percent distribution	share of total
Total people	**242,047**	**100.0%**	**11,873**	**100.0%**	**4.9%**
Never married	74,243	30.7	3,554	29.9	4.8
Married, spouse present	120,768	49.9	6,794	57.2	5.6
Married, spouse absent	3,415	1.4	314	2.6	9.2
Separated	5,539	2.3	159	1.3	2.9
Divorced	23,742	9.8	520	4.4	2.2
Widowed	14,341	5.9	533	4.5	3.7

Note: Asians are those who identify themselves as being of the race alone or of the race in combination with other races.
Source: Bureau of the Census, America's Families and Living Arrangements: 2010, Current Population Survey Annual Social and Economic Supplement, Internet site http://www.census.gov/population/www/socdemo/hh-fam/cps2010.html; calculations by New Strategist

Table 7.15 Marital Status of Asian Men by Age, 2010

(number and percent distribution of Asian men aged 18 or older by age and current marital status, 2010; numbers in thousands)

	total	never married	married, spouse present	married, spouse absent	separated	divorced	widowed
Total Asian men	**5,332**	**1,654**	**3,212**	**151**	**53**	**192**	**70**
Aged 18 to 19	203	200	2	1	0	0	0
Aged 20 to 24	525	488	27	4	6	1	0
Aged 25 to 29	591	414	143	12	6	6	10
Aged 30 to 34	624	203	385	13	2	19	2
Aged 35 to 39	616	121	437	20	6	33	0
Aged 40 to 44	553	87	434	17	2	12	1
Aged 45 to 49	501	59	387	21	0	30	3
Aged 50 to 54	464	25	374	22	8	30	4
Aged 55 to 64	680	38	572	18	10	36	6
Aged 65 or older	576	19	451	21	14	26	44
Total Asian men	**100.0%**	**31.0%**	**60.2%**	**2.8%**	**1.0%**	**3.6%**	**1.3%**
Aged 18 to 19	100.0	98.5	1.0	0.5	0.0	0.0	0.0
Aged 20 to 24	100.0	93.0	5.1	0.8	1.1	0.2	0.0
Aged 25 to 29	100.0	70.1	24.2	2.0	1.0	1.0	1.7
Aged 30 to 34	100.0	32.5	61.7	2.1	0.3	3.0	0.3
Aged 35 to 39	100.0	19.6	70.9	3.2	1.0	5.4	0.0
Aged 40 to 44	100.0	15.7	78.5	3.1	0.4	2.2	0.2
Aged 45 to 49	100.0	11.8	77.2	4.2	0.0	6.0	0.6
Aged 50 to 54	100.0	5.4	80.6	4.7	1.7	6.5	0.9
Aged 55 to 64	100.0	5.6	84.1	2.6	1.5	5.3	0.9
Aged 65 or older	100.0	3.3	78.3	3.6	2.4	4.5	7.6

Note: Asians are those who identify themselves as being of the race alone or of the race in combination with other races.
Source: Bureau of the Census, America's Families and Living Arrangements: 2010, Current Population Survey Annual Social and Economic Supplement, Internet site http://www.census.gov/population/www/socdemo/hh-fam/cps2010.html; calculations by New Strategist

Table 7.16 Marital Status of Asian Women by Age, 2010

(number and percent distribution of Asian women aged 18 or older by age and current marital status, 2010; numbers in thousands)

	total	never married	married, spouse present	married, spouse absent	separated	divorced	widowed
Total Asian women	**5,942**	**1,319**	**3,581**	**161**	**93**	**328**	**461**
Aged 18 to 19	155	150	0	0	2	2	2
Aged 20 to 24	510	421	73	10	4	2	0
Aged 25 to 29	637	278	333	8	6	10	2
Aged 30 to 34	662	126	492	8	10	24	2
Aged 35 to 39	681	97	514	11	10	45	5
Aged 40 to 44	620	65	459	20	16	47	14
Aged 45 to 49	583	50	414	38	9	51	19
Aged 50 to 54	485	30	368	15	7	48	17
Aged 55 to 64	807	59	567	27	14	62	78
Aged 65 or older	802	43	361	25	16	36	322
Total Asian women	**100.0%**	**22.2%**	**60.3%**	**2.7%**	**1.6%**	**5.5%**	**7.8%**
Aged 18 to 19	100.0	96.8	0.0	0.0	1.3	1.3	1.3
Aged 20 to 24	100.0	82.5	14.3	2.0	0.8	0.4	0.0
Aged 25 to 29	100.0	43.6	52.3	1.3	0.9	1.6	0.3
Aged 30 to 34	100.0	19.0	74.3	1.2	1.5	3.6	0.3
Aged 35 to 39	100.0	14.2	75.5	1.6	1.5	6.6	0.7
Aged 40 to 44	100.0	10.5	74.0	3.2	2.6	7.6	2.3
Aged 45 to 49	100.0	8.6	71.0	6.5	1.5	8.7	3.3
Aged 50 to 54	100.0	6.2	75.9	3.1	1.4	9.9	3.5
Aged 55 to 64	100.0	7.3	70.3	3.3	1.7	7.7	9.7
Aged 65 or older	100.0	5.4	45.0	3.1	2.0	4.5	40.1

Note: Asians are those who identify themselves as being of the race alone or of the race in combination with other races.
Source: Bureau of the Census, America's Families and Living Arrangements: 2010, Current Population Survey Annual Social and Economic Supplement, Internet site http://www.census.gov/population/www/socdemo/hh-fam/cps2010.html; calculations by New Strategist

Table 7.17 Marital History of Asian Men by Age, 2009

(number of Asian men aged 15 or older and percent distribution by marital history and age, 2009; numbers in thousands)

	total	15–19	20–24	25–29	30–34	35–39	40–49	50–59	60–69	70+
Total Asian men, number	**4,352**	**369**	**334**	**505**	**440**	**488**	**940**	**608**	**387**	**281**
Total Asian men, percent	**100.0%**	**100.0%**	**100.0%**	**100.0%**	**100.0%**	**100.0%**	**100.0%**	**100.0%**	**100.0%**	**100.0%**
Never married	33.0	97.1	94.8	70.9	30.6	17.1	13.7	6.4	0.0	5.8
Ever married	67.0	2.9	5.2	29.1	69.4	82.9	86.3	93.6	100.0	94.2
Married once	62.4	1.9	5.2	27.6	68.8	77.0	80.0	84.6	90.7	91.2
Still married	55.8	1.6	4.2	26.3	67.5	71.8	72.4	74.1	75.5	74.0
Married twice	4.3	0.9	0.0	1.5	0.6	5.2	6.0	9.0	7.3	3.0
Still married	3.7	0.0	0.0	0.7	0.6	5.2	5.5	7.4	7.3	1.9
Married three or more times	0.3	0.0	0.0	0.0	0.0	0.7	0.4	0.0	2.0	0.0
Still married	0.2	0.0	0.0	0.0	0.0	0.7	0.0	0.0	1.4	0.0
Ever divorced	8.2	0.9	0.0	1.5	1.8	10.7	11.3	17.3	14.2	6.3
Currently divorced	4.4	0.9	0.0	0.8	1.2	4.7	6.1	9.5	7.3	5.0
Ever widowed	2.1	0.0	0.0	0.9	0.0	0.0	1.0	1.6	7.8	13.7
Currently widowed	1.7	0.0	0.0	0.9	0.0	0.0	0.6	1.6	5.4	12.0

Note: Asians are those who identify themselves as being of the race alone.
Source: Bureau of the Census, Number, Timing, and Duration of Marriages and Divorces: 2009, Detailed Tables, Internet site http://www.census.gov/hhes/socdemo/marriage/data/sipp/index.html

Table 7.18 Marital History of Asian Women by Age, 2009

(number of Asian women aged 15 or older and percent distribution by marital history and age, 2009; numbers in thousands)

	total	15–19	20–24	25–29	30–34	35–39	40–49	50–59	60–69	70+
Total Asian women, number	**4,919**	**364**	**347**	**492**	**549**	**565**	**957**	**794**	**443**	**408**
Total Asian women, percent	**100.0%**	**100.0%**	**100.0%**	**100.0%**	**100.0%**	**100.0%**	**100.0%**	**100.0%**	**100.0%**	**100.0%**
Never married	23.8	96.5	85.2	51.6	11.8	10.2	6.6	5.8	7.1	1.3
Ever married	76.2	3.5	14.8	48.4	88.2	89.8	93.4	94.2	92.9	98.7
Married once	69.2	3.5	14.8	48.4	84.6	86.2	80.1	83.4	81.7	88.3
Still married	57.2	3.5	13.6	46.8	78.8	76.7	69.6	70.6	61.4	39.1
Married twice	6.4	0.0	0.0	0.0	3.0	3.3	12.0	10.1	10.2	9.6
Still married	5.0	0.0	0.0	0.0	3.0	2.8	11.4	7.0	7.7	4.0
Married three or more times	0.6	0.0	0.0	0.0	0.6	0.4	1.2	0.7	1.0	0.9
Still married	0.5	0.0	0.0	0.0	0.6	0.4	1.2	0.3	1.0	0.0
Ever divorced	11.1	0.0	0.7	0.6	6.9	11.9	19.2	17.4	14.8	11.2
Currently divorced	5.6	0.0	0.7	0.6	4.3	8.7	6.8	10.0	6.5	6.2
Ever widowed	7.1	0.0	0.0	0.0	1.3	0.6	1.7	5.5	17.2	49.9
Currently widowed	6.5	0.0	0.0	0.0	0.3	0.6	1.5	4.7	15.3	47.4

Note: Asians are those who identify themselves as being of the race alone.
Source: Bureau of the Census, Number, Timing, and Duration of Marriages and Divorces: 2009, Detailed Tables, Internet site http://www.census.gov/hhes/socdemo/marriage/data/sipp/index.html

CHAPTER
8

Population

■ The number of Asians in the United States grew 44 percent between 2000 and 2010, more than four times as fast as the population as a whole. Despite this rapid growth, Asians account for only 6 percent of the total U.S. population.

■ The Chinese are the largest ethnic group among Asians, accounting for 23 percent of the total. Asian Indians are number two at 19 percent, with Filipinos close behind at 18 percent.

■ Only 33 percent of Asians living in the United States were born here. Thirty-nine percent are naturalized citizens, and 28 percent are not citizens.

■ The West is home to 46 percent of the nation's Asian population. In the West, Asians account for 11 percent of the population—a far higher share than in any other region.

■ Nearly one-third (32 percent) of the nation's Asians live in California, where they account for 15 percent of the population.

■ Three metropolitan areas are home to at least 1 million Asians: New York, Los Angeles, and San Francisco.

The Number of Asians Is Growing Rapidly

The Asian population is growing faster than the Hispanic population.

The number of Asians in the United States grew 44 percent between 2000 and 2010, more than four times as fast as the population as a whole. The count of Asians ranges from 15 million who identify themselves as Asian and no other race (called Asian alone) to 17 million who identify themselves as Asian alone or in combination with other races. Beginning in 2000, Americans could identify themselves as being of more than one race, which increases the complexity of racial identification. In 2010, more than 1.6 million Asians identified themselves as both Asian and white, for example. Adding even more to the complexity is the fact that Hispanic is an ethnic identity rather than a race, meaning Asians can also be Hispanic. Two percent of the nation's Asians also identify themselves as Hispanic.

Despite the rapid growth of the Asian population, Asians account for just 6 percent of the total U.S. population. They are greatly outnumbered by Hispanics and blacks and will be for the foreseeable future.

- Immigration is fueling the growth of the Asian population.

Asians are outnumbered by blacks and Hispanics

(population by race and Hispanic origin, 2010)

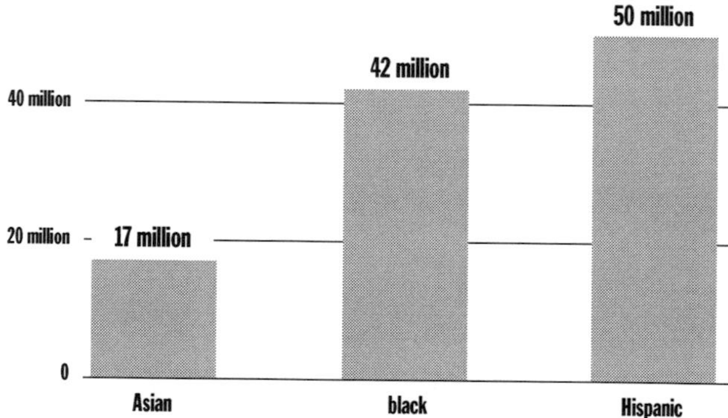

Table 8.1 Population by Race, 2000 and 2010

(number of people by race and Hispanic origin, 2000 and 2010; numerical and percent change, 2000–10)

	2010		2000		change	
	number	percent distribution	number	percent distribution	numerical	percent
Total population	**308,745,538**	**100.0%**	**281,421,906**	**100.0%**	**27,323,632**	**9.7%**
Race alone						
American Indian	2,932,248	0.9	2,475,956	0.9	456,292	18.4
Asian	14,674,252	4.8	10,242,998	3.6	4,431,254	43.3
Black	38,929,319	12.6	34,658,190	12.3	4,271,129	12.3
Native Hawaiian	540,013	0.2	398,835	0.1	141,178	35.4
White	223,553,265	72.4	211,460,626	75.1	12,092,639	5.7
Other race	19,107,368	6.2	15,359,073	5.5	3,748,295	24.4
Two or more races	**9,009,073**	**2.9**	**6,826,228**	**2.4**	**2,182,845**	**32.0**
Race alone or in combination						
American Indian	5,220,579	1.7	4,225,058	1.5	995,521	23.6
Asian	17,320,856	5.6	12,006,894	4.3	5,313,962	44.3
Black	42,020,743	13.6	37,104,248	13.2	4,916,495	13.3
Native Hawaiian	1,225,195	0.4	906,785	0.3	318,410	35.1
White	231,040,398	74.8	231,434,388	82.2	–393,990	–0.2
Hispanic	**50,477,594**	**16.3**	**35,305,818**	**12.5**	**15,171,776**	**43.0**
Non-Hispanic white	**196,817,552**	**63.7**	**194,552,774**	**69.1**	**2,264,778**	**1.2**

Note: Numbers by race in combination do not add to total because they include those who identify themselves as being of the race alone and those who identify themselves as being of the race in combination with other races. Hispanics may be of any race. Non-Hispanic whites are those who identify themselves as being white alone and not Hispanic. Numbers are for April 1 of each year.
Source: Bureau of the Census, An Overview: Race and Hispanic Origin and the 2010 Census, 2010 Census Briefs, Internet site http://2010.census.gov/2010census/data/; calculations by New Strategist

Table 8.2 Two-or-More-Races Population, 2010

(number and percent of people who identify themselves as being of two or more races, by racial identification, 2010)

	number	percent distribution
TOTAL POPULATION	**308,745,538**	**100.0%**
One race	**299,736,465**	**97.1**
White	223,553,265	72.4
Black	38,929,319	12.6
American Indian	2,932,248	0.9
Asian	14,674,252	4.8
Native Hawaiian	540,013	0.2
Other race	19,107,368	6.2
Two races	**8,265,318**	**2.7**
White and black	1,834,212	0.6
White and American Indian	1,432,309	0.5
White and Asian	1,623,234	0.5
White and Native Hawaiian	169,991	0.1
White and some other race	1,740,924	0.6
Black and American Indian	269,421	0.1
Black and Asian	185,595	0.1
Black and Native Hawaiian	50,308	0.0
Black and other race	314,571	0.1
American Indian and Asian	58,829	0.0
American Indian and Native Hawaiian	11,039	0.0
American Indian and other race	115,752	0.0
Asian and Native Hawaiian	165,690	0.1
Asian and other race	234,462	0.1
Native Hawaiian and other race	58,981	0.0
Three races	**676,469**	**0.2**
White, black, and American Indian	230,848	0.1
White, black, and Asian	61,511	0.0
White, black, and Native Hawaiian	9,245	0.0
White, black, and other race	46,641	0.0
White, American Indian, and Asian	45,960	0.0
White, American Indian, and Native Hawaiian	8,656	0.0
White, American Indian, and other race	30,941	0.0
White, Asian, and Native Hawaiian	143,126	0.0
White, Asian, and other race	35,786	0.0
White, Native Hawaiian, and other race	9,181	0.0
Black, American Indian, and Asian	9,460	0.0
Black, American Indian, and Native Hawaiian	2,142	0.0
Black, American Indian, and other race	8,236	0.0
Black, Asian, and Native Hawaiian	7,295	0.0
Black, Asian, and other race	8,122	0.0

	number	percent distribution
Black, Native Hawaiian, and other race	4,233	0.0%
American Indian, Asian, and Native Hawaiian	3,827	0.0
American Indian, Asian, and other race	3,785	0.0
American Indian, Native Hawaiian, and other race	2,000	0.0
Asian, Native Hawaiian, and other race	5,474	0.0
Four races	**57,875**	**0.0**
White, black, American Indian, and Asian	19,018	0.0
White, black, American Indian, and Native Hawaiian	2,673	0.0
White, black, American Indian, and other race	8,757	0.0
White, black, Asian, and Native Hawaiian	4,852	0.0
White, black, Asian, and other race	2,420	0.0
White, black, Native Hawaiian, and other race	560	0.0
White, American Indian, Asian, and Native Hawaiian	11,500	0.0
White, American Indian, Asian, and other race	1,535	0.0
White, American Indian, Native Hawaiian, and other race	454	0.0
White, Asian, Native Hawaiian, and other race	3,486	0.0
Black, American Indian, Asian, and Native Hawaiian	1,011	0.0
Black, American Indian, Asian, and other race	539	0.0
Black, American Indian, Native Hawaiian, and other race	212	0.0
Black, Asian, Native Hawaiian, and other race	574	0.0
American Indian, Asian, Native Hawaiian, and other race	284	0.0
Five races	**8,619**	**0.0**
White, black, American Indian, Asian, and Native Hawaiian	6,605	0.0
White, black, American Indian, Asian, and other race	1,023	0.0
White, black, American Indian, Native Hawaiian, and other race	182	0.0
White, black, Asian, Native Hawaiian, and other race	268	0.0
White, American Indian, Asian, Native Hawaiian, and other race	443	0.0
Black, American Indian, Asian, Native Hawaiian, and other race	98	0.0
Six races	**792**	**0.0**
White, black, American Indian, Asian, Native Hawaiian, and other race	792	0.0

Note: Most who identify themselves as "other race" are Hispanics who consider Hispanic a race rather than an ethnicity. Census racial categories are shown in the order provided by the Census Bureau. For readability, the names of some census racial categories have been shortened. Blacks include those who identify themselves as African American; American Indians include Alaska Natives; Native Hawaiians include other Pacific Islanders.
Source: Bureau of the Census, An Overview: Race and Hispanic Origin and the 2010 Census, 2010 Census Briefs, Internet site http://2010.census.gov/2010census/data/

Table 8.3 Asians by Racial Identification, 2000 and 2010

(total number of people, and number and percent distribution of Asians by racial identification, 2000 and 2010; percent change, 2000–10)

	2010		2000		
	number	percent distribution	number	percent distribution	percent change 2000–10
Total people	**308,745,538**	**100.0%**	**281,421,906**	**100.0%**	**9.7%**
Asian alone or in combination with one or more other races	17,320,856	5.6	12,006,894	4.3	44.3
Asian alone	14,674,252	4.8	10,242,998	3.6	43.3
Asian in combination	2,646,604	0.9	1,763,896	0.6	50.0

Source: Bureau of the Census, An Overview: Race and Hispanic Origin and the 2010 Census, 2010 Census Briefs, Internet site http://2010.census.gov/2010census/data/; calculations by New Strategist

Table 8.4 Asians by Hispanic Origin, 2010

(number and percent distribution of Asians by Hispanic origin and racial identification, 2010)

	Asian alone or in combination		Asian alone	
	number	percent distribution	number	percent distribution
Total Asians	**17,320,856**	**100.0%**	**14,674,252**	**100.0%**
Not Hispanic	16,931,838	97.8	14,465,124	98.6
Hispanic	389,018	2.2	209,128	1.4

Source: Bureau of the Census, An Overview: Race and Hispanic Origin and the 2010 Census, 2010 Census Briefs, Internet site http://2010.census.gov/2010census/data/; calculations by New Strategist

The Chinese Are the Largest Asian Ethnic Group

Asian Indians are the second-largest group.

The Asian population in the United States includes people from many different countries. The Chinese are the largest ethnic group among Asians, accounting for 23 percent of the total. Asian Indians are number two, accounting for 19 percent. Filipinos are close behind at 18 percent of Asians.

Among the nation's 14 million Asians in 2009, only one-third is native-born. Thirty-nine percent of the country's Asians are foreign-born naturalized citizens. A substantial 28 percent of Asians in the United States are not citizens.

Of the 10.7 million U.S. foreign-born who are from Asian countries, the largest percentage (19 percent) hail from China. Philippines is second with 16 percent, and India is third with a bit less than 16 percent.

■ Because so many Asians are immigrants, a change in the nation's immigration laws would profoundly affect the characteristics of Asians in the United States.

Just five ethnic groups account for 80 percent of Asians

(percent distribution of Asians by selected ethnic group, 2009)

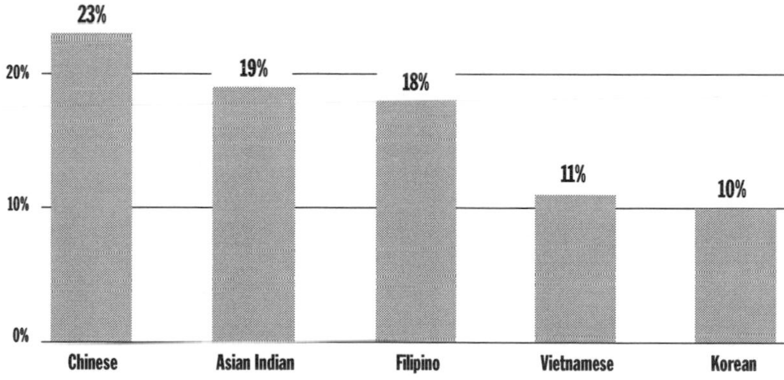

Table 8.5 Asians Ranked by Ethnic Group, 2009

(number and percent distribution of Asians by ethnic group, 2009)

	number	percent
Total Asians specifying an ethnic origin	**13,774,611**	**100.0%**
Chinese	3,106,005	22.5
Asian Indian	2,602,676	18.9
Filipino	2,475,794	18.0
Vietnamese	1,481,513	10.8
Korean	1,335,973	9.7
Japanese	766,875	5.6
Pakistani	333,064	2.4
Cambodian	241,520	1.8
Hmong	226,522	1.6
Laotian	199,433	1.4
Thai	165,371	1.2
Bangladeshi	102,983	0.7
Taiwanese	98,374	0.7
Indonesian	62,722	0.5
Sri Lankan	38,876	0.3
Malaysian	11,868	0.1
Other Asian	418,519	3.0
Other Asian, not specified	106,523	0.8

Note: Asians are those who identify themselves as being Asian alone.
Source: Bureau of the Census, 2009 American Community Survey, Internet site http://www.census.gov/acs/www/; calculations by New Strategist

Table 8.6 Asians by Citizenship Status, 2009

(total number of Asians, and number and percent distribution by foreign-born and citizenship status, by age, 2009)

	number	percent distribution
Total Asians	**13,774,611**	**100.0%**
Native-born	4,578,297	33.2
Foreign-born	9,196,314	66.8
Naturalized citizen	5,304,977	38.5
Not a citizen	3,891,337	28.3
Under age 18	**3,101,543**	**100.0**
Native-born	2,459,710	79.3
Foreign-born	641,833	20.7
Naturalized citizen	220,952	7.1
Not a citizen	420,881	13.6
Aged 18 or older	**10,673,068**	**100.0**
Native-born	2,118,587	19.8
Foreign-born	8,554,481	80.2
Naturalized citizen	5,084,025	47.6
Not a citizen	3,470,456	32.5

Note: Asians are those who identify themselves as being of the race alone.
Source: Bureau of the Census, 2009 American Community Survey, Internet site http://www.census.gov/acs/www/; calculations by New Strategist

Table 8.7 Population Born in Asia, 2009

(number and percent distribution of the population born in Asia, 2009)

	number	percent distribution
Total population	**307,006,556**	**100.0%**
Total foreign-born	38,517,104	12.5
Total born in Asia	10,652,379	3.5
Total born in Asia	**10,652,379**	**100.0**
Eastern Asia	3,334,141	31.3
China	1,990,381	18.7
Hong Kong	210,273	2.0
Taiwan	347,993	3.3
Japan	331,090	3.1
Korea	1,004,329	9.4
Other Eastern Asia	8,341	0.1
South Central Asia	2,713,675	25.5
Afghanistan	64,768	0.6
Bangladesh	151,091	1.4
India	1,665,219	15.6
Iran	362,699	3.4
Kazakhstan	25,389	0.2
Nepal	45,304	0.4
Pakistan	283,988	2.7
Sri Lanka	42,329	0.4
Uzbekistan	49,950	0.5
Other South Central Asia	22,938	0.2
Southeastern Asia	3,666,823	34.4
Burma	76,918	0.7
Cambodia	154,545	1.5
Indonesia	84,096	0.8
Laos	191,780	1.8
Malaysia	48,459	0.5
Philippines	1,725,894	16.2
Singapore	28,723	0.3
Thailand	203,384	1.9
Vietnam	1,152,384	10.8
Other Southeastern Asia	640	0.0
Western Asia	154,220	1.4
Armenia	82,651	0.8
Iraq	140,323	1.3
Israel	131,690	1.2
Jordan	60,406	0.6
Kuwait	21,467	0.2
Lebanon	123,614	1.2
Saudi Arabia	43,166	0.4
Syria	60,827	0.6
Turkey	105,350	1.0
Yeman	38,079	0.4
Other Western Asia	63,230	0.6
Other Asia	44,407	0.4

Source: Bureau of the Census, 2009 American Community Survey, Internet site http://www.census.gov/acs/www/; calculations by New Strategist

The Asian Population Is Aging

The number of older Asians is growing rapidly.

Asians accounted for 5 percent of the U.S. population, according to 2009 Census Bureau estimates (2010 census data by age was not available at the time of publication). The figure peaked at 7 percent in the 30-to-34 age group. The Asian share of the population falls with advancing age, to just 3 percent among people aged 65 or older.

The Asian population is getting older, just as is the U.S. population as a whole. Between 2000 and 2009, the Asian population grew 32 percent overall, but the increase was more than 45 percent among Asians aged 50 or older. Asian women outnumber Asian men beginning in the 25-to-29 age group. Among Asians aged 65 or older, there are only 76 Asian men per 100 Asian women.

■ The Asian share of the U.S. population peaks among 30-to-39-year-olds because many Asians are immigrants coming to the United States to work.

The number of older Asians is growing faster than average

(percent increase in total number of Asians and Asians aged 65 or older, 2000 to 2009)

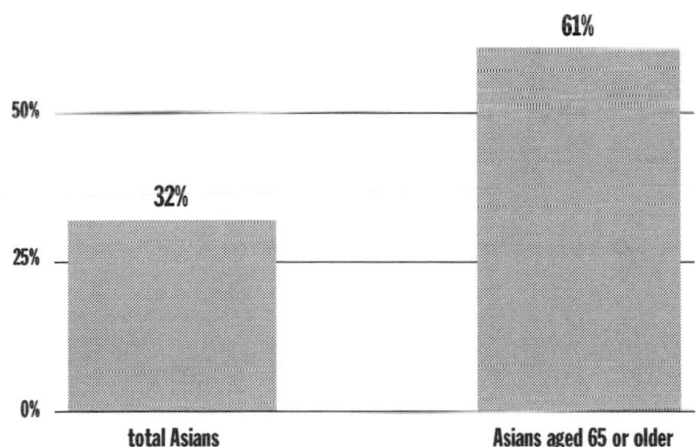

Table 8.8 Asian Share of Total Population by Age, 2009

(total number of people, number and percent distribution of Asians, and Asian share of total, by age, 2009)

		Asian		
	total	number	percent distribution	share of total
Total people	**307,006,550**	**15,989,876**	**100.0%**	**5.2%**
Under age 5	21,299,656	1,324,610	8.3	6.2
Aged 5 to 9	20,609,634	1,224,385	7.7	5.9
Aged 10 to 14	19,973,564	1,064,448	6.7	5.3
Aged 15 to 19	21,537,837	1,046,803	6.5	4.9
Aged 20 to 24	21,539,559	1,082,709	6.8	5.0
Aged 25 to 29	21,677,719	1,277,866	8.0	5.9
Aged 30 to 34	19,888,603	1,352,729	8.5	6.8
Aged 35 to 39	20,538,351	1,387,280	8.7	6.8
Aged 40 to 44	20,991,605	1,208,863	7.6	5.8
Aged 45 to 49	22,831,092	1,118,181	7.0	4.9
Aged 50 to 54	21,761,391	992,591	6.2	4.6
Aged 55 to 59	18,975,026	841,936	5.3	4.4
Aged 60 to 64	15,811,923	652,282	4.1	4.1
Aged 65 to 69	11,784,320	461,603	2.9	3.9
Aged 70 to 74	9,007,747	349,773	2.2	3.9
Aged 75 to 79	7,325,528	259,672	1.6	3.5
Aged 80 to 84	5,822,334	181,322	1.1	3.1
Aged 85 or older	5,630,661	162,823	1.0	2.9
Aged 18 to 24	30,412,035	1,505,431	9.4	5.0
Aged 18 or older	232,458,335	11,752,352	73.5	5.1
Aged 65 or older	39,570,590	1,415,193	8.9	3.6
Median age (years)	36.8	33.6	–	–

Note: Asians are those who identify themselves as being of the race alone or as being of the race in combination with other races. "–" means not applicable.
Source: Bureau of the Census, National Population Estimates, Internet site http://www.census.gov/popest/national/asrh/; calculations by New Strategist

Table 8.9 Asians by Age, 2000 and 2009

(number of Asians by age, 2000 and 2009; percent change, 2000–09)

	2009	2000	percent change
Total Asians	**15,989,876**	**12,119,307**	**31.9%**
Under age 5	1,324,610	941,956	40.6
Aged 5 to 9	1,224,385	913,553	34.0
Aged 10 to 14	1,064,448	890,497	19.5
Aged 15 to 19	1,046,803	928,545	12.7
Aged 20 to 24	1,082,709	979,807	10.5
Aged 25 to 29	1,277,866	1,133,074	12.8
Aged 30 to 34	1,352,729	1,086,187	24.5
Aged 35 to 39	1,387,280	1,030,574	34.6
Aged 40 to 44	1,208,863	954,768	26.6
Aged 45 to 49	1,118,181	833,815	34.1
Aged 50 to 54	992,591	695,060	42.8
Aged 55 to 59	841,936	478,488	76.0
Aged 60 to 64	652,282	376,365	73.3
Aged 65 to 69	461,603	298,802	54.5
Aged 70 to 74	349,773	240,102	45.7
Aged 75 to 79	259,672	170,813	52.0
Aged 80 to 84	181,322	97,273	86.4
Aged 85 or older	162,823	69,628	133.8
Aged 18 to 24	1,505,431	1,368,770	10.0
Aged 18 or older	11,752,352	8,833,719	33.0
Aged 65 or older	1,415,193	876,618	61.4

Note: Asians are those who identify themselves as being of the race alone or as being of the race in combination with other races. Numbers for 2000 and 2009 are July 1 estimates.
Source: Bureau of the Census, National Population Estimates, Internet site http://www.census.gov/popest/national/asrh/; calculations by New Strategist

Table 8.10 Asians by Age and Sex, 2009

(number of Asians by age and sex, and sex ratio by age, 2009)

	total	females	males	sex ratio
Total Asians	**15,989,876**	**8,232,261**	**7,757,615**	**94**
Under age 5	1,324,610	649,603	675,007	104
Aged 5 to 9	1,224,385	601,199	623,186	104
Aged 10 to 14	1,064,448	525,369	539,079	103
Aged 15 to 19	1,046,803	509,712	537,091	105
Aged 20 to 24	1,082,709	533,415	549,294	103
Aged 25 to 29	1,277,866	652,996	624,870	96
Aged 30 to 34	1,352,729	700,063	652,666	93
Aged 35 to 39	1,387,280	712,271	675,009	95
Aged 40 to 44	1,208,863	626,293	582,570	93
Aged 45 to 49	1,118,181	582,875	535,306	92
Aged 50 to 54	992,591	524,669	467,922	89
Aged 55 to 59	841,936	453,762	388,174	86
Aged 60 to 64	652,282	354,688	297,594	84
Aged 65 to 69	461,603	249,462	212,141	85
Aged 70 to 74	349,773	191,452	158,321	83
Aged 75 to 79	259,672	151,230	108,442	72
Aged 80 to 84	181,322	109,931	71,391	65
Aged 85 or older	162,823	103,271	59,552	58
Aged 18 to 24	1,505,431	739,253	766,178	104
Aged 18 or older	11,752,352	6,152,216	5,600,136	91
Aged 65 or older	1,415,193	805,346	609,847	76

Note: Asians are those who identify themselves as being of the race alone or as being of the race in combination with other races. The sex ratio is the number of males divided by the number of females multiplied by 100.
Source: Bureau of the Census, National Population Estimates, Internet site http://www.census.gov/popest/national/asrh/; calculations by New Strategist

Nearly Half of Asians Live in the West

California is home to nearly one in three.

The West is home to 46 percent of the nation's Asian population, according to the 2010 census. In the West, Asians account for 11 percent of the population—a far higher share than in any other region. In the Midwest and South, only 3 percent of the population is Asian.

Nearly one-third (32 percent) of the nation's Asians live in California, where they account for a substantial 15 percent of the state's population. California's Asian population grew 34 percent between 2000 and 2010. Among Asians in California, 26 percent are Chinese and 25 percent are Filipino, according to 2007–09 Census Bureau estimates.

The Asian (alone) share of the population reaches double digits in 10 metropolitan areas, according to the 2010 census: Honolulu (44 percent), San Jose (31 percent), San Francisco (23 percent), Vallejo, CA (15 percent), Los Angeles (15 percent), Sacramento (12 percent), Seattle (11 percent), San Diego (11 percent), Stockton, CA (14 percent), and Yuba City, CA (11 percent).

Because Asians are from many different nations, they speak a wide variety of languages—unlike Hispanics who share a common language. According to the Census Bureau, 2.5 million Americans speak Chinese languages at home. Among those speaking Chinese languages at home, the 55 percent majority speaks English less than very well.

■ New York is one of only three metropolitan areas in the nation (the others are Los Angeles and San Francisco) with more than 1 million Asians.

The Asian population is growing fastest in the South

(percent change in number of Asians by region, 2000 to 2010)

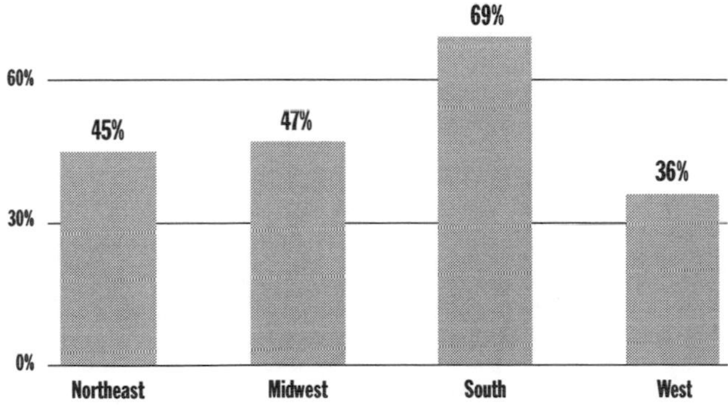

Table 8.11 Total and Asian Population by Region, 2010

(total number of people, number and percent distribution of Asians, and Asian share of total, by region, 2010)

		Asian		
	total	number	percent distribution	share of total
Total people	**308,745,538**	**17,320,856**	**100.0%**	**5.6%**
Northeast	55,317,240	3,428,624	19.8	6.2
Midwest	66,927,001	2,053,971	11.9	3.1
South	114,555,744	3,835,242	22.1	3.3
West	71,945,553	8,003,019	46.2	11.1

Note: Asians are those who identify themselves as being of the race alone or as being of the race in combination with other races.
Source: Bureau of the Census, 2010 Census, American Factfinder, Internet site http://factfinder2.census.gov/faces/nav/jsf/pages/index.xhtml; calculations by New Strategist

Table 8.12 Asians by Region, 2000 and 2010

(number of Asians by region, 2000 and 2010; percent change, 2000–10)

	2010	2000	percent change
Total Asians	**17,320,856**	**11,898,828**	**45.6%**
Northeast	3,428,624	2,368,297	44.8
Midwest	2,053,971	1,392,938	47.5
South	3,835,242	2,267,094	69.2
West	8,003,019	5,870,499	36.3

Note: Asians are those who identify themselves as being of the race alone or as being of the race in combination with other races. Total number of Asians in 2000 differs from the total in previous tables of this chapter because these are unadjusted census counts from April 1, 2000.
Source: Bureau of the Census, 2010 Census, American Factfinder, Internet site http://factfinder2.census.gov/faces/nav/jsf/pages/index.xhtml; calculations by New Strategist

Table 8.13 Total and Asian Population by State, 2010

(total number of people, number and percent distribution of Asians, and Asian share of total, by state, 2010)

		Asian		
	total	number	percent distribution	share of total
Total people	**308,745,538**	**17,320,856**	**100.0%**	**5.6%**
Alabama	4,779,736	67,036	0.4	1.4
Alaska	710,231	50,402	0.3	7.1
Arizona	6,392,017	230,907	1.3	3.6
Arkansas	2,915,918	44,943	0.3	1.5
California	37,253,956	5,556,592	32.1	14.9
Colorado	5,029,196	185,589	1.1	3.7
Connecticut	3,574,097	157,088	0.9	4.4
Delaware	897,934	33,701	0.2	3.8
District of Columbia	601,723	26,857	0.2	4.5
Florida	18,801,310	573,083	3.3	3.0
Georgia	9,687,653	365,497	2.1	3.8
Hawaii	1,360,301	780,968	4.5	57.4
Idaho	1,567,582	29,698	0.2	1.9
Illinois	12,830,632	668,694	3.9	5.2
Indiana	6,483,802	126,750	0.7	2.0
Iowa	3,046,355	64,512	0.4	2.1
Kansas	2,853,118	83,930	0.5	2.9
Kentucky	4,339,367	62,029	0.4	1.4
Louisiana	4,533,372	84,335	0.5	1.9
Maine	1,328,361	18,333	0.1	1.4
Maryland	5,773,552	370,044	2.1	6.4
Massachusetts	6,547,629	394,211	2.3	6.0
Michigan	9,883,640	289,607	1.7	2.9
Minnesota	5,303,925	247,132	1.4	4.7
Mississippi	2,967,297	32,560	0.2	1.1
Missouri	5,988,927	123,571	0.7	2.1
Montana	989,415	10,482	0.1	1.1
Nebraska	1,826,341	40,561	0.2	2.2
Nevada	2,700,551	242,916	1.4	9.0
New Hampshire	1,316,470	34,522	0.2	2.6
New Jersey	8,791,894	795,163	4.6	9.0
New Mexico	2,059,179	40,456	0.2	2.0
New York	19,378,102	1,579,494	9.1	8.2
North Carolina	9,535,483	252,585	1.5	2.6
North Dakota	672,591	9,193	0.1	1.4
Ohio	11,536,504	238,292	1.4	2.1
Oklahoma	3,751,351	84,170	0.5	2.2
Oregon	3,831,074	186,281	1.1	4.9
Pennsylvania	12,702,379	402,587	2.3	3.2
Rhode Island	1,052,567	36,763	0.2	3.5

	total	Asian number	Asian percent distribution	Asian share of total
South Carolina	4,625,364	75,674	0.4%	1.6%
South Dakota	814,180	10,216	0.1	1.3
Tennessee	6,346,105	113,398	0.7	1.8
Texas	25,145,561	1,110,666	6.4	4.4
Utah	2,763,885	77,748	0.4	2.8
Vermont	625,741	10,463	0.1	1.7
Virginia	8,001,024	522,199	3.0	6.5
Washington	6,724,540	604,251	3.5	9.0
West Virginia	1,852,994	16,465	0.1	0.9
Wisconsin	5,686,986	151,513	0.9	2.7
Wyoming	563,626	6,729	0.0	1.2

Note: Asians are those who identify themselves as being of the race alone and those who identify themselves as being of the race in combination with other races.
Source: Bureau of the Census, 2010 Census, American Factfinder, Internet site http://factfinder2.census.gov/faces/nav/jsf/pages/index.xhtml; calculations by New Strategist

Table 8.14 Asians by State, 2000 and 2010

(number of Asians by state, 2000 and 2010; percent change, 2000–10)

	2010	2000	percent change
Total Asians	**17,320,856**	**11,898,828**	**45.6%**
Alabama	67,036	39,458	69.9
Alaska	50,402	32,686	54.2
Arizona	230,907	118,672	94.6
Arkansas	44,943	25,401	76.9
California	5,556,592	4,155,685	33.7
Colorado	185,589	120,779	53.7
Connecticut	157,088	95,368	64.7
Delaware	33,701	18,944	77.9
District of Columbia	26,857	17,956	49.6
Florida	573,083	333,013	72.1
Georgia	365,497	199,812	82.9
Hawaii	780,968	703,232	11.1
Idaho	29,698	17,390	70.8
Illinois	668,694	473,649	41.2
Indiana	126,750	72,839	74.0
Iowa	64,512	43,119	49.6
Kansas	83,930	56,049	49.7
Kentucky	62,029	37,062	67.4
Louisiana	84,335	64,350	31.1
Maine	18,333	11,827	55.0
Maryland	370,044	238,408	55.2
Massachusetts	394,211	264,814	48.9
Michigan	289,607	208,329	39.0
Minnesota	247,132	162,414	52.2
Mississippi	32,560	23,281	39.9
Missouri	123,571	76,210	62.1
Montana	10,482	7,101	47.6
Nebraska	40,561	26,809	51.3
Nevada	242,916	112,456	116.0
New Hampshire	34,522	19,219	79.6
New Jersey	795,163	524,356	51.6
New Mexico	40,456	26,619	52.0
New York	1,579,494	1,169,200	35.1
North Carolina	252,585	136,212	85.4
North Dakota	9,193	4,967	85.1
Ohio	238,292	159,776	49.1
Oklahoma	84,170	58,723	43.3
Oregon	186,281	127,339	46.3
Pennsylvania	402,587	248,601	61.9
Rhode Island	36,763	28,290	30.0
South Carolina	75,674	44,931	68.4
South Dakota	10,216	6,009	70.0

	2010	2000	percent change
Tennessee	113,398	68,918	64.5%
Texas	1,110,666	644,193	72.4
Utah	77,748	48,692	59.7
Vermont	10,463	6,622	58.0
Virginia	522,199	304,559	71.5
Washington	604,251	395,741	52.7
West Virginia	16,465	11,873	38.7
Wisconsin	151,513	102,768	47.4
Wyoming	6,729	4,107	63.8

Note: Asians are those who identify themselves as being of the race alone or as being of the race in combination with other races. Total number of Asians in 2000 differs from the total in previous tables of this chapter because these are unadjusted census counts from April 1, 2000.
Source: Bureau of the Census, 2000 Census, The Asian Population 2000, Internet site http://www.census.gov/population/www/cen2000/briefs.html; and 2010 Census, American Factfinder, Internet site http://factfinder2.census.gov/faces/nav/jsf/pages/index.xhtml; calculations by New Strategist

Table 8.15 Asians by State and Ethnicity, 2007–09

(total number of Asians and percent distribution by state and ethnicity, 2007–09)

	total								
	number	percent	Chinese	Asian Indian	Filipino	Vietnamese	Korean	Japanese	other Asian
Total Asians	**13,500,734**	**100.0%**	**23.0%**	**19.1%**	**18.1%**	**10.9%**	**9.8%**	**5.7%**	**13.3%**
Alabama	48,458	100.0	20.2	23.7	10.2	12.0	14.4	6.5	13.1
Alaska	33,028	100.0	4.7	1.9	58.4	3.9	12.6	3.4	15.2
Arizona	159,998	100.0	19.4	20.9	20.2	12.8	8.8	6.3	11.6
Arkansas	34,978	100.0	11.7	15.4	11.6	16.2	10.1	4.3	30.6
California	4,544,779	100.0	25.7	10.5	25.4	11.9	9.1	6.1	11.2
Colorado	128,222	100.0	17.4	13.9	11.1	15.6	15.8	9.2	17.0
Connecticut	121,863	100.0	23.8	34.7	8.8	6.5	7.1	2.9	16.1
Delaware	26,305	100.0	22.7	38.6	14.6	7.4	5.4	2.2	9.1
District of Columbia	17,634	100.0	25.0	22.0	10.6	11.4	11.0	6.1	13.7
Florida	433,922	100.0	15.2	28.3	19.6	13.6	5.9	3.1	14.3
Georgia	280,706	100.0	15.1	29.1	6.2	16.0	17.4	2.9	13.2
Hawaii	485,088	100.0	10.8	0.4	35.8	1.9	4.8	37.2	9.2
Idaho	16,977	100.0	16.5	11.6	17.1	10.5	11.1	15.8	17.4
Illinois	552,581	100.0	17.6	32.4	19.9	4.5	11.5	3.1	11.0
Indiana	88,309	100.0	23.2	25.0	12.0	8.8	10.6	5.1	15.3
Iowa	46,663	100.0	18.6	17.5	6.6	21.8	13.7	3.0	18.8
Kansas	61,946	100.0	17.5	21.3	8.3	20.2	8.2	3.1	21.3
Kentucky	43,511	100.0	19.8	25.2	11.1	8.9	11.9	11.5	11.6
Louisiana	65,592	100.0	14.3	13.2	8.9	43.9	5.4	2.2	12.1
Maine	12,504	100.0	23.3	14.0	14.2	13.0	11.8	4.7	18.9
Maryland	284,521	100.0	22.0	24.7	13.5	9.0	15.7	2.3	12.8
Massachusetts	320,320	100.0	35.8	20.8	4.5	13.3	6.1	2.7	16.7
Michigan	238,580	100.0	18.4	32.9	9.9	7.3	10.1	5.7	15.7
Minnesota	191,384	100.0	10.7	15.4	4.6	11.8	8.9	2.1	46.6
Mississippi	24,578	100.0	19.0	20.8	16.0	23.5	7.5	2.3	10.9
Missouri	85,532	100.0	20.4	24.6	11.7	16.2	11.5	3.4	12.3
Montana	5,474	100.0	20.6	8.1	14.5	10.3	12.4	13.9	20.2
Nebraska	28,240	100.0	15.0	16.3	12.3	27.1	12.0	5.7	11.6
Nevada	166,945	100.0	15.8	5.2	51.2	4.6	6.3	6.2	10.6
New Hampshire	25,589	100.0	22.7	39.4	6.7	7.2	6.5	3.0	14.5
New Jersey	660,392	100.0	19.0	38.8	16.9	3.4	13.3	2.2	6.5
New Mexico	27,455	100.0	23.1	12.9	17.4	16.4	8.0	9.8	12.5
New York	1,345,871	100.0	40.3	24.9	8.1	2.5	9.5	3.0	11.7
North Carolina	180,301	100.0	16.5	27.0	9.4	13.6	10.2	3.4	19.9
North Dakota	5,617	100.0	31.3	15.6	12.6	13.2	7.2	4.8	15.5
Ohio	177,278	100.0	22.4	30.5	10.3	8.1	8.6	5.5	14.5
Oklahoma	57,924	100.0	14.6	15.7	10.3	27.3	9.9	3.9	18.4
Oregon	133,044	100.0	20.9	10.4	11.1	20.1	12.1	9.9	15.4
Pennsylvania	303,900	100.0	23.8	30.1	7.0	12.5	11.1	2.3	13.1
Rhode Island	30,023	100.0	21.2	11.6	12.1	3.9	7.8	1.7	41.7
South Carolina	54,974	100.0	16.4	22.8	17.2	12.3	9.1	5.6	16.6
South Dakota	6,755	100.0	9.6	12.2	21.8	20.6	15.8	3.2	16.8
Tennessee	84,717	100.0	16.6	23.6	11.7	10.8	12.4	5.4	19.5

	total			Asian					other
	number	percent	Chinese	Indian	Filipino	Vietnamese	Korean	Japanese	Asian
Texas	846,301	100.0%	17.0%	25.0%	11.1%	23.1%	7.1%	2.1%	14.7%
Utah	55,370	100.0	21.6	10.4	11.5	11.8	11.4	12.4	20.9
Vermont	6,922	100.0	27.6	18.7	3.3	12.7	14.4	7.1	16.3
Virginia	382,366	100.0	14.4	22.9	15.5	12.9	16.5	2.6	15.2
Washington	434,407	100.0	21.1	11.8	18.9	13.1	13.7	7.9	13.4
West Virginia	11,282	100.0	21.7	32.4	10.1	6.4	8.0	5.5	15.7
Wisconsin	118,069	100.0	14.2	16.8	6.7	3.9	7.2	2.2	49.1
Wyoming	3,539	100.0	20.5	8.9	29.3	4.4	12.2	12.3	12.4

Note: Asians are those who identify themselves as being of the race alone.
Source: Bureau of the Census, 2007-2009 American Community Survey 3-Year Estimates, Internet site http://www.census .gov/acs/www/; calculations by New Strategist

Table 8.16 People Who Speak Chinese Languages at Home, by State, 2007–09

(total number of people aged 5 or older, number and percent who speak Chinese languages at home, and number and percent of Chinese speakers who speak English less than very well, by state, 2007–09)

		speak Chinese languages at home			
				speak English less than very well	
	total people aged 5 or older	number	percent of total	number	percent of Chinese speakers
United States	**282,747,270**	**2,494,909**	**0.9%**	**1,382,340**	**55.4%**
Alabama	4,363,629	7,921	0.2	3,955	49.9
Alaska	636,921	1,075	0.2	571	53.1
Arizona	5,972,489	22,139	0.4	11,445	51.7
Arkansas	2,665,151	2,689	0.1	1,538	57.2
California	33,865,677	934,961	2.8	524,336	56.1
Colorado	4,576,380	15,330	0.3	7,436	48.5
Connecticut	3,291,944	23,250	0.7	11,177	48.1
Delaware	816,327	4,903	0.6	2,064	42.1
District of Columbia	555,412	2,407	0.4	1,180	49.0
Florida	17,253,500	47,586	0.3	25,484	53.6
Georgia	8,944,142	34,419	0.4	17,556	51.0
Hawaii	1,198,776	29,638	2.5	17,027	57.4
Idaho	1,401,660	1,982	0.1	1,053	53.1
Illinois	11,953,083	78,063	0.7	39,950	51.2
Indiana	5,940,354	16,276	0.3	8,827	54.2
Iowa	2,793,284	7,095	0.3	3,078	43.4
Kansas	2,595,844	8,824	0.3	4,957	56.2
Kentucky	3,999,541	6,445	0.2	3,456	53.6
Louisiana	4,127,403	7,685	0.2	4,292	55.8
Maine	1,247,671	2,354	0.2	1,281	54.4
Maryland	5,286,510	53,177	1.0	26,114	49.1
Massachusetts	6,161,389	91,483	1.5	45,098	49.3
Michigan	9,384,278	36,297	0.4	17,294	47.6
Minnesota	4,869,515	15,398	0.3	7,337	47.6
Mississippi	2,719,551	3,646	0.1	2,260	62.0
Missouri	5,551,344	13,714	0.2	8,197	59.8
Montana	905,718	996	0.1	621	62.3
Nebraska	1,650,973	2,978	0.2	1,672	56.1
Nevada	2,408,128	21,982	0.9	13,036	59.3
New Hampshire	1,245,974	4,384	0.4	2,188	49.9
New Jersey	8,111,099	99,359	1.2	45,501	45.8
New Mexico	1,840,935	4,656	0.3	2,248	48.3
New York	18,258,052	459,879	2.5	299,579	65.1
North Carolina	8,580,740	23,222	0.3	10,674	46.0
North Dakota	600,718	1,247	0.2	683	54.8
Ohio	10,790,145	31,999	0.3	16,538	51.7
Oklahoma	3,382,000	7,230	0.2	3,861	53.4
Oregon	3,537,689	21,411	0.6	11,158	52.1

	total people aged 5 or older	speak Chinese languages at home			
				speak English less than very well	
		number	percent of total	number	percent of Chinese speakers
Pennsylvania	11,820,455	58,520	0.5%	32,456	55.5%
Rhode Island	993,322	4,526	0.5	2,666	58.9
South Carolina	4,190,137	7,892	0.2	3,930	49.8
South Dakota	746,848	386	0.1	180	46.6
Tennessee	5,816,311	11,565	0.2	5,943	51.4
Texas	22,274,512	120,268	0.5	60,547	50.3
Utah	2,458,311	10,518	0.4	4,689	44.6
Vermont	588,388	1,574	0.3	746	47.4
Virginia	7,273,420	43,692	0.6	19,991	45.8
Washington	6,124,094	73,952	1.2	39,255	53.1
West Virginia	1,709,213	1,947	0.1	986	50.6
Wisconsin	5,268,313	11,969	0.2	6,229	52.0
Wyoming	–	–	–	–	–

Note: "–" means sample is too small to make a reliable estimate.
Source: Bureau of the Census, 2007-2009 American Community Survey 3-Year Estimates, Internet site http://www.census .gov/acs/www/; calculations by New Strategist

Table 8.17 Total and Asian Population by Metropolitan Area, 2010

(total number of people, number of Asians, and Asian share of total, for metropolitan areas, 2010)

	total population	Asian number	Asian share of total
Abilene, TX	165,252	2,209	1.3%
Akron, OH	703,200	14,190	2.0
Albany–Schenectady–Troy, NY	870,716	27,192	3.1
Albany, GA	157,308	1,481	0.9
Albuquerque, NM	887,077	17,924	2.0
Alexandria, LA	153,922	1,618	1.1
Allentown–Bethlehem–Easton, PA–NJ	821,173	20,434	2.5
Altoona, PA	127,089	706	0.6
Amarillo, TX	249,881	6,525	2.6
Ames, IA	89,542	5,383	6.0
Anchorage, AK	380,821	24,676	6.5
Anderson, IN	131,636	553	0.4
Anderson, SC	187,126	1,405	0.8
Ann Arbor, MI	344,791	27,109	7.9
Anniston–Oxford, AL	118,572	845	0.7
Appleton, WI	225,666	6,260	2.8
Asheville, NC	424,858	3,724	0.9
Athens–Clarke County, GA	192,541	6,134	3.2
Atlanta–Sandy Springs–Marietta, GA	5,268,860	254,307	4.8
Atlantic City–Hammonton, NJ	274,549	20,595	7.5
Auburn–Opelika, AL	140,247	3,658	2.6
Augusta–Richmond County, GA–SC	556,877	9,669	1.7
Austin–Round Rock–San Marcos, TX	1,716,289	82,433	4.8
Bakersfield–Delano, CA	839,631	34,846	4.2
Baltimore–Towson, MD	2,710,489	122,911	4.5
Bangor, ME	153,923	1,422	0.9
Barnstable Town, MA	215,888	2,287	1.1
Baton Rouge, LA	802,484	14,345	1.8
Battle Creek, MI	136,146	2,179	1.6
Bay City, MI	107,771	578	0.5
Beaumont–Port Arthur, TX	388,745	9,710	2.5
Bellingham, WA	201,140	7,090	3.5
Bend, OR	157,733	1,476	0.9
Billings, MT	158,050	961	0.6
Binghamton, NY	251,725	7,437	3.0
Birmingham–Hoover, AL	1,128,047	13,866	1.2
Bismarck, ND	108,779	446	0.4
Blacksburg–Christiansburg–Radford, VA	162,958	5,602	3.4
Bloomington–Normal, IL	169,572	7,227	4.3
Bloomington, IN	192,714	7,376	3.8
Boise City–Nampa, ID	616,561	11,101	1.8
Boston–Cambridge–Quincy, MA–NH	4,552,402	294,503	6.5
Boulder, CO	294,567	12,133	4.1
Bowling Green, KY	125,953	3,209	2.5
Bremerton–Silverdale, WA	251,133	12,396	4.9

	total population	Asian	
		number	share of total
Bridgeport–Stamford–Norwalk, CT	916,829	42,284	4.6%
Brownsville–Harlingen, TX	406,220	2,689	0.7
Brunswick, GA	112,370	1,004	0.9
Buffalo–Niagara Falls, NY	1,135,509	25,612	2.3
Burlington–South Burlington, VT	211,261	4,651	2.2
Burlington, NC	151,131	1,837	1.2
Canton–Massillon, OH	404,422	2,821	0.7
Cape Coral–Fort Myers, FL	618,754	8,461	1.4
Cape Girardeau–Jackson, MO–IL	96,275	940	1.0
Carson City, NV	55,274	1,181	2.1
Casper, WY	75,450	510	0.7
Cedar Rapids, IA	257,940	3,962	1.5
Champaign–Urbana, IL	231,891	18,057	7.8
Charleston–North Charleston–Summerville, SC	664,607	10,817	1.6
Charleston, WV	304,284	2,462	0.8
Charlotte–Gastonia–Rock Hill, NC–SC	1,758,038	55,315	3.1
Charlottesville, VA	201,559	7,869	3.9
Chattanooga, TN–GA	528,143	7,261	1.4
Cheyenne, WY	91,738	976	1.1
Chicago–Joliet–Naperville, IL–IN–WI	9,461,105	532,801	5.6
Chico, CA	220,000	9,057	4.1
Cincinnati–Middletown, OH–KY–IN	2,130,151	40,422	1.9
Clarksville, TN–KY	273,949	4,505	1.6
Cleveland–Elyria–Mentor, OH	2,077,240	40,522	2.0
Cleveland, TN	115,788	861	0.7
Coeur d'Alene, ID	138,494	961	0.7
College Station–Bryan, TX	228,660	10,214	4.5
Colorado Springs, CO	645,613	17,220	2.7
Columbia, MO	172,786	6,170	3.6
Columbia, SC	767,598	12,704	1.7
Columbus, GA–AL	294,865	4,975	1.7
Columbus, IN	76,794	2,632	3.4
Columbus, OH	1,836,536	57,274	3.1
Corpus Christi, TX	428,185	6,723	1.6
Corvallis, OR	85,579	4,429	5.2
Crestview–Fort Walton Beach–Destin, FL	180,822	5,328	2.9
Cumberland, MD–WV	103,299	678	0.7
Dallas–Fort Worth–Arlington, TX	6,371,773	341,503	5.4
Dalton, GA	142,227	1,446	1.0
Danville, IL	81,625	564	0.7
Danville, VA	106,561	584	0.5
Davenport–Moline–Rock Island, IA–IL	379,690	5,994	1.6
Dayton, OH	841,502	15,364	1.8
Decatur, AL	153,829	733	0.5
Decatur, IL	110,768	1,118	1.0
Deltona–Daytona Beach–Ormond Beach, FL	494,593	7,567	1.5
Denver–Aurora–Broomfield, CO	2,543,482	94,005	3.7
Des Moines–West Des Moines, IA	569,633	17,220	3.0
Detroit–Warren–Livonia, MI	4,296,250	141,316	3.3
Dothan, AL	145,639	941	0.6

	total population	Asian	
		number	share of total
Dover, DE	162,310	3,306	2.0%
Dubuque, IA	93,653	878	0.9
Duluth, MN–WI	279,771	2,310	0.8
Durham–Chapel Hill, NC	504,357	22,120	4.4
Eau Claire, WI	161,151	4,071	2.5
El Centro, CA	174,528	2,843	1.6
El Paso, TX	800,647	8,284	1.0
Elizabethtown, KY	119,736	2,129	1.8
Elkhart–Goshen, IN	197,559	1,915	1.0
Elmira, NY	88,830	1,057	1.2
Erie, PA	280,566	3,077	1.1
Eugene–Springfield, OR	351,715	8,322	2.4
Evansville, IN–KY	358,676	3,420	1.0
Fairbanks, AK	97,581	2,591	2.7
Fargo, ND–MN	208,777	4,378	2.1
Farmington, NM	130,044	484	0.4
Fayetteville–Springdale–Rogers, AR–MO	463,204	11,008	2.4
Fayetteville, NC	366,383	7,574	2.1
Flagstaff, AZ	134,421	1,846	1.4
Flint, MI	425,790	3,879	0.9
Florence–Muscle Shoals, AL	147,137	914	0.6
Florence, SC	205,566	1,874	0.9
Fond du Lac, WI	101,633	1,148	1.1
Fort Collins–Loveland, CO	299,630	5,800	1.9
Fort Smith, AR–OK	298,592	6,628	2.2
Fort Wayne, IN	416,257	9,933	2.4
Fresno, CA	930,450	89,357	9.6
Gadsden, AL	104,430	672	0.6
Gainesville, FL	264,275	13,295	5.0
Gainesville, GA	179,684	3,226	1.8
Glens Falls, NY	128,923	722	0.6
Goldsboro, NC	122,623	1,431	1.2
Grand Forks, ND–MN	98,461	1,510	1.5
Grand Junction, CO	146,723	1,121	0.8
Grand Rapids–Wyoming, MI	774,160	14,707	1.9
Great Falls, MT	81,327	684	0.8
Greeley, CO	252,825	3,022	1.2
Green Bay, WI	306,241	6,895	2.3
Greensboro–High Point, NC	723,801	21,037	2.9
Greenville–Mauldin–Easley, SC	636,986	10,945	1.7
Greenville, NC	189,510	2,685	1.4
Gulfport–Biloxi, MS	248,820	5,799	2.3
Hagerstown–Martinsburg, MD–WV	269,140	2,984	1.1
Hanford–Corcoran, CA	152,982	5,620	3.7
Harrisburg–Carlisle, PA	549,475	15,816	2.9
Harrisonburg, VA	125,228	2,178	1.7
Hartford–West Hartford–East Hartford, CT	1,212,381	47,339	3.9
Hattiesburg, MS	142,842	1,176	0.8
Hickory–Lenoir–Morganton, NC	365,497	9,325	2.6
Hinesville–Fort Stewart, GA	77,917	1,362	1.7

	total population	Asian	
		number	share of total
Holland–Grand Haven, MI	263,801	6,738	2.6%
Honolulu, HI	953,207	418,410	43.9
Hot Springs, AR	96,024	695	0.7
Houma–Bayou Cane–Thibodaux, LA	208,178	1,849	0.9
Houston–Sugar Land–Baytown, TX	5,946,800	389,007	6.5
Huntington–Ashland, WV–KY–OH	287,702	1,666	0.6
Huntsville, AL	417,593	9,189	2.2
Idaho Falls, ID	130,374	959	0.7
Indianapolis–Carmel, IN	1,756,241	39,576	2.3
Iowa City, IA	152,586	6,891	4.5
Ithaca, NY	101,564	8,737	8.6
Jackson, MI	160,248	1,137	0.7
Jackson, MS	539,057	5,664	1.1
Jackson, TN	115,425	978	0.8
Jacksonville, FL	1,345,596	46,181	3.4
Jacksonville, NC	177,772	3,355	1.9
Janesville, WI	160,331	1,630	1.0
Jefferson City, MO	149,807	1,281	0.9
Johnson City, TN	198,716	1,677	0.8
Johnstown, PA	143,679	729	0.5
Jonesboro, AR	121,026	1,120	0.9
Joplin, MO	175,518	1,937	1.1
Kalamazoo–Portage, MI	326,589	5,525	1.7
Kankakee–Bradley, IL	113,449	1,052	0.9
Kansas City, MO–KS	2,035,334	46,221	2.3
Kennewick–Pasco–Richland, WA	253,340	6,125	2.4
Killeen–Temple–Fort Hood, TX	405,300	10,372	2.6
Kingsport–Bristol–Bristol, TN–VA	309,544	1,523	0.5
Kingston, NY	182,493	3,106	1.7
Knoxville, TN	698,030	10,079	1.4
Kokomo, IN	98,688	805	0.8
La Crosse, WI–MN	133,665	4,831	3.6
Lafayette, IN	201,789	10,766	5.3
Lafayette, LA	273,738	3,728	1.4
Lake Charles, LA	199,607	2,079	1.0
Lake Havasu City–Kingman, AZ	200,186	2,103	1.1
Lakeland–Winter Haven, FL	602,095	9,760	1.6
Lancaster, PA	519,445	9,860	1.9
Lansing–East Lansing, MI	464,036	17,523	3.8
Laredo, TX	250,304	1,464	0.6
Las Cruces, NM	209,233	2,227	1.1
Las Vegas–Paradise, NV	1,951,269	168,831	8.7
Lawrence, KS	110,826	4,146	3.7
Lawton, OK	124,098	2,777	2.2
Lebanon, PA	133,568	1,533	1.1
Lewiston–Auburn, ME	107,702	778	0.7
Lewiston, ID–WA	60,888	396	0.7
Lexington–Fayette, KY	472,099	10,766	2.3
Lima, OH	106,331	740	0.7
Lincoln, NE	302,157	10,033	3.3

	total population	Asian number	Asian share of total
Little Rock–North Little Rock–Conway, AR	699,757	10,310	1.5%
Logan, UT–ID	125,442	2,137	1.7
Longview, TX	214,369	1,707	0.8
Longview, WA	102,410	1,500	1.5
Los Angeles–Long Beach–Santa Ana, CA	12,828,837	1,884,669	14.7
Louisville/Jefferson County, KY–IN	1,283,566	20,098	1.6
Lubbock, TX	284,890	5,759	2.0
Lynchburg, VA	252,634	3,351	1.3
Macon, GA	232,293	2,979	1.3
Madera–Chowchilla, CA	150,865	2,802	1.9
Madison, WI	568,593	23,465	4.1
Manchester–Nashua, NH	400,721	12,954	3.2
Manhattan, KS	127,081	4,241	3.3
Mankato–North Mankato, MN	96,740	1,680	1.7
Mansfield, OH	124,475	808	0.6
McAllen–Edinburg–Mission, TX	774,769	7,478	1.0
Medford, OR	203,206	2,364	1.2
Memphis, TN–MS–AR	1,316,100	24,479	1.9
Merced, CA	255,793	18,836	7.4
Miami–Fort Lauderdale–Pompano Beach, FL	5,564,635	125,564	2.3
Michigan City–La Porte, IN	111,467	583	0.5
Midland, TX	136,872	1,715	1.3
Milwaukee–Waukesha–West Allis, WI	1,555,908	46,067	3.0
Minneapolis–St. Paul–Bloomington, MN–WI	3,279,833	188,018	5.7
Missoula, MT	109,299	1,236	1.1
Mobile, AL	412,992	7,561	1.8
Modesto, CA	514,453	26,090	5.1
Monroe, LA	176,441	1,487	0.8
Monroe, MI	152,021	842	0.6
Montgomery, AL	374,536	5,827	1.6
Morgantown, WV	129,709	2,989	2.3
Morristown, TN	136,608	703	0.5
Mount Vernon–Anacortes, WA	116,901	2,080	1.8
Muncie, IN	117,671	1,144	1.0
Muskegon–Norton Shores, MI	172,188	941	0.5
Myrtle Beach–North Myrtle Beach–Conway, SC	269,291	2,816	1.0
Napa, CA	136,484	9,223	6.8
Naples–Marco Island, FL	321,520	3,507	1.1
Nashville–Davidson–Murfreesboro–Franklin, TN	1,589,934	36,306	2.3
New Haven–Milford, CT	862,477	30,263	3.5
New Orleans–Metairie–Kenner, LA	1,167,764	31,808	2.7
New York–Northern New Jersey–Long Island, NY–NJ–PA	18,897,109	1,878,261	9.9
Niles–Benton Harbor, MI	156,813	2,451	1.6
North Port–Bradenton–Sarasota, FL	702,281	10,178	1.4
Norwich–New London, CT	274,055	11,383	4.2
Ocala, FL	331,298	4,407	1.3
Ocean City, NJ	97,265	834	0.9
Odessa, TX	137,130	1,080	0.8
Ogden–Clearfield, UT	547,184	8,361	1.5

	total population	Asian	
		number	share of total
Oklahoma City, OK	1,252,987	35,218	2.8%
Olympia, WA	252,264	13,037	5.2
Omaha–Council Bluffs, NE–IA	865,350	17,997	2.1
Orlando–Kissimmee–Sanford, FL	2,134,411	84,852	4.0
Oshkosh–Neenah, WI	166,994	3,822	2.3
Owensboro, KY	114,752	714	0.6
Oxnard–Thousand Oaks–Ventura, CA	823,318	55,446	6.7
Palm Bay–Melbourne–Titusville, FL	543,376	11,349	2.1
Palm Coast, FL	95,696	2,046	2.1
Panama City–Lynn Haven–Panama City Beach, FL	168,852	3,353	2.0
Parkersburg–Marietta–Vienna, WV–OH	162,056	831	0.5
Pascagoula, MS	162,246	3,070	1.9
Pensacola–Ferry Pass–Brent, FL	448,991	10,933	2.4
Peoria, IL	379,186	7,132	1.9
Philadelphia–Camden–Wilmington, PA–NJ–DE–MD	5,965,343	295,766	5.0
Phoenix–Mesa–Glendale, AZ	4,192,887	138,717	3.3
Pine Bluff, AR	100,258	638	0.6
Pittsburgh, PA	2,356,285	41,238	1.8
Pittsfield, MA	131,219	1,611	1.2
Pocatello, ID	90,656	1,111	1.2
Port St. Lucie, FL	424,107	5,874	1.4
Portland–South Portland–Biddeford, ME	514,098	8,134	1.6
Portland–Vancouver–Hillsboro, OR–WA	2,226,009	126,965	5.7
Poughkeepsie–Newburgh–Middletown, NY	670,301	19,332	2.9
Prescott, AZ	211,033	1,785	0.8
Providence–New Bedford–Fall River, RI–MA	1,600,852	40,699	2.5
Provo–Orem, UT	526,810	7,054	1.3
Pueblo, CO	159,063	1,258	0.8
Punta Gorda, FL	159,978	1,912	1.2
Racine, WI	195,408	2,121	1.1
Raleigh–Cary, NC	1,130,490	49,862	4.4
Rapid City, SD	126,382	1,217	1.0
Reading, PA	411,442	5,385	1.3
Redding, CA	177,223	4,391	2.5
Reno–Sparks, NV	425,417	21,856	5.1
Richmond, VA	1,258,251	39,265	3.1
Riverside–San Bernardino–Ontario, CA	4,224,851	259,071	6.1
Roanoke, VA	308,707	5,007	1.6
Rochester, MN	186,011	7,993	4.3
Rochester, NY	1,054,323	26,844	2.5
Rockford, IL	349,431	7,496	2.1
Rocky Mount, NC	152,392	860	0.6
Rome, GA	96,317	1,253	1.3
Sacramento–Arden-Arcade–Roseville, CA	2,149,127	255,995	11.9
Saginaw–Saginaw Township North, MI	200,169	2,108	1.1
Salem, OR	390,738	7,430	1.9
Salinas, CA	415,057	25,258	6.1
Salisbury, MD	125,203	2,655	2.1
Salt Lake City, UT	1,124,197	34,807	3.1
San Angelo, TX	111,823	1,121	1.0

	total population	Asian number	Asian share of total
San Antonio–New Braunfels, TX	2,142,508	45,330	2.1%
San Diego–Carlsbad–San Marcos, CA	3,095,313	336,091	10.9
San Francisco–Oakland–Fremont, CA	4,335,391	1,005,823	23.2
San Jose–Sunnyvale–Santa Clara, CA	1,836,911	571,967	31.1
San Luis Obispo–Paso Robles, CA	269,637	8,507	3.2
Sandusky, OH	77,079	463	0.6
Santa Barbara–Santa Maria–Goleta, CA	423,895	20,665	4.9
Santa Cruz–Watsonville, CA	262,382	11,112	4.2
Santa Fe, NM	144,170	1,672	1.2
Santa Rosa–Petaluma, CA	483,878	18,341	3.8
Savannah, GA	347,611	7,224	2.1
Scranton–Wilkes-Barre, PA	563,631	6,874	1.2
Seattle–Tacoma–Bellevue, WA	3,439,809	392,961	11.4
Sebastian–Vero Beach, FL	138,028	1,666	1.2
Sheboygan, WI	115,507	5,310	4.6
Sherman–Denison, TX	120,877	1,046	0.9
Shreveport–Bossier City, LA	398,604	4,652	1.2
Sioux City, IA–NE–SD	143,577	3,193	2.2
Sioux Falls, SD	228,261	2,996	1.3
South Bend–Mishawaka, IN–MI	319,224	5,375	1.7
Spartanburg, SC	284,307	5,746	2.0
Spokane, WA	471,221	9,957	2.1
Springfield, IL	210,170	3,250	1.5
Springfield, MA	692,942	17,198	2.5
Springfield, MO	436,712	5,147	1.2
Springfield, OH	138,333	858	0.6
St. Cloud, MN	189,093	3,407	1.8
St. George, UT	138,115	982	0.7
St. Joseph, MO–KS	127,329	845	0.7
St. Louis, MO–IL	2,812,896	60,072	2.1
State College, PA	153,990	7,986	5.2
Steubenville–Weirton, OH–WV	124,454	470	0.4
Stockton, CA	685,306	98,472	14.4
Sumter, SC	107,456	1,188	1.1
Syracuse, NY	662,577	15,760	2.4
Tallahassee, FL	367,413	8,509	2.3
Tampa–St. Petersburg–Clearwater, FL	2,783,243	80,879	2.9
Terre Haute, IN	172,425	1,912	1.1
Texarkana, TX–Texarkana, AR	136,027	932	0.7
Toledo, OH	651,429	9,006	1.4
Topeka, KS	233,870	2,219	0.9
Trenton–Ewing, NJ	366,513	32,752	8.9
Tucson, AZ	980,263	25,731	2.6
Tulsa, OK	937,478	16,546	1.8
Tuscaloosa, AL	219,461	2,356	1.1
Tyler, TX	209,714	2,597	1.2
Utica–Rome, NY	299,397	6,897	2.3
Valdosta, GA	139,588	1,758	1.3
Vallejo–Fairfield, CA	413,344	60,473	14.6
Victoria, TX	115,384	1,862	1.6

	total population	Asian	
		number	share of total
Vineland–Millville–Bridgeton, NJ	156,898	1,907	1.2%
Virginia Beach–Norfolk–Newport News, VA–NC	1,671,683	58,017	3.5
Visalia–Porterville, CA	442,179	15,176	3.4
Waco, TX	234,906	3,220	1.4
Warner Robins, GA	139,900	3,403	2.4
Washington–Arlington–Alexandria, DC–VA–MD–WV	5,582,170	517,458	9.3
Waterloo–Cedar Falls, IA	167,819	1,908	1.1
Wausau, WI	134,063	7,146	5.3
Wenatchee–East Wenatchee, WA	110,884	871	0.8
Wheeling, WV–OH	147,950	748	0.5
Wichita Falls, TX	151,306	2,715	1.8
Wichita, KS	623,061	21,164	3.4
Williamsport, PA	116,111	671	0.6
Wilmington, NC	362,315	3,196	0.9
Winchester, VA–WV	128,472	1,631	1.3
Winston-Salem, NC	477,717	6,937	1.5
Worcester, MA	798,552	31,815	4.0
Yakima, WA	243,231	2,560	1.1
York–Hanover, PA	434,972	5,407	1.2
Youngstown–Warren–Boardman, OH–PA	565,773	3,394	0.6
Yuba City, CA	166,892	18,525	11.1
Yuma, AZ	195,751	2,324	1.2

Note: Asians are those who identify themselves as being of the race alone.
Source: Bureau of the Census, 2010 Census, Internet site, http://factfinder2.census.gov/faces/nav/jsf/pages/index.xhtml; calculations by New Strategist

CHAPTER
9

Spending

■ The nation's 4.6 million Asian households spent an average of $56,308 in 2009, or 15 percent more than the $49,067 spent by the average household.

■ Asian households spend more than twice the average on education and account for a disproportionate share of the market. Asians also spend more than average on restaurant meals, airline fares, and books.

■ Asian spending is above average because they are highly educated, which boosts their incomes.

Asian Households Spend the Most

Their spending is above average on most products and services.

Asian households spent $56,308 in 2009—15 percent more than the average household, according to the Consumer Expenditure Survey. The reasons for the higher spending of Asians are their higher incomes (due in part to their higher level of education) and their larger household size. The Asian investment in education is revealed in these statistics. Asian households spend more than twice as much as the average household on education and account for a disproportionate share of the market.

Asians spend well above average on a number of products and services. They spend twice as much as the average household on fish and seafood, 40 percent more than average on food away from home (mostly restaurant meals), 31 percent more than average on owned homes and 54 percent more than average on rented homes. Asian households spend more than twice the average on public transportation.

■ Asian spending is above average because most Asian households are headed by college graduates.

Asian households spend 15 percent more than the average household

(average annual spending of total and Asian consumer units, 2009)

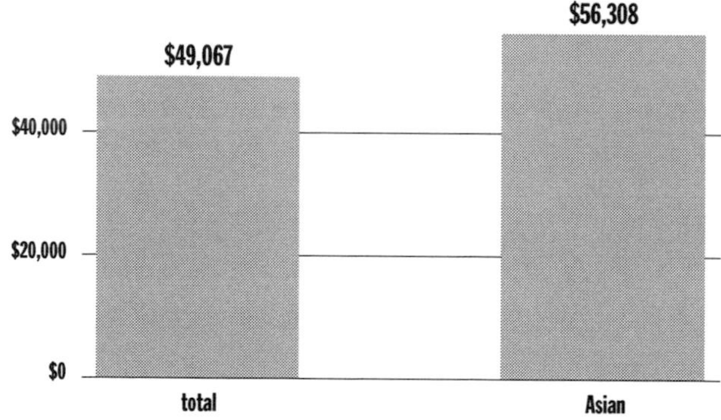

Table 9.1 Average Spending by Race and Hispanic Origin of Householder, 2009

(average annual spending of households by product and service category and by race and Hispanic origin of householder, 2009)

	total households	Asian	black	Hispanic	non-Hispanic white and other
Number of households (in 000s)	**120,847**	**4,584**	**14,659**	**14,295**	**92,119**
Average number of persons per household	**2.5**	**2.7**	**2.6**	**3.3**	**2.4**
Average annual household spending	**$49,067**	**$56,308**	**$35,311**	**$41,981**	**$52,320**
FOOD	**6,372**	**7,565**	**4,524**	**6,094**	**6,696**
Food at home	**3,753**	**3,905**	**2,880**	**3,784**	**3,882**
Cereals and bakery products	506	520	390	479	529
Cereals and cereal products	173	215	149	184	174
Bakery products	334	305	241	294	354
Meats, poultry, fish, and eggs	841	966	845	955	823
Beef	226	186	191	252	227
Pork	168	172	193	202	160
Other meats	114	82	91	110	118
Poultry	154	184	183	192	144
Fish and seafood	135	274	144	141	133
Eggs	44	67	42	58	42
Dairy products	406	346	258	403	429
Fresh milk and cream	144	152	105	171	146
Other dairy products	262	195	153	232	283
Fruits and vegetables	656	903	484	734	671
Fresh fruits	220	310	151	256	225
Fresh vegetables	209	385	136	240	216
Processed fruits	118	117	105	121	120
Processed vegetables	110	91	92	117	111
Other food at home	1,343	1,169	903	1,213	1,430
Sugar and other sweets	141	106	88	109	153
Fats and oils	102	99	82	105	105
Miscellaneous foods	715	646	462	617	768
Nonalcoholic beverages	337	267	253	348	348
Food prepared by consumer unit on trips	49	52	17	33	56
Restaurants and other food away from home	**2,619**	**3,660**	**1,645**	**2,310**	**2,814**
ALCOHOLIC BEVERAGES	**435**	**350**	**201**	**267**	**496**
HOUSING	**16,895**	**20,395**	**13,503**	**15,983**	**17,579**
Shelter	**10,075**	**13,571**	**7,919**	**10,043**	**10,429**
Owned dwellings	6,543	8,543	3,632	5,298	7,198
Mortgage interest and charges	3,594	5,349	2,220	3,454	3,837
Property taxes	1,811	2,334	912	1,368	2,021
Maintenance, repair, insurance, other expenses	1,138	860	500	476	1,340
Rented dwellings	2,860	4,411	4,046	4,415	2,437
Other lodging	672	616	241	330	794

	total households	Asian	black	Hispanic	non-Hispanic white and other
Utilities, fuels, and public services	**$3,645**	**$3,270**	**$3,668**	**$3,532**	**$3,660**
Natural gas	483	499	517	389	493
Electricity	1,377	1,056	1,462	1,339	1,369
Fuel oil and other fuels	141	48	50	47	171
Telephone services	1,162	1,123	1,224	1,272	1,135
Water and other public services	481	544	415	485	492
Household services	**1,011**	**1,347**	**633**	**714**	**1,119**
Personal services	389	688	281	334	417
Other household services	622	659	352	380	702
Housekeeping supplies	**659**	**536**	**429**	**517**	**714**
Laundry and cleaning supplies	156	130	124	194	155
Other household products	360	292	224	233	399
Postage and stationery	143	113	81	91	160
Household furnishings and equipment	**1,506**	**1,671**	**854**	**1,177**	**1,657**
Household textiles	124	187	79	101	134
Furniture	343	304	271	331	357
Floor coverings	30	13	7	7	37
Major appliances	194	183	127	146	212
Small appliances and miscellaneous housewares	93	134	51	80	102
Miscellaneous household equipment	721	848	319	513	814
APPAREL AND RELATED SERVICES	**1,725**	**2,150**	**1,755**	**2,002**	**1,678**
Men and boys	**383**	**427**	**388**	**432**	**375**
Men, aged 16 or older	304	335	303	323	302
Boys, aged 2 to 15	79	91	86	109	73
Women and girls	**678**	**913**	**629**	**693**	**682**
Women, aged 16 or older	561	789	504	509	576
Girls, aged 2 to 15	118	124	126	185	106
Children under age 2	**91**	**122**	**75**	**147**	**85**
Footwear	**323**	**344**	**430**	**472**	**285**
Other apparel products and services	**249**	**344**	**231**	**258**	**251**
TRANSPORTATION	**7,658**	**8,784**	**5,302**	**7,156**	**8,109**
Vehicle purchases	**2,657**	**2,582**	**1,489**	**2,333**	**2,897**
Cars and trucks, new	1,297	1,131	568	1,010	1,460
Cars and trucks, used	1,304	1,451	910	1,293	1,371
Gasoline and motor oil	**1,986**	**1,871**	**1,618**	**2,104**	**2,026**
Other vehicle expenses	**2,536**	**3,153**	**1,876**	**2,309**	**2,670**
Vehicle finance charges	281	208	242	278	288
Maintenance and repairs	733	713	504	584	791
Vehicle insurance	1,075	1,610	859	1,049	1,109
Vehicle rentals, leases, licenses, other charges	447	623	270	398	482
Public transportation	**479**	**1,178**	**319**	**410**	**516**
HEALTH CARE	**3,126**	**2,498**	**1,763**	**1,568**	**3,581**
Health insurance	1,785	1,509	1,133	848	2,033
Medical services	736	575	294	418	855
Drugs	486	307	279	241	556
Medical supplies	119	107	57	61	137

	total households	Asian	black	Hispanic	non-Hispanic white and other
ENTERTAINMENT	**$2,693**	**$2,270**	**$1,404**	**$1,664**	**$3,050**
Fees and admissions	628	848	223	302	742
Audio and visual equipment and services	975	924	840	818	1,020
Pets, toys, and playground equipment	690	295	242	391	804
Other entertainment products and services	400	202	99	153	485
PERSONAL CARE PRODUCTS, SERVICES	**596**	**557**	**536**	**532**	**614**
READING	**110**	**111**	**46**	**36**	**131**
EDUCATION	**1,068**	**2,327**	**591**	**707**	**1,197**
TOBACCO PRODUCTS AND SMOKING SUPPLIES	**380**	**122**	**230**	**182**	**434**
MISCELLANEOUS	**816**	**611**	**626**	**544**	**887**
CASH CONTRIBUTIONS	**1,723**	**1,452**	**1,280**	**1,015**	**1,903**
PERSONAL INSURANCE AND PENSIONS	**5,471**	**7,117**	**3,550**	**4,230**	**5,966**
Life and other personal insurance	309	283	235	119	350
Pensions and Social Security	5,162	6,834	3,315	4,111	5,616
PERSONAL TAXES	**2,104**	**3,526**	**743**	**745**	**2,525**
Federal income taxes	1,404	2,541	378	421	1,716
State and local income taxes	524	787	291	230	605
Other taxes	177	198	74	95	205
GIFTS FOR PEOPLE IN OTHER HOUSEHOLDS	**1,067**	**1,153**	**570**	**743**	**1,193**

Note: "Asian" and "black" include Hispanics and non-Hispanics who identify themselves as being of the respective race alone. "Hispanic" includes people of any race who identify themselves as Hispanic. "Other" includes people who identify themselves as non-Hispanic and as Alaska Native, American Indian, Asian (who are also included in the Asian column), Native Hawaiian or other Pacific Islander, as well as non-Hispanics reporting more than one race. Spending by category does not add to total spending because gift spending is also included in the preceding product and service categories and personal taxes are not included in the total.

Source: Bureau of Labor Statistics, 2009 Consumer Expenditure Survey, Internet site http://www.bls.gov/cex/

Table 9.2 Indexed Spending by Race and Hispanic Origin of Householder, 2009

(indexed average annual spending of households by product and service category and by race and Hispanic origin of householder, 2009; index definition: an index of 100 is the average for all households; an index of 150 means that spending by households in that group is 50 percent above the average for all households; an index of 50 indicates spending that is 50 percent below the average for all households)

	total households	Asian	black	Hispanic	non-Hispanic white and other
Average household spending, total	**$49,067**	**$56,308**	**$35,311**	**$41,981**	**$52,320**
Average household spending, index	**100**	**115**	**72**	**86**	**107**
FOOD	**100**	**119**	**71**	**96**	**105**
Food at home	**100**	**104**	**77**	**101**	**103**
Cereals and bakery products	100	103	77	95	105
Cereals and cereal products	100	124	86	106	101
Bakery products	100	91	72	88	106
Meats, poultry, fish, and eggs	100	115	100	114	98
Beef	100	82	85	112	100
Pork	100	102	115	120	95
Other meats	100	72	80	96	104
Poultry	100	119	119	125	94
Fish and seafood	100	203	107	104	99
Eggs	100	152	95	132	95
Dairy products	100	85	64	99	106
Fresh milk and cream	100	106	73	119	101
Other dairy products	100	74	58	89	108
Fruits and vegetables	100	138	74	112	102
Fresh fruits	100	141	69	116	102
Fresh vegetables	100	184	65	115	103
Processed fruits	100	99	89	103	102
Processed vegetables	100	83	84	106	101
Other food at home	100	87	67	90	106
Sugar and other sweets	100	75	62	77	109
Fats and oils	100	97	80	103	103
Miscellaneous foods	100	90	65	86	107
Nonalcoholic beverages	100	79	75	103	103
Food prepared by consumer unit on trips	100	106	35	67	114
Restaurants and other food away from home	**100**	**140**	**63**	**88**	**107**
ALCOHOLIC BEVERAGES	**100**	**80**	**46**	**61**	**114**
HOUSING	**100**	**121**	**80**	**95**	**104**
Shelter	**100**	**135**	**79**	**100**	**104**
Owned dwellings	100	131	56	81	110
Mortgage interest and charges	100	149	62	96	107
Property taxes	100	129	50	76	112
Maintenance, repair, insurance, other expenses	100	76	44	42	118
Rented dwellings	100	154	141	154	85
Other lodging	100	92	36	49	118

	total households	Asian	black	Hispanic	non-Hispanic white and other
Utilities, fuels, and public services	**100**	**90**	**101**	**97**	**100**
Natural gas	100	103	107	81	102
Electricity	100	77	106	97	99
Fuel oil and other fuels	100	34	35	33	121
Telephone services	100	97	105	109	98
Water and other public services	100	113	86	101	102
Household services	**100**	**133**	**63**	**71**	**111**
Personal services	100	177	72	86	107
Other household services	100	106	57	61	113
Housekeeping supplies	**100**	**81**	**65**	**78**	**108**
Laundry and cleaning supplies	100	83	79	124	99
Other household products	100	81	62	65	111
Postage and stationery	100	79	57	64	112
Household furnishings and equipment	**100**	**111**	**57**	**78**	**110**
Household textiles	100	151	64	81	108
Furniture	100	89	79	97	104
Floor coverings	100	43	23	23	123
Major appliances	100	94	65	75	109
Small appliances and miscellaneous housewares	100	144	55	86	110
Miscellaneous household equipment	100	118	44	71	113
APPAREL AND RELATED SERVICES	**100**	**125**	**102**	**116**	**97**
Men and boys	**100**	**111**	**101**	**113**	**98**
Men, aged 16 or older	100	110	100	106	99
Boys, aged 2 to 15	100	115	109	138	92
Women and girls	**100**	**135**	**93**	**102**	**101**
Women, aged 16 or older	100	141	90	91	103
Girls, aged 2 to 15	100	105	107	157	90
Children under age 2	**100**	**134**	**82**	**162**	**93**
Footwear	**100**	**107**	**133**	**146**	**88**
Other apparel products and services	**100**	**138**	**93**	**104**	**101**
TRANSPORTATION	**100**	**115**	**69**	**93**	**106**
Vehicle purchases	**100**	**97**	**56**	**88**	**109**
Cars and trucks, new	100	87	44	78	113
Cars and trucks, used	100	111	70	99	105
Gasoline and motor oil	**100**	**94**	**81**	**106**	**102**
Other vehicle expenses	**100**	**124**	**74**	**91**	**105**
Vehicle finance charges	100	74	86	99	102
Maintenance and repairs	100	97	69	80	108
Vehicle insurance	100	150	80	98	103
Vehicle rentals, leases, licenses, other charges	100	139	60	89	108
Public transportation	**100**	**246**	**67**	**86**	**108**
HEALTH CARE	**100**	**80**	**56**	**50**	**115**
Health insurance	100	85	63	48	114
Medical services	100	78	40	57	116
Drugs	100	63	57	50	114
Medical supplies	100	90	48	51	115

	total households	Asian	black	Hispanic	non-Hispanic white and other
ENTERTAINMENT	**100**	**84**	**52**	**62**	**113**
Fees and admissions	100	135	36	48	118
Audio and visual equipment and services	100	95	86	84	105
Pets, toys, and playground equipment	100	43	35	57	117
Other entertainment products and services	100	51	25	38	121
PERSONAL CARE PRODUCTS, SERVICES	**100**	**93**	**90**	**89**	**103**
READING	**100**	**101**	**42**	**33**	**119**
EDUCATION	**100**	**218**	**55**	**66**	**112**
TOBACCO PRODUCTS AND SMOKING SUPPLIES	**100**	**32**	**61**	**48**	**114**
MISCELLANEOUS	**100**	**75**	**77**	**67**	**109**
CASH CONTRIBUTIONS	**100**	**84**	**74**	**59**	**110**
PERSONAL INSURANCE AND PENSIONS	**100**	**130**	**65**	**77**	**109**
Life and other personal insurance	100	92	76	39	113
Pensions and Social Security	100	132	64	80	109
PERSONAL TAXES	**100**	**168**	**35**	**35**	**120**
Federal income taxes	100	181	27	30	122
State and local income taxes	100	150	56	44	115
Other taxes	100	112	42	54	116
GIFTS FOR PEOPLE IN OTHER HOUSEHOLDS	**100**	**108**	**53**	**70**	**112**

Note: "Asian" and "black" include Hispanics and non-Hispanics who identify themselves as being of the respective race alone. "Hispanic" includes people of any race who identify themselves as Hispanic. "Other" includes people who identify themselves as non-Hispanic and as Alaska Native, American Indian, Asian (who are also included in the Asian column), Native Hawaiian or other Pacific Islander, as well as non-Hispanics reporting more than one race.
Source: Calculations by New Strategist based on the Bureau of Labor Statistics' 2009 Consumer Expenditure Survey

Table 9.3 Total Spending by Race and Hispanic Origin of Householder, 2009

(total annual spending by race and Hispanic origin groups, 2009; households and dollars in thousands)

	total households	Asian	black	Hispanic	non-Hispanic white and other
Number of households	**120,847**	**4,584**	**14,659**	**14,295**	**92,119**
Total spending of all households	**$5,929,599,749**	**$258,115,872**	**$517,623,949**	**$600,118,395**	**$4,819,666,080**
FOOD	**770,037,084**	**34,677,960**	**66,317,316**	**87,113,730**	**616,828,824**
Groceries	**453,538,791**	**17,900,520**	**42,217,920**	**54,092,280**	**357,605,958**
Cereals and bakery products	61,148,582	2,383,680	5,717,010	6,847,305	48,730,951
Cereals and cereal products	20,906,531	985,560	2,184,191	2,630,280	16,028,706
Bakery products	40,362,898	1,398,120	3,532,819	4,202,730	32,610,126
Meats, poultry, fish, and eggs	101,632,327	4,428,144	12,386,855	13,651,725	75,813,937
Beef	27,311,422	852,624	2,799,869	3,602,340	20,911,013
Pork	20,302,296	788,448	2,829,187	2,887,590	14,739,040
Other meats	13,776,558	375,888	1,333,969	1,572,450	10,870,042
Poultry	18,610,438	843,456	2,682,597	2,744,640	13,265,136
Fish and seafood	16,314,345	1,256,016	2,110,896	2,015,595	12,251,827
Eggs	5,317,268	307,128	615,678	829,110	3,868,998
Dairy products	49,063,882	1,586,064	3,782,022	5,760,885	39,519,051
Fresh milk and cream	17,401,968	696,768	1,539,195	2,444,445	13,449,374
Other dairy products	31,661,914	893,880	2,242,827	3,316,440	26,069,677
Fruits and vegetables	79,275,632	4,139,352	7,094,956	10,492,530	61,811,849
Fresh fruits	26,586,340	1,421,040	2,213,509	3,659,520	20,726,775
Fresh vegetables	25,257,023	1,764,840	1,993,624	3,430,800	19,897,704
Processed fruits	14,259,946	536,328	1,539,195	1,729,695	11,054,280
Processed vegetables	13,293,170	417,144	1,348,628	1,672,515	10,225,209
Other food at home	162,297,521	5,358,696	13,237,077	17,339,835	131,730,170
Sugar and other sweets	17,039,427	485,904	1,289,992	1,558,155	14,094,207
Fats and oils	12,326,394	453,816	1,202,038	1,500,975	9,672,495
Miscellaneous foods	86,405,605	2,961,264	6,772,458	8,820,015	70,747,392
Nonalcoholic beverages	40,725,439	1,223,928	3,708,727	4,974,660	32,057,412
Food prepared by consumer unit on trips	5,921,503	238,368	249,203	471,735	5,158,664
Restaurants and other food away from home	**316,498,293**	**16,777,440**	**24,114,055**	**33,021,450**	**259,222,866**
ALCOHOLIC BEVERAGES	**52,568,445**	**1,604,400**	**2,946,459**	**3,816,765**	**45,691,024**
HOUSING	**2,041,710,065**	**93,490,680**	**197,940,477**	**228,476,985**	**1,619,359,901**
Shelter	**1,217,533,525**	**62,209,464**	**116,084,621**	**143,564,685**	**960,709,051**
Owned dwellings	790,701,921	39,161,112	53,241,488	75,734,910	663,072,562
Mortgage interest and charges	434,324,118	24,519,816	32,542,980	49,374,930	353,460,603
Property taxes	218,853,917	10,699,056	13,369,008	19,555,560	186,172,499
Maintenance, repair, insurance, other expenses	137,523,886	3,942,240	7,329,500	6,804,420	123,439,460
Rented dwellings	345,622,420	20,220,024	59,310,314	63,112,425	224,494,003
Other lodging	81,209,184	2,823,744	3,532,819	4,717,350	73,142,486

	total households	Asian	black	Hispanic	non-Hispanic white and other
Utilities, fuels, and public services	**$440,487,315**	**$14,989,680**	**$53,769,212**	**$50,489,940**	**$337,155,540**
Natural gas	58,369,101	2,287,416	7,578,703	5,560,755	45,414,667
Electricity	166,406,319	4,840,704	21,431,458	19,141,005	126,110,911
Fuel oil and other fuels	17,039,427	220,032	732,950	671,865	15,752,349
Telephone	140,424,214	5,147,832	17,942,616	18,183,240	104,555,065
Water and other public services	58,127,407	2,493,696	6,083,485	6,933,075	45,322,548
Household services	**122,176,317**	**6,174,648**	**9,279,147**	**10,206,630**	**103,081,161**
Personal services	47,009,483	3,153,792	4,119,179	4,774,530	38,413,623
Other household services	75,166,834	3,020,856	5,159,968	5,432,100	64,667,538
Housekeeping supplies	**79,638,173**	**2,457,024**	**6,288,711**	**7,390,515**	**65,772,966**
Laundry and cleaning supplies	18,852,132	595,920	1,817,716	2,773,230	14,278,445
Other household products	43,504,920	1,338,528	3,283,616	3,330,735	36,755,481
Postage and stationery	17,281,121	517,992	1,187,379	1,300,845	14,739,040
Household furnishings, equipment	**181,995,582**	**7,659,864**	**12,518,786**	**16,825,215**	**152,641,183**
Household textiles	14,985,028	857,208	1,158,061	1,443,795	12,343,946
Furniture	41,450,521	1,393,536	3,972,589	4,731,645	32,886,483
Floor coverings	3,625,410	59,592	102,613	100,065	3,408,403
Major appliances	23,444,318	838,872	1,861,693	2,087,070	19,529,228
Small appliances and misc. housewares	11,238,771	614,256	747,609	1,143,600	9,396,138
Miscellaneous household equipment	87,130,687	3,887,232	4,676,221	7,333,335	74,984,866
APPAREL, RELATED SERVICES	**208,461,075**	**9,855,600**	**25,726,545**	**28,618,590**	**154,575,682**
Men and boys	**46,284,401**	**1,957,368**	**5,687,692**	**6,175,440**	**34,544,625**
Men, aged 16 or older	36,737,488	1,535,640	4,441,677	4,617,285	27,819,938
Boys, aged 2 to 15	9,546,913	417,144	1,260,674	1,558,155	6,724,687
Women and girls	**81,934,266**	**4,185,192**	**9,220,511**	**9,906,435**	**62,825,158**
Women, aged 16 or older	67,795,167	3,616,776	7,388,136	7,276,155	53,060,544
Girls, aged 2 to 15	14,259,946	568,416	1,847,034	2,644,575	9,764,614
Children under age 2	**10,997,077**	**559,248**	**1,099,425**	**2,101,365**	**7,830,115**
Footwear	**39,033,581**	**1,576,896**	**6,303,370**	**6,747,240**	**26,253,915**
Other apparel products and services	**30,090,903**	**1,576,896**	**3,386,229**	**3,688,110**	**23,121,869**
TRANSPORTATION	**925,446,326**	**40,265,856**	**77,722,018**	**102,295,020**	**746,992,971**
Vehicle purchases	**321,090,479**	**11,835,888**	**21,827,251**	**33,350,235**	**266,868,743**
Cars and trucks, new	156,738,559	5,184,504	8,326,312	14,437,950	134,493,740
Cars and trucks, used	157,584,488	6,651,384	13,339,690	18,483,435	126,295,149
Gasoline and motor oil	**240,002,142**	**8,576,664**	**23,718,262**	**30,076,680**	**186,633,094**
Other vehicle expenses	**306,467,992**	**14,453,352**	**27,500,284**	**33,007,155**	**245,957,730**
Vehicle finance charges	33,958,007	953,472	3,547,478	3,974,010	26,530,272
Maintenance and repairs	88,580,851	3,268,392	7,388,136	8,348,280	72,866,129
Vehicle insurance	129,910,525	7,380,240	12,592,081	14,995,455	102,159,971
Vehicle rentals, leases, licenses, other charges	54,018,609	2,855,832	3,957,930	5,689,410	44,401,358
Public transportation	**57,885,713**	**5,399,952**	**4,676,221**	**5,860,950**	**47,533,404**
HEALTH CARE	**377,767,722**	**11,450,832**	**25,843,817**	**22,414,560**	**329,878,139**
Health insurance	215,711,895	6,917,256	16,608,647	12,122,160	187,277,927
Medical services	88,943,392	2,635,800	4,309,746	5,975,310	78,761,745
Drugs	58,731,642	1,407,288	4,089,861	3,445,095	51,218,164
Medical supplies	14,380,793	490,488	835,563	871,995	12,620,303

	total households	Asian	black	Hispanic	non-Hispanic white and other
ENTERTAINMENT	**$325,440,971**	**$10,405,680**	**$20,581,236**	**$23,786,880**	**$280,962,950**
Fees and admissions	75,891,916	3,887,232	3,268,957	4,317,090	68,352,298
Audio and visual equipment, services	117,825,825	4,235,616	12,313,560	11,693,310	93,961,380
Pets, toys, hobbies, and playground equipment	83,384,430	1,352,280	3,547,478	5,589,345	74,063,676
Other entertainment products and services	48,338,800	925,968	1,451,241	2,187,135	44,677,715
PERSONAL CARE PRODUCTS AND SERVICES	**72,024,812**	**2,553,288**	**7,857,224**	**7,604,940**	**56,561,066**
READING	**13,293,170**	**508,824**	**674,314**	**514,620**	**12,067,589**
EDUCATION	**129,064,596**	**10,666,968**	**8,663,469**	**10,106,565**	**110,266,443**
TOBACCO PRODUCTS AND SMOKING SUPPLIES	**45,921,860**	**559,248**	**3,371,570**	**2,601,690**	**39,979,646**
MISCELLANEOUS	**98,611,152**	**2,800,824**	**9,176,534**	**7,776,480**	**81,709,553**
CASH CONTRIBUTIONS	**208,219,381**	**6,655,968**	**18,763,520**	**14,509,425**	**175,302,457**
PERSONAL INSURANCE AND PENSIONS	**661,153,937**	**32,624,328**	**52,039,450**	**60,467,850**	**549,581,954**
Life and other personal insurance	37,341,723	1,297,272	3,444,865	1,701,105	32,241,650
Pensions and Social Security	623,812,214	31,327,056	48,594,585	58,766,745	517,340,304
PERSONAL TAXES	**254,262,088**	**16,163,184**	**10,891,637**	**10,649,775**	**232,600,475**
Federal income taxes	169,669,188	11,647,944	5,541,102	6,018,195	158,076,204
State and local income taxes	63,323,828	3,607,608	4,265,769	3,287,850	55,731,995
Other taxes	21,389,919	907,632	1,084,766	1,358,025	18,884,395
GIFTS FOR PEOPLE IN OTHER HOUSEHOLDS	**128,943,749**	**5,285,352**	**8,355,630**	**10,621,185**	**109,897,967**

Note: "Asian" and "black" include Hispanics and non-Hispanics who identify themselves as being of the respective race alone. "Hispanic" includes people of any race who identify themselves as Hispanic. "Other" includes people who identify themselves as non-Hispanic and as Alaska Native, American Indian, Asian (who are also included in the Asian column), Native Hawaiian or other Pacific Islander, as well as non-Hispanics reporting more than one race. Spending by category does not add to total spending because gift spending is also included in the preceding product and service categories and personal taxes are not included in the total.
Source: Calculations by New Strategist based on the Bureau of Labor Statistics' 2009 Consumer Expenditure Survey

Table 9.4 Market Shares by Race and Hispanic Origin of Householder, 2009

(percentage of total annual spending accounted for by race and Hispanic origin groups, 2009)

	total households	Asian	black	Hispanic	non-Hispanic white and other
Share of total households	**100.0%**	**3.8%**	**12.1%**	**11.8%**	**76.2%**
Share of total spending	**100.0**	**4.4**	**8.7**	**10.1**	**81.3**
FOOD	**100.0**	**4.5**	**8.6**	**11.3**	**80.1**
Groceries	**100.0**	**3.9**	**9.3**	**11.9**	**78.8**
Cereals and bakery products	100.0	3.9	9.3	11.2	79.7
Cereals and cereal products	100.0	4.7	10.4	12.6	76.7
Bakery products	100.0	3.5	8.8	10.4	80.8
Meats, poultry, fish, and eggs	100.0	4.4	12.2	13.4	74.6
Beef	100.0	3.1	10.3	13.2	76.6
Pork	100.0	3.9	13.9	14.2	72.6
Other meats	100.0	2.7	9.7	11.4	78.9
Poultry	100.0	4.5	14.4	14.7	71.3
Fish and seafood	100.0	7.7	12.9	12.4	75.1
Eggs	100.0	5.8	11.6	15.6	72.8
Dairy products	100.0	3.2	7.7	11.7	80.5
Fresh milk and cream	100.0	4.0	8.8	14.0	77.3
Other dairy products	100.0	2.8	7.1	10.5	82.3
Fruits and vegetables	100.0	5.2	8.9	13.2	78.0
Fresh fruits	100.0	5.3	8.3	13.8	78.0
Fresh vegetables	100.0	7.0	7.9	13.6	78.8
Processed fruits	100.0	3.8	10.8	12.1	77.5
Processed vegetables	100.0	3.1	10.1	12.6	76.9
Other food at home	100.0	3.3	8.2	10.7	81.2
Sugar and other sweets	100.0	2.9	7.6	9.1	82.7
Fats and oils	100.0	3.7	9.8	12.2	78.5
Miscellaneous foods	100.0	3.4	7.8	10.2	81.9
Nonalcoholic beverages	100.0	3.0	9.1	12.2	78.7
Food prepared by consumer unit on trips	100.0	4.0	4.2	8.0	87.1
Restaurants and other food away from home	**100.0**	**5.3**	**7.6**	**10.4**	**81.9**
ALCOHOLIC BEVERAGES	**100.0**	**3.1**	**5.6**	**7.3**	**86.9**
HOUSING	**100.0**	**4.6**	**9.7**	**11.2**	**79.3**
Shelter	**100.0**	**5.1**	**9.5**	**11.8**	**78.9**
Owned dwellings	100.0	5.0	6.7	9.6	83.9
Mortgage interest and charges	100.0	5.6	7.5	11.4	81.4
Property taxes	100.0	4.9	6.1	8.9	85.1
Maintenance, repair, insurance, other expenses	100.0	2.9	5.3	4.9	89.8
Rented dwellings	100.0	5.9	17.2	18.3	65.0
Other lodging	100.0	3.5	4.4	5.8	90.1

	total households	Asian	black	Hispanic	non-Hispanic white and other
Utilities, fuels, and public services	**100.0%**	**3.4%**	**12.2%**	**11.5%**	**76.5%**
Natural gas	100.0	3.9	13.0	9.5	77.8
Electricity	100.0	2.9	12.9	11.5	75.8
Fuel oil and other fuels	100.0	1.3	4.3	3.9	92.4
Telephone	100.0	3.7	12.8	12.9	74.5
Water and other public services	**100.0**	**4.3**	**10.5**	**11.9**	**78.0**
Household services	100.0	5.1	7.6	8.4	84.4
Personal services	100.0	6.7	8.8	10.2	81.7
Other household services	100.0	4.0	6.9	7.2	86.0
Housekeeping supplies	**100.0**	**3.1**	**7.9**	**9.3**	**82.6**
Laundry and cleaning supplies	100.0	3.2	9.6	14.7	75.7
Other household products	100.0	3.1	7.5	7.7	84.5
Postage and stationery	100.0	3.0	6.9	7.5	85.3
Household furnishings and equipment	**100.0**	**4.2**	**6.9**	**9.2**	**83.9**
Household textiles	100.0	5.7	7.7	9.6	82.4
Furniture	100.0	3.4	9.6	11.4	79.3
Floor coverings	100.0	1.6	2.8	2.8	94.0
Major appliances	100.0	3.6	7.9	8.9	83.3
Small appliances and miscellaneous housewares	100.0	5.5	6.7	10.2	83.6
Miscellaneous household equipment	100.0	4.5	5.4	8.4	86.1
APPAREL AND RELATED SERVICES	**100.0**	**4.7**	**12.3**	**13.7**	**74.2**
Men and boys	**100.0**	**4.2**	**12.3**	**13.3**	**74.6**
Men, aged 16 or older	100.0	4.2	12.1	12.6	75.7
Boys, aged 2 to 15	100.0	4.4	13.2	16.3	70.4
Women and girls	**100.0**	**5.1**	**11.3**	**12.1**	**76.7**
Women, aged 16 or older	100.0	5.3	10.9	10.7	78.3
Girls, aged 2 to 15	100.0	4.0	13.0	18.5	68.5
Children under age 2	**100.0**	**5.1**	**10.0**	**19.1**	**71.2**
Footwear	**100.0**	**4.0**	**16.1**	**17.3**	**67.3**
Other apparel products and services	**100.0**	**5.2**	**11.3**	**12.3**	**76.8**
TRANSPORTATION	**100.0**	**4.4**	**8.4**	**11.1**	**80.7**
Vehicle purchases	**100.0**	**3.7**	**6.8**	**10.4**	**83.1**
Cars and trucks, new	100.0	3.3	5.3	9.2	85.8
Cars and trucks, used	100.0	4.2	8.5	11.7	80.1
Gasoline and motor oil	**100.0**	**3.6**	**9.9**	**12.5**	**77.8**
Other vehicle expenses	**100.0**	**4.7**	**9.0**	**10.8**	**80.3**
Vehicle finance charges	100.0	2.8	10.4	11.7	78.1
Maintenance and repairs	100.0	3.7	8.3	9.4	82.3
Vehicle insurance	100.0	5.7	9.7	11.5	78.6
Vehicle rentals, leases, licenses, other charges	100.0	5.3	7.3	10.5	82.2
Public transportation	**100.0**	**9.3**	**8.1**	**10.1**	**82.1**
HEALTH CARE	**100.0**	**3.0**	**6.8**	**5.9**	**87.3**
Health insurance	100.0	3.2	7.7	5.6	86.8
Medical services	100.0	3.0	4.8	6.7	88.6
Drugs	100.0	2.4	7.0	5.9	87.2
Medical supplies	100.0	3.4	5.8	6.1	87.8

	total households	Asian	black	Hispanic	non-Hispanic white and other
ENTERTAINMENT	**100.0%**	**3.2%**	**6.3%**	**7.3%**	**86.3%**
Fees and admissions	100.0	5.1	4.3	5.7	90.1
Audio and visual equipment and services	100.0	3.6	10.5	9.9	79.7
Pets, toys, hobbies, and playground equipment	100.0	1.6	4.3	6.7	88.8
Other entertainment products and services	100.0	1.9	3.0	4.5	92.4
PERSONAL CARE PRODUCTS, SERVICES	**100.0**	**3.5**	**10.9**	**10.6**	**78.5**
READING	**100.0**	**3.8**	**5.1**	**3.9**	**90.8**
EDUCATION	**100.0**	**8.3**	**6.7**	**7.8**	**85.4**
TOBACCO PRODUCTS AND SMOKING SUPPLIES	**100.0**	**1.2**	**7.3**	**5.7**	**87.1**
MISCELLANEOUS	**100.0**	**2.8**	**9.3**	**7.9**	**82.9**
CASH CONTRIBUTIONS	**100.0**	**3.2**	**9.0**	**7.0**	**84.2**
PERSONAL INSURANCE AND PENSIONS	**100.0**	**4.9**	**7.9**	**9.1**	**83.1**
Life and other personal insurance	100.0	3.5	9.2	4.6	86.3
Pensions and Social Security	100.0	5.0	7.8	9.4	82.9
PERSONAL TAXES	**100.0**	**6.4**	**4.3**	**4.2**	**91.5**
Federal income taxes	100.0	6.9	3.3	3.5	93.2
State and local income taxes	100.0	5.7	6.7	5.2	88.0
Other taxes	100.0	4.2	5.1	6.3	88.3
GIFTS FOR PEOPLE IN OTHER HOUSEHOLDS	**100.0**	**4.1**	**6.5**	**8.2**	**85.2**

Note: "Asian" and "black" include Hispanics and non-Hispanics who identify themselves as being of the respective race alone. "Hispanic" includes people of any race who identify themselves as Hispanic. "Other" includes people who identify themselves as non-Hispanic and as Alaska Native, American Indian, Asian (who are also included in the Asian column), Native Hawaiian or other Pacific Islander, as well as non-Hispanics reporting more than one race.
Source: Calculations by New Strategist based on the Bureau of Labor Statistics' 2009 Consumer Expenditure Survey

Asians Spend Much More than Average on College Tuition and Air Fares

Asian spending is above average on most items because their households have more earners, which boosts incomes.

Asian households have above-average incomes because most are headed by college graduates. Not surprisingly, their spending on college tuition is more than twice the average, and their spending on technical school tuition is eight times the average. They also spend more than twice the average on fees for recreational lessons and 24 percent more than average on books.

Asians spend only 4 percent more than the average household on groceries overall, but nearly four times the average on rice. They also spend 70 to 71 percent more than average on lunch and dinners at full-service restaurants.

Asian households spend more than twice the average on airline fares and mass transit. They spend less than average on cable television service and pets.

■ Asians spend 19 percent less than the average household on alcoholic beverages.

Asians spend more than average on books

(indexed spending by Asian households on selected items, 2009)

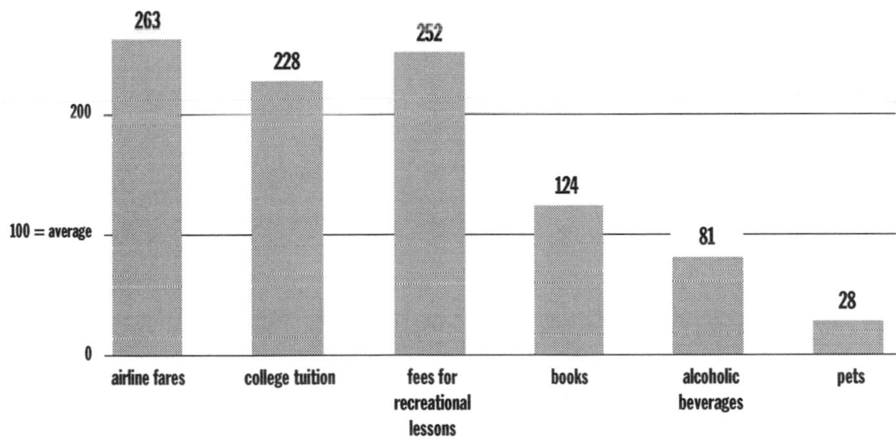

Table 9.5 Spending on Alcoholic Beverages by Asian Households, 2009

(average annual, indexed, aggregate, and market share of spending by Asian households on alcoholic beverages, 2009)

	Asian average	index	aggregate (in 000s)	market share
ALCOHOLIC BEVERAGES, TOTAL	**$350.45**	**81**	**$1,606,463**	**3.1%**
At home	**174.17**	**71**	**798,395**	**2.7**
Beer and ale	67.93	59	311,391	2.2
Whiskey	9.66	95	44,281	3.6
Wine	77.16	76	353,701	2.9
Other alcoholic beverages	19.43	100	89,067	3.8
Away from home	**176.28**	**93**	**808,068**	**3.5**
Beer and ale	57.35	82	262,892	3.1
Wine	47.98	155	219,940	5.9
Other alcoholic beverages	35.98	78	164,932	2.9
Alcoholic beverages purchased on trips	34.97	84	160,302	3.2

Note: The index is calculated by dividing Asian spending on each item by average household spending on the item and multiplying by 100. Subcategories may not add to total because some are not shown.
Source: Bureau of Labor Statistics, unpublished data from the 2009 Consumer Expenditure Survey; calculations by New Strategist

Table 9.6 Spending on Apparel by Asian Households, 2009

(average annual, indexed, aggregate, and market share of spending by Asian households on apparel, accessories, and related services, 2009)

	Asian average	index	aggregate (in 000s)	market share
APPAREL, TOTAL	$2,149.75	125	$9,854,454	4.7%
Men's apparel	**335.40**	**110**	**1,537,474**	**4.2**
Suits	13.94	78	63,901	3.0
Sport coats and tailored jackets	7.76	114	35,572	4.3
Coats and jackets	28.71	82	131,607	3.1
Underwear	19.37	122	88,792	4.6
Hosiery	10.55	89	48,361	3.4
Nightwear	0.61	36	2,796	1.4
Accessories	26.32	92	120,651	3.5
Sweaters and vests	25.88	179	118,634	6.8
Active sportswear	13.72	81	62,892	3.1
Shirts	95.10	113	435,938	4.3
Pants and shorts	91.97	136	421,590	5.2
Uniforms	0.80	29	3,667	1.1
Costumes	0.69	96	3,163	3.6
Boys' (aged 2 to 15) apparel	**91.41**	**116**	**419,023**	**4.4**
Coats and jackets	8.18	188	37,497	7.1
Sweaters	3.06	165	14,027	6.2
Shirts	25.16	104	115,333	4.0
Underwear	13.42	221	61,517	8.4
Nightwear	0.86	80	3,942	3.0
Hosiery	9.90	206	45,382	7.8
Accessories	4.00	93	18,336	3.5
Suits, sport coats, and vests	2.75	296	12,606	11.2
Pants and shorts	19.90	77	91,222	2.9
Uniforms	3.34	99	15,311	3.8
Active sportswear	0.54	45	2,475	1.7
Costumes	0.29	39	1,329	1.5
Women's apparel	**788.62**	**141**	**3,615,034**	**5.3**
Coats and jackets	78.17	186	358,331	7.1
Dresses	121.48	168	556,864	6.4
Sport coats and tailored jackets	7.74	163	35,480	6.2
Sweaters and vests	62.42	142	286,133	5.4
Shirts, blouses, and tops	156.21	141	716,067	5.3
Skirts	21.73	236	99,610	8.9
Pants and shorts	83.08	90	380,839	3.4
Active sportswear	38.16	138	174,925	5.3
Nightwear	25.54	118	117,075	4.5
Undergarments	43.01	119	197,158	4.5
Hosiery	29.09	165	133,349	6.2
Suits	10.40	92	47,674	3.5
Accessories	102.32	161	469,035	6.1
Uniforms	6.59	104	30,209	3.9
Costumes	2.68	166	12,285	6.3

	Asian average	index	aggregate (in 000s)	market share
Girls' (aged 2 to 15) apparel	**$124.18**	**106**	**$569,241**	**4.0%**
Coats and jackets	13.22	186	60,600	7.1
Dresses and suits	12.48	96	57,208	3.6
Shirts, blouses, and sweaters	26.70	86	122,393	3.3
Skirts, pants, and shorts	23.70	89	108,641	3.4
Active sportswear	12.68	109	58,125	4.1
Underwear and nightwear	13.92	123	63,809	4.7
Hosiery	5.13	97	23,516	3.7
Accessories	8.42	132	38,597	5.0
Uniforms	5.78	176	26,496	6.7
Costumes	2.14	117	9,810	4.4
Children's (under age 2) apparel	**121.63**	**133**	**557,552**	**5.1**
Coats, jackets, and snowsuits	5.25	194	24,066	7.3
Outerwear including dresses	20.23	96	92,734	3.6
Underwear	73.91	134	338,803	5.1
Nightwear and loungewear	4.70	98	21,545	3.7
Accessories	17.54	236	80,403	9.0
Footwear	**344.15**	**107**	**1,577,584**	**4.0**
Men's	97.24	104	445,748	4.0
Boys'	57.66	134	264,313	5.1
Women's	167.20	111	766,445	4.2
Girls'	22.05	61	101,077	2.3
Other apparel products and services	**344.37**	**138**	**1,578,592**	**5.2**
Material for making clothes	23.11	239	105,936	9.1
Sewing patterns and notions	3.65	65	16,732	2.5
Watches	27.74	111	127,160	4.2
Jewelry	141.88	145	650,378	5.5
Shoe repair and other shoe services	0.87	73	3,988	2.8
Coin-operated apparel laundry, dry cleaning	64.55	156	295,897	5.9
Apparel alteration, repair, tailoring services	8.66	151	39,697	5.7
Clothing rental	3.71	157	17,007	5.9
Watch and jewelry repair	2.29	65	10,497	2.4
Professional laundry, dry cleaning	67.64	122	310,062	4.6
Clothing storage	0.28	17	1,284	0.7

Note: The index is calculated by dividing Asian spending on each item by average household spending on the item and multiplying by 100. Subcategories may not add to total because some are not shown.
Source: Bureau of Labor Statistics, unpublished data from the 2009 Consumer Expenditure Survey; calculations by New Strategist

Table 9.7 Spending on Entertainment by Asian Households, 2009

(average annual, indexed, aggregate, and market share of spending by Asian households on entertainment, 2009)

	Asian average	index	aggregate (in 000s)	market share
ENTERTAINMENT, TOTAL	**$2,269.55**	**84**	**$10,403,617**	**3.2%**
Fees and admission	**847.96**	**135**	**3,887,049**	**5.1**
Recreation expenses on trips	25.38	128	116,342	4.9
Social, recreation, civic club membership	116.32	101	533,211	3.8
Fees for participant sports	141.07	114	646,665	4.3
Participant sports on trips	35.81	163	164,153	6.2
Movie, theater, amusement park, and other admissions	128.82	107	590,511	4.1
Movie, other admissions on trips	70.36	172	322,530	6.5
Admission to sports events	25.51	50	116,938	1.9
Admission to sports events on trips	23.44	172	107,449	6.5
Fees for recreational lessons	255.85	252	1,172,816	9.5
Other entertainment services on trips	25.38	128	116,342	4.9
Audio and visual equipment and services	**924.49**	**95**	**4,237,862**	**3.6**
Radios	0.54	24	2,475	0.9
Television sets	140.46	100	643,869	3.8
Tape recorders and players	–	–	–	–
Cable and satellite television services	462.10	77	2,118,266	2.9
Miscellaneous sound equipment	3.21	292	14,715	11.1
Miscellaneous video equipment	4.82	132	22,095	5.0
Satellite radio service	10.74	77	49,232	2.9
Sound equipment accessories	9.52	89	43,640	3.4
Online gaming services	1.07	49	4,905	1.8
VCRs and video disc players	13.03	105	59,730	4.0
Video game hardware and software	89.24	167	409,076	6.3
Video cassettes, tapes, and discs	19.57	65	89,709	2.5
Streaming and downloading video	1.34	96	6,143	3.6
Repair of TV, radio, and sound equipment	2.06	62	9,443	2.4
Rental of television sets	–	–	–	–
Personal digital audio players	17.39	134	79,716	5.1
Sound components and component systems	2.23	19	10,222	0.7
Satellite dishes	2.37	224	10,864	8.5
Compact discs, records, and audio tapes	16.28	88	74,628	3.3
Streaming and downloading audio	4.51	80	20,674	3.0
Rental of VCR, radio, and sound equipment	–	–	–	–
Musical instruments and accessories	98.16	421	449,965	16.0
Rental and repair of musical instruments	2.12	133	9,718	5.1
Rental of video cassettes, tapes, discs, films	21.58	85	98,923	3.2
Rental of computer and video game hardware and software	0.94	409	4,309	15.5
Installation of televisions	1.20	176	5,501	6.7

	Asian average	index	aggregate (in 000s)	market share
Pets, toys, hobbies, playground equipment	**$294.86**	**43**	**$1,351,638**	**1.6%**
Pets	154.00	28	705,936	1.1
Pet food	76.00	45	348,384	1.7
Pet purchase, supplies, and medicines	49.56	30	227,183	1.1
Pet services	11.01	25	50,470	1.0
Veterinarian services	17.43	11	79,899	0.4
Toys, games, hobbies, and tricycles	138.36	99	634,242	3.8
Stamp and coin collecting	1.63	30	7,472	1.1
Playground equipment	0.87	36	3,988	1.3
Other entertainment supplies, equipment, services	**202.24**	**51**	**927,068**	**1.9**
Unmotored recreational vehicles	–	–	–	–
Motorized recreational vehicles	–	–	–	–
Rental of recreational vehicles	5.46	84	25,029	3.2
Docking and landing fees	–	–	–	–
Sports, recreation, exercise equipment	107.96	83	494,889	3.2
Athletic gear, game tables, exercise equip.	26.46	51	121,293	1.9
Bicycles	7.59	55	34,793	2.1
Camping equipment	18.12	169	83,062	6.4
Hunting and fishing equipment	3.37	11	15,448	0.4
Winter sports equipment	6.06	157	27,779	6.0
Water sports equipment	2.39	79	10,956	3.0
Other sports equipment	4.29	72	19,665	2.7
Global positioning system devices	38.78	486	177,768	18.4
Rental and repair of misc. sports equipment	0.90	33	4,126	1.3
Photographic equipment and supplies	69.57	118	318,909	4.5
Film	1.12	65	5,134	2.5
Photo processing	8.75	68	40,110	2.6
Repair and rental of photographic equipment	2.58	437	11,827	16.6
Photographic equipment	49.49	180	226,862	6.8
Photographer fees	7.61	53	34,884	2.0
Fireworks	–	–	–	–
Souvenirs	0.19	7	871	0.3
Visual goods	–	–	–	–
Pinball, electronic video games	3.44	132	15,769	5.0
Live entertainment at catered affairs	1.82	21	8,343	0.8
Rental of party supplies for catered affairs	13.81	98	63,305	3.7

Note: The index is calculated by dividing Asian spending on each item by average household spending on the item and multiplying by 100. Subcategories may not add to total because some are not shown. "–" means sample is too small to make a reliable estimate.

Source: Bureau of Labor Statistics, unpublished data from the 2009 Consumer Expenditure Survey; calculations by New Strategist

Table 9.8 Spending on Financial Products and Services by Asian Households, 2009

(average annual, indexed, aggregate, and market share of spending by Asian households on financial products and services, cash contributions, insurance, pensions, and taxes, 2009)

	Asian average	index	aggregate (in 000s)	market share
FINANCIAL PRODUCTS, SERVICES, TOTAL	**$610.84**	**75**	**$2,800,091**	**2.8%**
Lottery and gambling losses	52.54	70	240,843	2.7
Legal fees	65.57	41	300,573	1.5
Funeral expenses	11.72	25	53,724	0.9
Safe deposit box rental	2.96	78	13,569	3.0
Checking accounts, other bank service charges	18.24	78	83,612	2.9
Cemetery lots, vaults, and maintenance fees	5.41	39	24,799	1.5
Accounting fees	49.02	83	224,708	3.2
Miscellaneous personal services	45.11	109	206,784	4.1
Dating services	0.42	111	1,925	4.2
Finance charges, except mortgage, vehicles	204.66	101	938,161	3.8
Occupational expenses	64.16	113	294,109	4.3
Expenses for other properties	73.68	68	337,749	2.6
Credit card memberships	3.57	189	16,365	7.2
Shopping club membership fees	12.67	134	58,079	5.1
Vacation clubs	1.11	18	5,088	0.7
CASH CONTRIBUTIONS, TOTAL	**1,451.58**	**84**	**6,654,043**	**3.2**
Support for college students	155.40	143	712,354	5.4
Alimony expenditures	144.83	314	663,901	11.9
Child support expenditures	107.92	50	494,705	1.9
Gifts of stocks, bonds, and mutual funds for people in other households	10.20	81	46,757	3.1
Cash contributions to charities and other organizations	170.65	82	782,260	3.1
Cash contributions to church, religious organizations	511.07	71	2,342,745	2.7
Cash contributions to educational institutions	10.76	35	49,324	1.3
Cash contributions to political organizations	0.60	8	2,750	0.3
Other cash gifts	340.15	92	1,559,248	3.5
PERSONAL INSURANCE AND PENSIONS, TOTAL	**7,117.02**	**130**	**32,624,420**	**4.9**
Life and other personal insurance	**282.84**	**92**	**1,296,539**	**3.5**
Life, endowment, annuity, other personal insurance	276.70	95	1,268,393	3.6
Other nonhealth insurance	6.14	36	28,146	1.4
Pensions and Social Security	**6,834.18**	**132**	**31,327,881**	**5.0**
Deductions for government retirement	117.67	147	539,399	5.6
Deductions for private pensions	993.97	159	4,556,358	6.0
Nonpayroll deposit to retirement plans	456.32	99	2,091,771	3.8
Deductions for Social Security	5,266.22	132	24,140,352	5.0

	Asian average	index	aggregate (in 000s)	market share
PERSONAL TAXES, TOTAL	**$3,525.97**	**168**	**$16,163,046**	**6.4%**
Federal income taxes	2,540.54	181	11,645,835	6.9
State and local income taxes	787.39	150	3,609,396	5.7
Other taxes	198.04	112	907,815	4.3

Note: The index is calculated by dividing Asian spending on each item by average household spending on the item and multiplying by 100. Subcategories may not add to total because some are not shown.
Source: Bureau of Labor Statistics, unpublished data from the 2009 Consumer Expenditure Survey; calculations by New Strategist

Table 9.9 Spending on Gifts for People in Other Households by Asian Households, 2009

(average annual, indexed, aggregate, and market share of spending by Asian households on gifts for people in other households, 2009)

	Asian average	index	aggregate (in 000s)	market share
GIFTS, TOTAL	**$1,153.21**	**108**	**$5,286,315**	**4.1%**
Food	**77.05**	**80**	**353,197**	**3.0**
Candy and chewing gum	2.54	34	11,643	1.3
Alcoholic beverages	**22.26**	**254**	**102,040**	**9.6**
Housing	**145.28**	**72**	**665,964**	**2.7**
Housekeeping supplies	32.49	105	148,934	4.0
Postage and stationery	26.03	124	119,322	4.7
Household textiles	3.61	41	16,548	1.5
Appliances and miscellaneous housewares	15.24	99	69,860	3.7
Major appliances	0.47	11	2,154	0.4
Small appliances and misc. housewares	14.77	135	67,706	5.1
Miscellaneous household equipment	36.44	88	167,041	3.3
Decorative items for the home	12.53	122	57,438	4.6
Plants and fresh flowers, indoor	6.87	78	31,492	3.0
Other housing	57.50	54	263,580	2.1
Apparel and services	**245.32**	**104**	**1,124,547**	**3.9**
Males, aged 2 and over	58.33	110	267,385	4.2
Females, aged 2 and over	88.59	103	406,097	3.9
Children under age 2	43.56	91	199,679	3.4
Other apparel products and services	54.84	111	251,387	4.2
Jewelry	3.84	29	17,603	1.1
Transportation	**211.74**	**246**	**970,616**	**9.3**
Airline fares	18.53	190	84,942	7.2
Ship fares	13.44	172	61,609	6.5
Health care	**15.17**	**54**	**69,539**	**2.1**
Entertainment	**68.37**	**75**	**313,408**	**2.8**
Toys and games, arts and crafts, tricycles	19.90	59	91,222	2.2
Other entertainment	48.47	84	222,186	3.2
Personal care products and services	**12.86**	**105**	**58,950**	**4.0**
Cosmetics, perfume, and bath products	9.96	116	45,657	4.4
Education	**291.84**	**128**	**1,337,795**	**4.8**
College tuition	181.10	96	830,162	3.6
All other gifts	**63.32**	**83**	**290,259**	**3.2**
Gift of trip expenses	53.09	117	243,365	4.4

Note: The index is calculated by dividing Asian spending on each item by average household spending on the item and multiplying by 100. Spending on gifts is also included in the product and service categories in other tables. Subcategories may not add to total because some are not shown.
Source: Bureau of Labor Statistics, unpublished data from the 2009 Consumer Expenditure Survey; calculations by New Strategist

Table 9.10 Spending on Groceries by Asian Households, 2009

(average annual, indexed, aggregate, and market share of spending by Asian households on groceries, 2009)

	Asian average	index	aggregate (in 000s)	market share
GROCERIES, TOTAL	**$3,904.64**	**104**	**$17,898,870**	**3.9%**
Cereals and bakery products	**520.18**	**103**	**2,384,505**	**3.9**
Cereals and cereal products	215.37	125	987,256	4.7
Flour	11.26	130	51,616	4.9
Prepared flour mixes	8.26	57	37,864	2.2
Ready-to-eat and cooked cereals	58.87	63	269,860	2.4
Rice	93.95	392	430,667	14.9
Pasta, cornmeal, other cereal products	43.03	135	197,250	5.1
Bakery products	304.81	91	1,397,249	3.5
Bread	93.32	99	427,779	3.7
White bread	35.79	106	164,061	4.0
Bread, other than white	57.53	95	263,718	3.6
Cookies and crackers	66.15	79	303,232	3.0
Cookies	43.37	92	198,808	3.5
Crackers	22.78	62	104,424	2.3
Frozen and refrigerated bakery products	18.39	67	84,300	2.5
Other bakery products	126.95	100	581,939	3.8
Biscuits and rolls	46.32	95	212,331	3.6
Cakes and cupcakes	46.79	125	214,485	4.7
Bread and cracker products	3.73	71	17,098	2.7
Sweetrolls, coffee cakes, doughnuts	18.46	85	84,621	3.2
Pies, tarts, turnovers	11.65	82	53,404	3.1
Meats, poultry, fish, and eggs	**965.65**	**115**	**4,426,540**	**4.4**
Beef	186.21	82	853,587	3.1
Ground beef	61.65	69	282,604	2.6
Roast	34.83	100	159,661	3.8
Chuck roast	10.93	117	50,103	4.4
Round roast	3.54	64	16,227	2.4
Other roast	20.35	103	93,284	3.9
Steak	66.20	80	303,461	3.0
Round steak	8.85	83	40,568	3.2
Sirloin steak	24.58	110	112,675	4.2
Other steak	32.77	65	150,218	2.5
Other beef	23.53	121	107,862	4.6
Pork	171.65	102	786,844	3.9
Bacon	34.89	108	159,936	4.1
Pork chops	25.49	87	116,846	3.3
Ham	21.92	58	100,481	2.2
Ham, not canned	21.62	58	99,106	2.2
Canned ham	0.30	29	1,375	1.1
Sausage	21.13	76	96,860	2.9
Other pork	68.21	167	312,675	6.4
Other meats	82.34	73	377,447	2.8
Frankfurters	11.32	50	51,891	1.9
Lunch meats (cold cuts)	48.10	60	220,490	2.3
Bologna, liverwurst, salami	9.48	50	43,456	1.9
Other lunch meats	38.62	63	177,034	2.4
Lamb, organ meats, and others	22.93	217	105,111	8.2

	Asian average	index	aggregate (in 000s)	market share
Poultry	$184.28	120	$844,740	4.5%
Fresh and frozen chicken	157.33	130	721,201	4.9
Fresh and frozen whole chicken	56.88	186	260,738	7.1
Fresh and frozen chicken parts	100.45	112	460,463	4.2
Other poultry	26.95	81	123,539	3.1
Fish and seafood	274.46	203	1,258,125	7.7
Canned fish and seafood	22.72	124	104,148	4.7
Fresh fish and shellfish	157.86	221	723,630	8.4
Frozen fish and shellfish	93.88	207	430,346	7.9
Eggs	66.71	152	305,799	5.8
Dairy products	**346.43**	**85**	**1,588,035**	**3.2**
Fresh milk and cream	151.63	105	695,072	4.0
Fresh milk, all types	143.51	113	657,850	4.3
Cream	8.11	47	37,176	1.8
Other dairy products	194.81	74	893,009	2.8
Butter	16.82	78	77,103	2.9
Cheese	77.08	58	353,335	2.2
Ice cream and related products	51.96	83	238,185	3.2
Miscellaneous dairy products	48.95	108	224,387	4.1
Fruits and vegetables	**903.31**	**138**	**4,140,773**	**5.2**
Fresh fruits	309.96	141	1,420,857	5.4
Apples	49.91	136	228,787	5.2
Bananas	42.94	129	196,837	4.9
Oranges	48.73	201	223,378	7.6
Citrus fruits, excluding oranges	30.54	157	139,995	5.9
Other fresh fruits	137.84	130	631,859	4.9
Fresh vegetables	385.15	184	1,765,528	7.0
Potatoes	60.66	164	278,065	6.2
Lettuce	42.54	160	195,003	6.1
Tomatoes	56.43	157	258,675	5.9
Other fresh vegetables	225.52	206	1,033,784	7.8
Processed fruits	117.15	99	537,016	3.8
Frozen fruits and fruit juices	6.93	60	31,767	2.3
Frozen orange juice	2.32	83	10,635	3.1
Frozen fruits	3.29	54	15,081	2.0
Frozen fruit juices, excluding orange	1.32	49	6,051	1.9
Canned fruits	20.41	100	93,559	3.8
Dried fruits	8.34	98	38,231	3.7
Fresh fruit juice	27.08	140	124,135	5.3
Canned and bottled fruit juice	54.38	94	249,278	3.5
Processed vegetables	91.05	83	417,373	3.2
Frozen vegetables	27.74	79	127,160	3.0
Canned and dried vegetables and juices	63.31	85	290,213	3.2
Canned beans	8.37	53	38,368	2.0
Canned corn	6.15	95	28,192	3.6
Canned miscellaneous vegetables	16.51	71	75,682	2.7
Dried peas	0.34	79	1,559	3.0
Dried beans	3.68	94	16,869	3.6
Dried miscellaneous vegetables	10.67	115	48,911	4.4
Fresh and canned vegetable juices	17.52	119	80,312	4.5

	Asian average	index	aggregate (in 000s)	market share
Sugar and other sweets	**$105.82**	**75**	**$485,079**	**2.9%**
Candy and chewing gum	62.41	72	286,087	2.7
Sugar	19.72	104	90,396	4.0
Artificial sweeteners	2.84	47	13,019	1.8
Jams, preserves, other sweets	20.84	71	95,531	2.7
Fats and oils	**98.78**	**97**	**452,808**	**3.7**
Margarine	3.27	40	14,990	1.5
Fats and oils	58.81	165	269,585	6.3
Salad dressings	19.15	67	87,784	2.5
Nondairy cream and imitation milk	7.95	49	36,443	1.9
Peanut butter	9.60	69	44,006	2.6
Miscellaneous foods	**645.70**	**90**	**2,959,889**	**3.4**
Frozen prepared foods	93.60	63	429,062	2.4
Frozen meals	38.53	56	176,622	2.1
Other frozen prepared foods	55.08	70	252,487	2.7
Canned and packaged soups	49.54	105	227,091	4.0
Potato chips, nuts, and other snacks	108.02	73	495,164	2.8
Potato chips and other snacks	72.14	67	330,690	2.5
Nuts	35.88	91	164,474	3.5
Condiments and seasonings	130.15	100	596,608	3.8
Salt, spices, and other seasonings	48.12	154	220,582	5.8
Olives, pickles, relishes	6.77	43	31,034	1.6
Sauces and gravies	54.52	99	249,920	3.7
Baking needs and miscellaneous products	20.74	75	95,072	2.8
Other canned or packaged prepared foods	264.38	109	1,211,918	4.1
Prepared salads	25.78	77	118,176	2.9
Prepared desserts	7.83	57	35,893	2.2
Baby food	62.04	188	284,391	7.1
Miscellaneous prepared foods	159.37	99	730,552	3.8
Nonalcoholic beverages	**266.52**	**79**	**1,221,728**	**3.0**
Cola	51.81	59	237,497	2.2
Other carbonated drinks	26.74	54	122,576	2.1
Tea	23.73	81	108,778	3.1
Coffee	49.77	86	228,146	3.3
Roasted coffee	33.84	88	155,123	3.3
Instant and freeze-dried coffee	15.93	83	73,023	3.2
Noncarbonated fruit-flavored drinks	15.67	64	71,831	2.4
Other nonalcoholic beverages and ice	8.60	67	39,422	2.5
Bottled water	65.26	115	299,152	4.4
Sports drinks	24.96	139	114,417	5.3
Groceries purchased on trips	**52.24**	**108**	**239,468**	**4.1**

Note: The index is calculated by dividing Asian spending on each item by average household spending on the item and multiplying by 100. Subcategories may not add to total because some are not shown.
Source: Bureau of Labor Statistics, unpublished data from the 2009 Consumer Expenditure Survey; calculations by New Strategist

Table 9.11 Out-of-Pocket Spending on Health Care by Asian Households, 2009

(average annual, indexed, aggregate, and market share of spending by Asian households on out-of-pocket health care costs, 2009)

	Asian average	index	aggregate (in 000s)	market share
HEALTH CARE, TOTAL	**$2,498.29**	**80**	**$11,452,161**	**3.0%**
Health insurance	**1,509.30**	**85**	**6,918,631**	**3.2**
Commercial health insurance	276.18	80	1,266,009	3.0
Traditional fee-for-service health plan (not BCBS)	46.56	55	213,431	2.1
Preferred-provider health plan (not BCBS)	229.62	89	1,052,578	3.4
Blue Cross, Blue Shield	387.73	74	1,777,354	2.8
Traditional fee-for-service health plan	34.96	40	160,257	1.5
Preferred-provider health plan	145.24	68	665,780	2.6
Health maintenance organization	172.93	102	792,711	3.9
Commercial Medicare supplement	24.14	53	110,658	2.0
Other BCBS health insurance	10.45	111	47,903	4.2
Health maintenance plans (HMOs)	423.36	148	1,940,682	5.6
Medicare payments	207.82	60	952,647	2.3
Medicare prescription drug premium	30.61	49	140,316	1.9
Commercial Medicare supplements and other health insurance	123.56	80	566,399	3.0
Commercial Medicare supplement (not BCBS)	68.01	67	311,758	2.5
Other health insurance (not BCBS)	55.54	107	254,595	4.1
Long term care insurance	60.03	95	275,178	3.6
Medical services	**574.68**	**78**	**2,634,333**	**3.0**
Physician's services	118.12	64	541,462	2.4
Dental services	270.71	101	1,240,935	3.8
Eye care services	22.39	56	102,636	2.1
Service by professionals other than physician	43.92	89	201,329	3.4
Lab tests, X-rays	32.37	67	148,384	2.5
Hospital room and services	80.81	77	370,433	2.9
Care in convalescent or nursing home	–	–	–	–
Other medical services	6.37	29	29,200	1.1
Drugs	**307.46**	**63**	**1,409,397**	**2.4**
Nonprescription drugs	95.67	117	438,551	4.4
Nonprescription vitamins	35.46	83	162,549	3.1
Prescription drugs	176.33	49	808,297	1.8
Medical supplies	**106.84**	**90**	**489,755**	**3.4**
Eyeglasses and contact lenses	53.05	89	243,181	3.4
Hearing aids	0.67	4	3,071	0.2
Topicals and dressings	52.56	165	240,935	6.3
Medical equipment for general use	0.10	4	458	0.1
Supportive and convalescent medical equipment	–	–	–	–
Rental of medical equipment	0.20	18	917	0.7
Rental of supportive, convalescent medical equip.	0.26	11	1,192	0.4

Note: The index is calculated by dividing Asian spending on each item by average household spending on the item and multiplying by 100. Subcategories may not add to total because some are not shown. "–" means sample is too small to make a reliable estimate.

Source: Bureau of Labor Statistics, unpublished data from the 2009 Consumer Expenditure Survey; calculations by New Strategist

Table 9.12 Spending on Household Operations by Asian Households, 2009

(average annual, indexed, aggregate, and market share of spending by Asian households on household services, supplies, furnishings, and equipment, 2009)

	Asian average	index	aggregate (in 000s)	market share
HOUSEHOLD SERVICES, TOTAL	**$1,347.26**	**133**	**$6,175,840**	**5.1%**
Personal services	**688.32**	**177**	**3,155,259**	**6.7**
Babysitting and child care in own home	64.74	138	296,768	5.2
Babysitting and child care in someone else's home	47.71	148	218,703	5.6
Care for elderly, invalids, handicapped, etc.	108.64	236	498,006	8.9
Day care centers, nurseries, preschools	467.23	180	2,141,782	6.8
Other household services	**658.93**	**106**	**3,020,535**	**4.0**
Housekeeping services	118.03	105	541,050	4.0
Gardening, lawn care service	107.81	100	494,201	3.8
Water-softening service	4.73	119	21,682	4.5
Nonclothing laundry, dry cleaning, sent out	0.31	30	1,421	1.1
Nonclothing laundry and dry cleaning, coin-operated	4.78	133	21,912	5.1
Termite and pest control services	16.69	90	76,507	3.4
Home security system service fee	20.12	96	92,230	3.6
Other home services	35.05	177	160,669	6.7
Termite and pest control products	1.72	60	7,884	2.3
Moving, storage, and freight express	44.04	120	201,879	4.5
Appliance repair, including at service center	17.60	106	80,678	4.0
Reupholstering and furniture repair	–	–	–	–
Repairs and rentals of lawn and garden equipment, hand and power tools, etc.	2.77	47	12,698	1.8
Appliance rental	0.45	33	2,063	1.3
Repair of office equipment for nonbusiness use	0.32	42	1,467	1.6
Repair of misc. household equip., furnishings	–	–	–	–
Repair of computer systems, nonbusiness use	4.57	68	20,949	2.6
Computer information services	279.87	110	1,282,924	4.2
HOUSEKEEPING SUPPLIES, TOTAL	**535.63**	**81**	**2,455,328**	**3.1**
Laundry and cleaning supplies	**130.21**	**84**	**596,883**	**3.2**
Soaps and detergents	76.75	90	351,822	3.4
Other laundry cleaning products	53.46	76	245,061	2.9
Other household products	**292.05**	**81**	**1,338,757**	**3.1**
Cleansing and toilet tissue, paper towels, and napkins	96.59	87	442,769	3.3
Miscellaneous household products	130.96	95	600,321	3.6
Lawn and garden supplies	64.50	58	295,668	2.2
Postage and stationery	**113.36**	**79**	**519,642**	**3.0**
Stationery, stationery supplies, giftwrap	43.87	59	201,100	2.2
Postage	66.92	104	306,761	3.9
Delivery services	2.58	65	11,827	2.5

	Asian average	index	aggregate (in 000s)	market share
HOUSEHOLD FURNISHINGS AND EQUIPMENT, TOTAL	**$1,670.90**	**111**	**$7,659,406**	**4.2%**
Household textiles	**187.47**	**151**	**859,362**	**5.7**
Bathroom linens	30.07	163	137,841	6.2
Bedroom linens	119.72	175	548,796	6.7
Kitchen and dining room linens	5.51	90	25,258	3.4
Curtains and draperies	20.70	121	94,889	4.6
Slipcovers and decorative pillows	2.01	58	9,214	2.2
Sewing materials for household items	8.44	87	38,689	3.3
Other linens	1.03	90	4,722	3.4
Furniture	**304.10**	**89**	**1,393,994**	**3.4**
Mattresses and springs	37.18	66	170,433	2.5
Other bedroom furniture	65.99	108	302,498	4.1
Sofas	106.19	128	486,775	4.8
Living room chairs	11.64	34	53,358	1.3
Living room tables	6.02	52	27,596	2.0
Kitchen and dining room furniture	23.01	72	105,478	2.7
Infants' furniture	12.36	155	56,658	5.9
Outdoor furniture	4.11	22	18,840	0.8
Wall units, cabinets, and other furniture	37.60	100	172,358	3.8
Floor coverings	**13.09**	**43**	**60,005**	**1.6**
Wall-to-wall carpeting	–	–	–	–
Floor coverings, nonpermanent	13.09	79	60,005	3.0
Major appliances	**183.49**	**95**	**841,118**	**3.6**
Dishwashers (built-in), garbage disposals, range hoods	17.45	131	79,991	5.0
Refrigerators and freezers	46.37	82	212,560	3.1
Washing machines	22.27	69	102,086	2.6
Clothes dryers	19.01	80	87,142	3.0
Cooking stoves, ovens	46.55	171	213,385	6.5
Microwave ovens	11.09	113	50,837	4.3
Window air conditioners	7.42	227	34,013	8.6
Electric floor-cleaning equipment	5.87	41	26,908	1.6
Sewing machines	7.44	91	34,105	3.4
Small appliances and misc. housewares	**134.41**	**144**	**616,135**	**5.5**
Housewares	106.63	167	488,792	6.3
Plastic dinnerware	3.56	143	16,319	5.4
China and other dinnerware	2.59	53	11,873	2.0
Flatware	4.91	134	22,507	5.1
Glassware	7.36	65	33,738	2.5
Silver serving pieces	0.53	19	2,430	0.7
Other serving pieces	2.95	166	13,523	6.3
Nonelectric cookware	52.98	396	242,860	15.0
Tableware, nonelectric kitchenware	31.75	134	145,542	5.1
Small appliances	27.78	94	127,344	3.6
Small electric kitchen appliances	22.96	111	105,249	4.2
Portable heating and cooling equipment	4.82	55	22,095	2.1

	Asian average	index	aggregate (in 000s)	market share
Miscellaneous household equipment	**$848.34**	**118**	**$3,888,791**	**4.5%**
Window coverings	39.49	192	181,022	7.3
Infants' equipment	3.97	29	18,198	1.1
Laundry and cleaning equipment	14.21	86	65,139	3.3
Outdoor equipment	18.91	112	86,683	4.2
Lamps and lighting fixtures	16.14	57	73,986	2.1
Household decorative items (including clocks)	104.29	81	478,065	3.1
Telephones and accessories	46.01	98	210,910	3.7
Lawn and garden equipment	31.77	56	145,634	2.1
Power tools	62.93	178	288,471	6.8
Office furniture for home use	8.44	113	38,689	4.3
Hand tools	11.67	88	53,495	3.3
Indoor plants and fresh flowers	140.29	280	643,089	10.6
Closet and storage items	15.12	103	69,310	3.9
Rental of furniture	0.20	10	917	0.4
Luggage	13.06	120	59,867	4.5
Computers and computer hardware for nonbusiness use	213.47	136	978,546	5.2
Portable memory	11.69	152	53,587	5.8
Computer software and accessories for nonbusiness use	22.08	108	101,215	4.1
Personal digital assistants	1.98	71	9,076	2.7
Internet services away from home	2.19	100	10,039	3.8
Telephone answering devices	0.15	33	688	1.3
Business equipment for home use	4.47	159	20,490	6.0
Other hardware	15.94	122	73,069	4.6
Smoke alarms	1.47	111	6,738	4.2
Other household appliances	9.41	107	43,135	4.1
Miscellaneous household equipment and parts	38.99	93	178,730	3.5

Note: The index is calculated by dividing Asian spending on each item by average household spending on the item and multiplying by 100. Subcategories may not add to total because some are not shown. "–" means sample is too small to make a reliable estimate.

Source: Bureau of Labor Statistics, unpublished data from the 2009 Consumer Expenditure Survey; calculations by New Strategist

Table 9.13 Spending on Personal Care, Reading, Education, and Tobacco by Asian Households, 2009

(average annual, indexed, aggregate, and market share of spending by Asian households on personal care, reading, education, and tobacco products, 2009)

	Asian average	index	aggregate (in 000s)	market share
PERSONAL CARE PRODUCTS AND SERVICES, TOTAL	**$557.40**	**94**	**$2,555,122**	**3.6%**
Personal care products	**335.70**	**110**	**1,538,849**	**4.2**
Hair care products	63.51	97	291,130	3.7
Hair accessories	11.55	181	52,945	6.9
Wigs and hairpieces	0.18	6	825	0.2
Oral hygiene products	34.74	119	159,248	4.5
Shaving products	5.67	35	25,991	1.3
Cosmetics, perfume, and bath products	188.23	131	862,846	5.0
Deodorants, feminine hygiene, misc. products	28.50	87	130,644	3.3
Electric personal care appliances	3.33	38	15,265	1.5
Personal care services	**221.70**	**76**	**1,016,273**	**2.9**
READING, TOTAL	**110.86**	**101**	**508,182**	**3.8**
Newspaper and magazine subscriptions	37.59	87	172,313	3.3
Newspapers and magazines, nonsubscription	10.92	73	50,057	2.8
Books	62.19	124	285,079	4.7
EDUCATION, TOTAL	**2,326.53**	**218**	**10,664,814**	**8.3**
College tuition	1,605.84	228	7,361,171	8.7
Elementary and high school tuition	358.48	221	1,643,272	8.4
Technical and vocational school tuition	110.82	840	507,999	31.9
Test preparation and tutoring services	14.02	161	64,268	6.1
Other school tuition	15.17	186	69,539	7.1
Other school expenses including rentals	50.38	142	230,942	5.4
Books, supplies for college	101.37	152	464,680	5.8
Books, supplies for elementary, high school	26.47	142	121,338	5.4
Books, supplies for technical and vocational school	1.45	254	6,647	9.6
Books, supplies for day care, nursery school	–	–	–	–
Books, supplies for others schools	2.40	160	11,002	6.1
Miscellaneous school expenses and supplies	40.13	81	183,956	3.1
TOBACCO PRODUCTS AND SMOKING SUPPLIES, TOTAL	**122.49**	**32**	**561,494**	**1.2**
Cigarettes	114.26	33	523,768	1.2
Other tobacco products	7.83	26	35,893	1.0
Smoking accessories	0.40	21	1,834	0.8

Note: The index is calculated by dividing Asian spending on each item by average household spending on the item and multiplying by 100. Subcategories may not add to total because some are not shown. "–" means sample is too small to make a reliable estimate.

Source: Bureau of Labor Statistics, unpublished data from the 2009 Consumer Expenditure Survey; calculations by New Strategist

Table 9.14 Spending on Restaurant Meals by Asian Households, 2009

(average annual, indexed, aggregate, and market share of spending by Asian households on restaurant meals and other food away from home, 2009)

	Asian average	index	aggregate (in 000s)	market share
FOOD AWAY FROM HOME, TOTAL	**$3,660.50**	**140**	**$16,779,732**	**5.3%**
Meals at restaurants	**3,153.32**	**144**	**14,454,819**	**5.5**
Lunch	1,074.73	147	4,926,562	5.6
At fast-food restaurants*	456.63	129	2,093,192	4.9
At full-service restaurants	493.12	170	2,260,462	6.5
At vending machines, mobile vendors	11.26	131	51,616	5.0
At employer and school cafeterias	113.72	142	521,292	5.4
Dinner	1,632.50	154	7,483,380	5.8
At fast-food restaurants*	416.27	119	1,908,182	4.5
At full-service restaurants	1,199.60	171	5,498,966	6.5
At vending machines, mobile vendors	3.81	135	17,465	5.1
At employer and school cafeterias	12.83	183	58,813	6.9
Snacks and nonalcoholic beverages	190.51	114	873,298	4.3
At fast-food restaurants*	124.25	113	569,562	4.3
At full-service restaurants	32.87	107	150,676	4.0
At vending machines, mobile vendors	25.61	121	117,396	4.6
At employer and school cafeterias	7.78	141	35,664	5.4
Breakfast and brunch	255.58	112	1,171,579	4.3
At fast-food restaurants*	127.06	109	582,443	4.1
At full-service restaurants	99.77	104	457,346	3.9
At vending machines, mobile vendors	4.91	179	22,507	6.8
At employer and school cafeterias	23.85	206	109,328	7.8
Board (including at school)	**50.96**	**112**	**233,601**	**4.3**
Catered affairs	**81.83**	**116**	**375,109**	**4.4**
Restaurant meals on trips	**269.25**	**121**	**1,234,242**	**4.6**
School lunches	**63.53**	**98**	**291,222**	**3.7**
Meals as pay	**41.61**	**157**	**190,740**	**5.9**

** The category fast-food restaurants also includes take-out, delivery, concession stands, buffets, and cafeterias other than employer and school.*
Note: The index is calculated by dividing Asian spending on each item by average household spending on the item and multiplying by 100. Subcategories may not add to total because some are not shown.
Source: Bureau of Labor Statistics, unpublished data from the 2009 Consumer Expenditure Survey; calculations by New Strategist

Table 9.15 Spending on Shelter and Utilities by Asian Households, 2009

(average annual, indexed, aggregate, and market share of spending by Asian households on shelter and utilities, 2009)

	Asian average	index	aggregate (in 000s)	market share
SHELTER, TOTAL	**$13,571.34**	**135**	**$62,211,023**	**5.1%**
Owned dwellings*	**8,543.45**	**131**	**39,163,175**	**5.0**
Mortgage interest and charges	5,349.38	149	24,521,558	5.6
Mortgage interest	5,080.40	150	23,288,554	5.7
Interest paid, home equity loan	74.23	94	340,270	3.6
Interest paid, home equity line of credit	194.75	148	892,734	5.6
Property taxes	2,334.48	129	10,701,256	4.9
Maintenance, repairs, insurance, other expenses	859.59	76	3,940,361	2.9
Homeowner's insurance	269.08	79	1,233,463	3.0
Ground rent	3.99	8	18,290	0.3
Maintenance and repair services	435.18	72	1,994,865	2.7
Painting and papering	45.96	59	210,681	2.2
Plumbing and water heating	86.51	149	396,562	5.7
Heat, air conditioning, electrical work	93.71	83	429,567	3.1
Roofing and gutters	32.16	28	147,421	1.1
Other repair and maintenance services	134.83	71	618,061	2.7
Repair, replacement of hard-surface flooring	37.83	74	173,413	2.8
Repair of built-in appliances	4.17	196	19,115	7.4
Maintenance and repair materials	34.14	46	156,498	1.8
Paints, wallpaper, and supplies	9.73	75	44,602	2.9
Tools, equipment for painting, wallpapering	1.05	76	4,813	2.9
Plumbing supplies and equipment	3.93	71	18,015	2.7
Electrical supplies, heating, cooling equipment	4.06	66	18,611	2.5
Hard-surface flooring, repair and replacement	–	–	–	–
Roofing and gutters	0.82	11	3,759	0.4
Plaster, paneling, siding, windows, doors, screens, awnings	7.82	56	35,847	2.1
Patio, walk, fence, driveway, masonry, brick, and stucco materials	0.10	14	458	0.5
Miscellaneous supplies and equipment	6.64	36	30,438	1.4
Property management and security	101.58	177	465,643	6.7
Property management	92.62	187	424,570	7.1
Management and upkeep services for security	8.96	111	41,073	4.2
Parking	15.62	248	71,602	9.4
Rented dwellings	**4,411.41**	**154**	**20,221,903**	**5.9**
Rent	4,324.19	158	19,822,087	6.0
Rent as pay	63.02	79	288,884	3.0
Maintenance, insurance, and other expenses	24.21	57	110,979	2.2
Tenant's insurance	9.71	78	44,511	3.0
Maintenance and repair services	7.21	36	33,051	1.4
Maintenance and repair materials	7.29	74	33,417	2.8

	Asian average	index	aggregate (in 000s)	market share
Other lodging	**$616.48**	**92**	**$2,825,944**	**3.5%**
Owned vacation homes	194.87	64	893,284	2.4
Mortgage interest and charges	107.56	79	493,055	3.0
Property taxes	57.41	54	263,167	2.1
Maintenance, insurance, and other expenses	29.90	50	137,062	1.9
Housing while attending school	80.13	117	367,316	4.4
Lodging on trips	341.48	114	1,565,344	4.3
UTILITIES, FUELS, AND PUBLIC SERVICES, TOTAL	**3,269.60**	**90**	**14,987,846**	**3.4**
Natural gas	**498.96**	**103**	**2,287,233**	**3.9**
Electricity	**1,056.26**	**77**	**4,841,896**	**2.9**
Fuel oil and other fuels	**48.07**	**34**	**220,353**	**1.3**
Fuel oil	28.32	37	129,819	1.4
Coal, wood, and other fuels	3.76	35	17,236	1.3
Bottled gas	16.00	30	73,344	1.1
Telephone services	**1,122.52**	**97**	**5,145,632**	**3.7**
Residential telephone and pay phones	362.88	84	1,663,442	3.2
Cellular phone service	722.09	101	3,310,061	3.8
Phone cards	32.02	335	146,780	12.7
Voice over IP	5.53	78	25,350	3.0
Water and other public services	**543.78**	**113**	**2,492,688**	**4.3**
Water and sewerage maintenance	388.87	111	1,782,580	4.2
Trash and garbage collection	151.88	120	696,218	4.6
Septic tank cleaning	3.04	69	13,935	2.6

** The amount paid in mortgage principal is not shown here because it is considered an asset.*
Note: The index is calculated by dividing Asian spending on each item by average household spending on the item and multiplying by 100. Subcategories may not add to total because some are not shown. "–" means sample is too small to make a reliable estimate.
Source: Bureau of Labor Statistics, unpublished data from the 2009 Consumer Expenditure Survey; calculations by New Strategist

Table 9.16 Spending on Transportation by Asian Households, 2009

(average annual, indexed, aggregate, and market share of spending by Asian households on transportation, 2009)

	Asian average	index	aggregate (in 000s)	market share
TRANSPORTATION, TOTAL	**$8,783.81**	**115**	**$40,264,985**	**4.4%**
Vehicle purchases	**2,581.76**	**97**	**11,834,788**	**3.7**
Cars and trucks, new	1,130.73	87	5,183,266	3.3
New cars	397.83	57	1,823,653	2.2
New trucks	732.90	122	3,359,614	4.6
Cars and trucks, used	1,451.03	111	6,651,522	4.2
Used cars	1,251.35	181	5,736,188	6.9
Used trucks	199.68	33	915,333	1.2
Other vehicles	–	–	–	–
New motorcycles	–	–	–	–
Used motorcycles	–	–	–	–
Gasoline and motor oil	**1,870.66**	**94**	**8,575,105**	**3.6**
Gasoline	1,783.50	97	8,175,564	3.7
Diesel fuel	3.60	10	16,502	0.4
Gasoline on trips	78.66	72	360,577	2.7
Motor oil	4.11	42	18,840	1.6
Motor oil on trips	0.79	72	3,621	2.7
Other vehicle expenses	**3,153.46**	**124**	**14,455,461**	**4.7**
Vehicle finance charges	207.68	74	952,005	2.8
Automobile finance charges	106.73	89	489,250	3.4
Truck finance charges	90.79	67	416,181	2.5
Motorcycle and plane finance charges	1.59	33	7,289	1.2
Other vehicle finance charges	8.57	43	39,285	1.6
Maintenance and repairs	713.03	97	3,268,530	3.7
Coolant, additives, brake, transmission fluids	3.32	85	15,219	3.2
Tires—purchased, replaced, installed	115.07	97	527,481	3.7
Parts, equipment, and accessories	34.67	79	158,927	3.0
Vehicle audio equipment	2.83	125	12,973	4.7
Vehicle products and cleaning services	6.04	120	27,687	4.6
Vehicle video equipment	2.21	111	10,131	4.2
Miscellaneous auto repair, servicing	70.84	128	324,731	4.8
Body work and painting	35.99	133	164,978	5.1
Clutch and transmission repair	23.57	69	108,045	2.6
Drive shaft and rear-end repair	2.33	45	10,681	1.7
Brake work	73.11	112	335,136	4.2
Repair to steering or front-end	6.52	37	29,888	1.4
Repair to engine cooling system	22.65	101	103,828	3.8
Motor tune-up	59.36	129	272,106	4.9
Lube, oil change, and oil filters	70.45	94	322,943	3.6
Front-end alignment, wheel balance, rotation	9.03	70	41,394	2.7
Shock absorber replacement	3.07	54	14,073	2.1

	Asian average	index	aggregate (in 000s)	market share
Tire repair and other repair work	$39.62	80	$181,618	3.0%
Vehicle air conditioning repair	7.77	62	35,618	2.4
Exhaust system repair	10.53	101	48,270	3.8
Electrical system repair	26.45	86	121,247	3.3
Motor repair, replacement	85.82	125	393,399	4.7
Auto repair service policy	1.79	10	8,205	0.4
Vehicle insurance	1,609.97	150	7,380,102	5.7
Vehicle rental, leases, licenses, other charges	622.78	139	2,854,824	5.3
Leased and rented vehicles	341.71	147	1,566,399	5.6
Rented vehicles	47.14	143	216,090	5.4
Auto rental	11.06	222	50,699	8.4
Auto rental on trips	35.21	149	161,403	5.6
Truck rental	0.65	29	2,980	1.1
Truck rental on trips	0.22	13	1,008	0.5
Leased vehicles	294.56	147	1,350,263	5.6
Car lease payments	139.70	131	640,385	5.0
Truck lease payments	112.52	137	515,792	5.2
Vehicle registration, state	108.75	114	498,510	4.3
Vehicle registration, local	10.98	136	50,332	5.1
Driver's license	7.63	97	34,976	3.7
Vehicle inspection	14.07	124	64,497	4.7
Parking fees	71.63	180	328,352	6.8
Parking fees in home city, excl. residence	63.78	194	292,368	7.4
Parking fees on trips	7.85	113	35,984	4.3
Tolls	46.39	208	212,652	7.9
Tolls on trips	4.19	93	19,207	3.5
Towing charges	1.36	29	6,234	1.1
Global positioning services	0.99	52	4,538	2.0
Automobile service clubs	15.08	86	69,127	3.3
Public transportation	**1,177.93**	**246**	**5,399,631**	**9.3**
Airline fares	791.86	263	3,629,886	10.0
Intercity bus fares	15.70	170	71,969	6.5
Intracity mass transit fares	175.01	269	802,246	10.2
Local transportation on trips	17.44	163	79,945	6.2
Taxi fares and limousine service on trips	10.24	163	46,940	6.2
Taxi fares and limousine service	49.82	212	228,375	8.0
Intercity train fares	25.72	172	117,900	6.5
Ship fares	90.76	188	416,044	7.1
School bus	1.38	418	6,326	15.9

Note: The index is calculated by dividing Asian spending on each item by average household spending on the item and multiplying by 100. Subcategories may not add to total because some are not shown. "–" means sample is too small to make a reliable estimate.

Source: Bureau of Labor Statistics, unpublished data from the 2009 Consumer Expenditure Survey; calculations by New Strategist

CHAPTER

10

Time Use

■ Asians spend 55 percent more time than the average person caring for household children as a primary activity on an average day. They spend 15 percent more time working and 19 percent more time eating and drinking.

■ Asian men are 24 percent less likely than the average man to participate in household activities on an average day and 10 percent less likely to shop. That may be because they are 11 percent more likely to work.

■ Asian women are far more likely than the average woman to care for household children on an average day (36 versus 26 percent). They are more likely than the average woman to work, but less likely to socialize, do housework, or watch television.

Work Ranks Second in Time Use among Asians

Watching television is third.

We know how Asians prioritize their time thanks to the American Time Use Survey (ATUS), first introduced by the Bureau of Labor Statistics in 2003. The survey collects data on how Americans spend their time during an average day. ATUS data are published annually, allowing social scientists to better understand our economy, our lifestyles, and the way policy decisions affect our lives. Through telephone interviews with a nationally representative sample of Americans aged 15 or older, ATUS asks survey respondents what they did minute by minute during the previous 24 hours—or diary day.

In 2009, the average Asian aged 15 or older spent 3.75 hours a day in work and work-related activities and another 3.73 hours a day in leisure pursuits. The amount of time Asians spend working appears low because the average includes weekdays and weekends, people of working-age and retirees. Fifty-one percent of Asians participated in work or work-related activities on diary day, and those who worked spent 7.31 hours doing so.

Everyone spends more time sleeping than doing anything else. Among Asians aged 15 or older, sleep consumes 8.64 hours a day, on average. Television is the third most time-consuming activity for Asians. The average Asian spends 2.12 hours a day watching television as a primary activity.

■ The 60 percent majority of Asian men engage in work and work-related activities on an average day compared with a smaller 43 percent of Asian women.

Half of Asians work on an average day

(percent of Asians aged 15 or older who participated in selected primary activities on an average day, 2009)

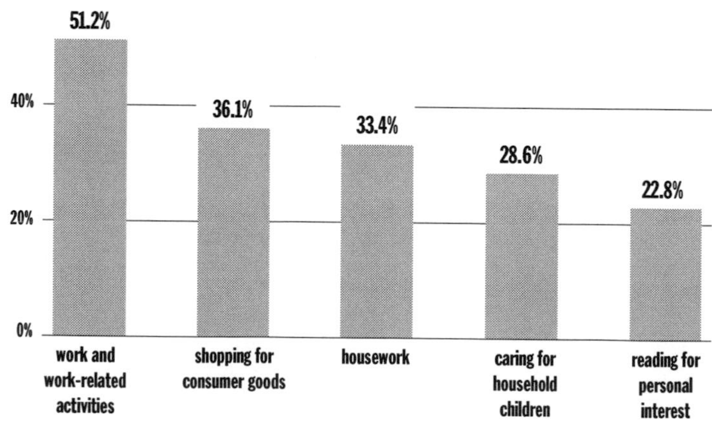

Table 10.1 Time Use of Total Asians, 2009

(number and percent of total Asians aged 15 or older participating in primary activities on an average day, hours spent doing activity by the average Asian aged 15 or older and by Asians aged 15 or older who participated in the activity, 2009; numbers of participants in thousands)

	total Asians participating		time spent doing activity (hours)	
	number	percent	average Asian	Asian participants
Total, all activities	**7,368**	**100.0%**	**24.00**	**24.00**
Personal care	7,368	100.0	9.28	9.28
Sleeping	7,368	100.0	8.64	8.64
Grooming	5,648	76.7	0.60	0.79
Household activities	5,254	71.3	1.75	2.45
Housework	2,463	33.4	0.53	1.58
Food preparation and cleanup	3,937	53.4	0.78	1.45
Household management	1,923	26.1	0.20	0.78
Caring for and helping household members	2,388	32.4	0.68	2.10
Caring for and helping household children	2,106	28.6	0.59	2.06
Work and work-related activities	3,775	51.2	3.75	7.31
Working	3,621	49.1	3.71	7.56
Education	1,014	13.8	0.79	–
Consumer purchases (store, telephone, Internet)	2,657	36.1	0.41	1.13
Eating and drinking	7,205	97.8	1.32	1.35
Socializing, relaxing, and leisure	7,016	95.2	3.73	3.92
Socializing and communicating	2,309	31.3	0.42	1.35
Watching television	5,656	76.8	2.12	2.76
Computer use for leisure (excluding games)	1,065	14.5	0.24	1.69
Reading for personal interest	1,682	22.8	0.28	1.22
Sports, exercise, recreation	1,893	25.7	0.35	1.34
Religious and spiritual activities	910	12.4	0.17	–
Volunteer activities	408	5.5	0.11	–
Telephone calls	1,089	14.8	0.09	0.62
Traveling	6,469	87.8	1.20	1.37

Note: Primary activities are those respondents identified as their main activity. Other activities done simultaneously, such as eating while watching TV, are not included. Numbers may not add to total because not all categories are shown. "–" means data are not available. Asians are those who identify themselves as being of the race alone.
Source: Bureau of Labor Statistics, unpublished tables from the 2009 American Time Use Survey, Internet site http://www.bls.gov/tus/home.htm; calculations by New Strategist

Table 10.2 Time Use of Asian Men, 2009

(number and percent of Asian men aged 15 or older participating in primary activities on an average day, hours spent doing activity by the average Asian man aged 15 or older and by Asian men aged 15 or older who participated in the activity, 2009; numbers of participants in thousands)

	Asian men participating		time spent doing activity (hours)	
	number	percent	average Asian man	Asian men participating
Total, all activities	**3,560**	**100.0%**	**24.00**	**24.00**
Personal care	3,560	100.0	9.23	9.23
Sleeping	3,560	100.0	8.63	8.63
Grooming	2,615	73.5	0.54	0.73
Household activities	2,124	59.7	1.02	1.72
Housework	718	20.2	0.23	–
Food preparation and cleanup	1,130	31.7	0.31	0.97
Household management	945	26.5	0.21	–
Caring for and helping household members	915	25.7	0.35	–
Caring for and helping household children	727	20.4	0.30	–
Work and work-related activities	2,131	59.9	4.34	7.25
Working	2,014	56.6	4.29	7.58
Education	523	14.7	0.87	–
Consumer purchases (store, telephone, Internet)	1,039	29.2	0.27	0.91
Eating and drinking	3,429	96.3	1.33	1.38
Socializing, relaxing, and leisure	3,422	96.1	4.35	4.53
Socializing and communicating	1,006	28.3	0.42	–
Watching television	2,790	78.4	2.49	3.17
Computer use for leisure (excluding games)	654	18.4	0.32	–
Reading for personal interest	735	20.6	0.24	–
Sports, exercise, recreation	1,019	28.6	0.43	–
Religious and spiritual activities	328	9.2	0.12	–
Volunteer activities	222	6.2	0.13	–
Telephone calls	463	13.0	0.10	–
Traveling	3,129	87.9	1.22	1.39

Note: Primary activities are those respondents identified as their main activity. Other activities done simultaneously, such as eating while watching TV, are not included. Numbers may not add to total because not all categories are shown. "–" means data are not available. Asians are those who identify themselves as being of the race alone.
Source: Bureau of Labor Statistics, unpublished tables from the 2009 American Time Use Survey, Internet site http://www.bls.gov/tus/home.htm; calculations by New Strategist

Table 10.3 Time Use of Asian Women, 2009

(number and percent of Asian women aged 15 or older participating in primary activities on an average day, hours spent doing activity by the average Asian woman aged 15 or older and by Asian women aged 15 or older who participated in the activity, 2009; numbers of participants in thousands)

	Asian women participating		time spent doing activity (hours)	
	number	percent	average Asian woman	Asian women participating
Total, all activities	**3,808**	**100.0%**	**24.00**	**24.00**
Personal care	3,808	100.0	9.33	9.33
Sleeping	3,808	100.0	8.64	8.64
Grooming	3,033	79.6	0.67	0.84
Household activities	3,130	82.2	2.43	2.95
Housework	1,746	45.9	0.81	1.76
Food preparation and cleanup	2,807	73.7	1.21	1.65
Household management	978	25.7	0.20	0.76
Caring for and helping household members	1,473	38.7	0.99	2.56
Caring for and helping household children	1,380	36.2	0.85	2.36
Work and work-related activities	1,644	43.2	3.19	7.40
Working	1,607	42.2	3.18	7.53
Education	491	12.9	0.72	–
Consumer purchases (store, telephone, Internet)	1,618	42.5	0.54	1.26
Eating and drinking	3,776	99.2	1.31	1.32
Socializing, relaxing, and leisure	3,594	94.4	3.15	3.34
Socializing and communicating	1,303	34.2	0.42	1.24
Watching television	2,866	75.3	1.77	2.36
Computer use for leisure (excluding games)	412	10.8	0.18	–
Reading for personal interest	947	24.9	0.32	–
Sports, exercise, recreation	874	23.0	0.26	–
Religious and spiritual activities	582	15.3	0.22	–
Volunteer activities	186	4.9	0.09	–
Telephone calls	626	16.4	0.08	–
Traveling	3,340	87.7	1.18	1.34

Note: Primary activities are those respondents identified as their main activity. Other activities done simultaneously, such as eating while watching TV, are not included. Numbers may not add to total because not all categories are shown. "–" means data are not available. Asians are those who identify themselves as being of the race alone.

Source: Bureau of Labor Statistics, unpublished tables from the 2009 American Time Use Survey, Internet site http://www.bls.gov/tus/home.htm; calculations by New Strategist

Asians Spend More Time Working than the Average Person

They also spend more time eating and drinking.

Asian time use differs in a number of ways from the average, reflecting their more youthful population and their higher incomes and educational attainment. The biggest difference is in the amount of time devoted to caring for household children. Asians spend 55 percent more time than the average person caring for household children as a primary activity on an average day. They spend 15 percent more time working, and 19 percent more time eating and drinking.

On an average day, Asian men spend 11 percent more time working than the average man. They spend 18 percent more time eating and drinking. Asian women spend 70 percent more time than the average woman caring for household children, 57 percent more time preparing meals, and 21 percent more time eating and drinking.

■ Asian women spend much more time than Asian men preparing meals, shopping, and caring for children.

Asians spend less time than the average person watching television

(index of Asian to total people aged 15 or older in time spent doing selected primary activities on an average day, 2009)

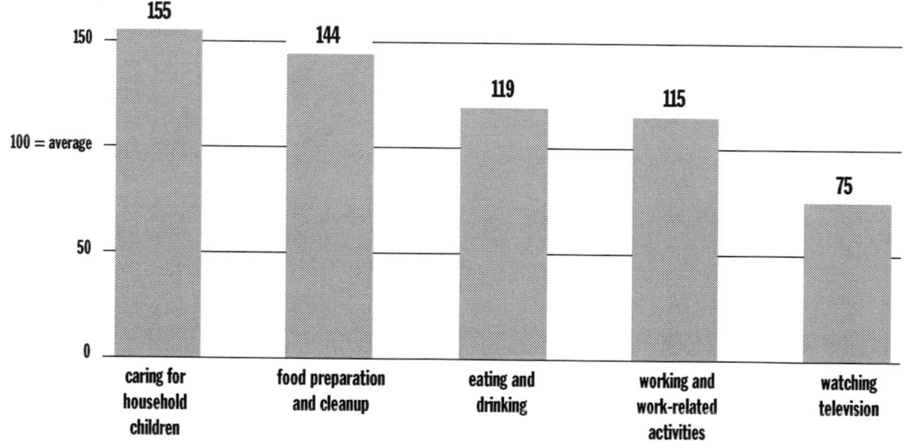

Table 10.4 Indexed Time Use of Total Asians, 2009

(hours spent doing primary activities on an average day by total people and Asians aged 15 or older, and index of time spent by Asians to total people, 2009)

	average hours		index, Asians
	total	Asians	to total people
Total, all activities	**24.00**	**24.00**	**100**
Personal care	9.43	9.28	98
Sleeping	8.67	8.64	100
Grooming	0.67	0.60	90
Household activities	1.83	1.75	96
Housework	0.60	0.53	88
Food preparation and cleanup	0.54	0.78	144
Household management	0.21	0.20	95
Caring for and helping household members	0.46	0.68	148
Caring for and helping household children	0.38	0.59	155
Work and work-related activities	3.25	3.75	115
Working	3.18	3.71	117
Education	0.44	0.79	180
Consumer purchases (store, telephone, Internet)	0.38	0.41	108
Eating and drinking	1.11	1.32	119
Socializing, relaxing, and leisure	4.69	3.73	80
Socializing and communicating	0.63	0.42	67
Watching television	2.82	2.12	75
Computer use for leisure (excluding games)	0.16	0.24	150
Reading for personal interest	0.34	0.28	82
Sports, exercise, recreation	0.33	0.35	106
Religious and spiritual activities	0.15	0.17	113
Volunteer activities	0.15	0.11	73
Telephone calls	0.11	0.09	82
Traveling	1.20	1.20	100

Note: Primary activities are those respondents identified as their main activity. Other activities done simultaneously, such as eating while watching TV, are not included. Numbers may not add to total because not all categories are shown. Asians are those who identify themselves as being of the race alone.
Source: Bureau of Labor Statistics, unpublished tables from the 2009 American Time Use Survey, Internet site http://www.bls.gov/tus/home.htm; calculations by New Strategist

Table 10.5 Indexed Time Use of Asian Men, 2009

(hours spent doing primary activities on an average day by total and Asian men aged 15 or older, and index of time spent by Asian men to total men, 2009)

	average hours		index, Asian men
	total men	Asian men	to total men
Total, all activities	**24.00**	**24.00**	**100**
Personal care	9.24	9.23	100
Sleeping	8.62	8.63	100
Grooming	0.54	0.54	100
Household activities	1.35	1.02	76
Housework	0.26	0.23	88
Food preparation and cleanup	0.29	0.31	107
Household management	0.21	0.21	100
Caring for and helping household members	0.31	0.35	113
Caring for and helping household children	0.26	0.30	115
Work and work-related activities	3.90	4.34	111
Working	3.81	4.29	113
Education	0.40	0.87	218
Consumer purchases (store, telephone, Internet)	0.30	0.27	90
Eating and drinking	1.13	1.33	118
Socializing, relaxing, and leisure	4.91	4.35	89
Socializing and communicating	0.56	0.42	75
Watching television	3.09	2.49	81
Computer use for leisure (excluding games)	0.20	0.32	160
Reading for personal interest	0.27	0.24	89
Sports, exercise, recreation	0.44	0.43	98
Religious and spiritual activities	0.12	0.12	100
Volunteer activities	0.15	0.13	87
Telephone calls	0.07	0.10	143
Traveling	1.24	1.22	98

Note: The index is calculated by dividing the average time spent by Asian men doing primary activity by average time spent by total men doing primary activity and °multiplying by 100. Primary activities are those respondents identified as their main activity. Other activities done simultaneously, such as eating while watching TV, are not included. Numbers may not add to total because not all categories are shown. Asians are those who identify themselves as being of the race alone.
Source: Bureau of Labor Statistics, unpublished tables from the 2009 American Time Use Survey, Internet site http://www.bls.gov/tus/home.htm; calculations by New Strategist

Table 10.6 Indexed Time Use of Asian Women, 2009

(hours spent doing primary activities on an average day by total and Asian women aged 15 or older, and index of time spent by Asian women to total women, 2009)

	average hours		index, Asian women
	total women	Asian women	to total women
Total, all activities	**24.00**	**24.00**	**100**
Personal care	9.61	9.33	97
Sleeping	8.73	8.64	99
Grooming	0.79	0.67	85
Household activities	2.28	2.43	107
Housework	0.92	0.81	88
Food preparation and cleanup	0.77	1.21	157
Household management	0.25	0.20	80
Caring for and helping household members	0.60	0.99	165
Caring for and helping household children	0.50	0.85	170
Work and work-related activities	2.65	3.19	120
Working	2.58	3.18	123
Education	0.47	0.72	153
Consumer purchases (store, telephone, Internet)	0.46	0.54	117
Eating and drinking	1.08	1.31	121
Socializing, relaxing, and leisure	4.48	3.15	70
Socializing and communicating	0.69	0.42	61
Watching television	2.56	1.77	69
Computer use for leisure (excluding games)	0.13	0.18	138
Reading for personal interest	0.42	0.32	76
Sports, exercise, recreation	0.23	0.26	113
Religious and spiritual activities	0.17	0.22	129
Volunteer activities	0.15	0.09	60
Telephone calls	0.15	0.08	53
Traveling	1.17	1.18	101

Note: The index is calculated by dividing the average time spent by Asian women doing primary activity by average time spent by total women doing primary activity and multiplying by 100. Primary activities are those respondents identified as their main activity. Other activities done simultaneously, such as eating while watching TV, are not included. Numbers may not add to total because not all categories are shown. Asians are those who identify themselves as being of the race alone.
Source: Bureau of Labor Statistics, unpublished tables from the 2009 American Time Use Survey, Internet site http://www.bls.gov/tus/home.htm; calculations by New Strategist

Table 10.7 Indexed Time Use of Asians by Sex, 2009

(average hours spent by Asians aged 15 or older doing primary activities on an average day by sex, and index of Asian women's time to Asian men's, 2009)

	Asians aged 15 or older, average hours		index of women to men
	Asian men	Asian women	
Total, all activities	**24.00**	**24.00**	**100**
Personal care	9.23	9.33	101
Sleeping	8.63	8.64	100
Grooming	0.54	0.67	124
Household activities	1.02	2.43	238
Housework	0.23	0.81	352
Food preparation and cleanup	0.31	1.21	390
Household management	0.21	0.20	95
Caring for and helping household members	0.35	0.99	283
Caring for and helping household children	0.30	0.85	283
Work and work-related activities	4.34	3.19	74
Working	4.29	3.18	74
Education	0.87	0.72	83
Consumer purchases (store, telephone, Internet)	0.27	0.54	200
Eating and drinking	1.33	1.31	98
Socializing, relaxing, and leisure	4.35	3.15	72
Socializing and communicating	0.42	0.42	100
Watching television	2.49	1.77	71
Computer use for leisure (excluding games)	0.32	0.18	56
Reading for personal interest	0.24	0.32	133
Sports, exercise, recreation	0.43	0.26	60
Religious and spiritual activities	0.12	0.22	183
Volunteer activities	0.13	0.09	69
Telephone calls	0.10	0.08	80
Traveling	1.22	1.18	97

Note: The index is calculated by dividing women's time by men's and multiplying by 100. Primary activities are those respondents identified as their main activity. Other activities done simultaneously, such as eating while watching TV, are not included. Numbers may not add to total because not all categories are shown. Asians are those who identify themselves as being of the race alone.

Source: Bureau of Labor Statistics, unpublished tables from the 2009 American Time Use Survey, Internet site http://www.bls.gov/tus/home.htm; calculations by New Strategist

Asians Are More Likely to Participate in Sports and Exercise

They are less likely to socialize on an average day.

Asian participation in many activities is below average. On an average day, they are 8 percent less likely than the average person to do housework, and 10 percent less likely to shop. Only 31 percent socialize or communicate as a primary activity on an average day compared with 38 percent of all Americans aged 15 or older. But Asians are more likely than average to participate in sports and exercise, more likely to work, care for household children, and use a computer for leisure.

Asian men's participation in some activities is well below average. They are 14 percent less likely than the average man to participate in household activities and 18 percent less likely to shop on an average day. That may be because they are 16 percent more likely to work. Asian women are far more likely than the average woman to care for household children (36 versus 26 percent). They are also more likely than the average woman to work, but less likely to socialize, do housework, or watch television.

■ Forty-two percent of Asian women, but only 29 percent of Asian men, shop for consumer goods on an average day.

More than 25 percent of Asians participate in sports and exercise on an average day

(percent of Asians and total people aged 15 or older who participated in sports and exercise on an average day, 2009)

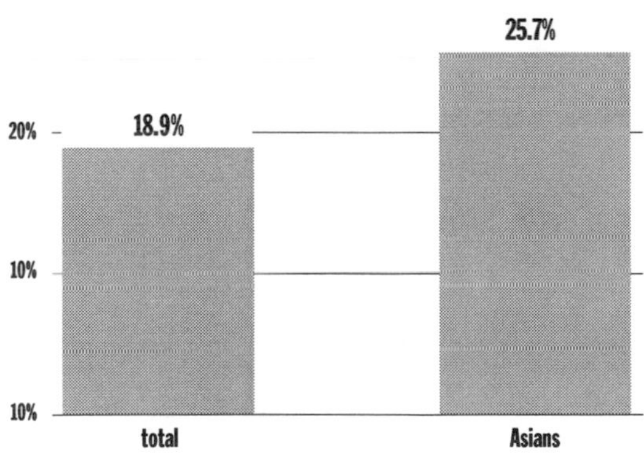

Table 10.8 Indexed Participation in Primary Activities: Total Asians, 2009

(percent of total people and Asians aged 15 or older participating in primary activities on an average day, and index of participation by Asians to total people, 2009)

	percent participating		index, Asians to total people
	total	Asians	
Total, all activities	**100.0%**	**100.0%**	**100**
Personal care	100.0	100.0	100
Sleeping	99.9	100.0	100
Grooming	78.4	76.7	98
Household activities	78.2	71.3	91
Housework	36.3	33.4	92
Food preparation and cleanup	54.6	53.4	98
Household management	28.9	26.1	90
Caring for and helping household members	25.2	32.4	129
Caring for and helping household children	21.1	28.6	136
Work and work-related activities	45.3	51.2	113
Working	42.7	49.1	115
Education	8.2	13.8	169
Consumer purchases (store, telephone, Internet)	40.2	36.1	90
Eating and drinking	96.4	97.8	101
Socializing, relaxing, and leisure	95.1	95.2	100
Socializing and communicating	37.7	31.3	83
Watching television	81.8	76.8	94
Computer use for leisure (excluding games)	10.9	14.5	132
Reading for personal interest	24.2	22.8	94
Sports, exercise, recreation	18.9	25.7	136
Religious and spiritual activities	9.0	12.4	138
Volunteer activities	7.0	5.5	79
Telephone calls	15.4	14.8	96
Traveling	87.0	87.8	101

Note: The index is calculated by dividing percent of Asians doing primary activity by percent of total people doing primary activity and multiplying by 100. Primary activities are those respondents identified as their main activity. Other activities done simultaneously, such as eating while watching TV, are not included. Asians are those who identify themselves as being of the race alone.

Source: Bureau of Labor Statistics, unpublished tables from the 2009 American Time Use Survey, Internet site http://www.bls.gov/tus/home.htm; calculations by New Strategist

Table 10.9 Indexed Participation in Primary Activities: Asian Men, 2009

(percent of total and Asian men aged 15 or older participating in primary activities on an average day, and index of participation by Asian men to total men, 2009)

	percent participating		index, Asian men
	total men	Asian men	to total men
Total, all activities	**100.0%**	**100.0%**	**100**
Personal care	100.0	100.0	100
Sleeping	99.8	100.0	100
Grooming	74.6	73.5	99
Household activities	69.0	59.7	86
Housework	20.2	20.2	100
Food preparation and cleanup	39.9	31.7	80
Household management	25.1	26.5	106
Caring for and helping household members	20.2	25.7	127
Caring for and helping household children	15.9	20.4	129
Work and work-related activities	51.8	59.9	116
Working	48.4	56.6	117
Education	7.4	14.7	199
Consumer purchases (store, telephone, Internet)	35.8	29.2	82
Eating and drinking	96.1	96.3	100
Socializing, relaxing, and leisure	94.6	96.1	102
Socializing and communicating	33.4	28.3	85
Watching television	82.7	78.4	95
Computer use for leisure (excluding games)	11.9	18.4	154
Reading for personal interest	20.8	20.6	99
Sports, exercise, recreation	21.7	28.6	132
Religious and spiritual activities	7.0	9.2	132
Volunteer activities	7.0	6.2	89
Telephone calls	10.4	13.0	125
Traveling	88.4	87.9	99

Note: The index is calculated by dividing percent of Asians doing primary activity by percent of total people doing primary activity and multiplying by 100. Primary activities are those respondents identified as their main activity. Other activities done simultaneously, such as eating while watching TV, are not included. Asians are those who identify themselves as being of the race alone.

Source: Bureau of Labor Statistics, unpublished tables from the 2009 American Time Use Survey, Internet site http://www.bls.gov/tus/home.htm; calculations by New Strategist

Table 10.10 Indexed Participation in Primary Activities: Asian Women, 2009

(percent of total and Asian women aged 15 or older participating in primary activities on an average day, and index of participation by Asian women to total women, 2009)

	percent participating		index, Asian women to total women
	total women	Asian women	
Total, all activities	**100.0%**	**100.0%**	**100**
Personal care	100.0	100.0	100
Sleeping	100.0	100.0	100
Grooming	82.1	79.6	97
Household activities	86.7	82.2	95
Housework	51.3	45.9	89
Food preparation and cleanup	68.3	73.7	108
Household management	32.5	25.7	79
Caring for and helping household members	29.9	38.7	130
Caring for and helping household children	25.9	36.2	140
Work and work-related activities	39.2	43.2	110
Working	37.3	42.2	113
Education	8.9	12.9	145
Consumer purchases (store, telephone, Internet)	44.4	42.5	96
Eating and drinking	96.7	99.2	102
Socializing, relaxing, and leisure	95.6	94.4	99
Socializing and communicating	41.8	34.2	82
Watching television	80.9	75.3	93
Computer use for leisure (excluding games)	10.1	10.8	108
Reading for personal interest	27.3	24.9	91
Sports, exercise, recreation	16.3	23.0	141
Religious and spiritual activities	10.8	15.3	141
Volunteer activities	7.1	4.9	69
Telephone calls	20.0	16.4	82
Traveling	85.6	87.7	102

Note: The index is calculated by dividing percent of Asians doing primary activity by percent of total people doing primary activity and multiplying by 100. Primary activities are those respondents identified as their main activity. Other activities done simultaneously, such as eating while watching TV, are not included. Asians are those who identify themselves as being of the race alone.
Source: Bureau of Labor Statistics, unpublished tables from the 2009 American Time Use Survey, Internet site http://www.bls.gov/tus/home.htm; calculations by New Strategist

Table 10.11 Indexed Participation in Primary Activities: Asians by Sex, 2009

(percent of Asians aged 15 or older participating in primary activities on an average day by sex, and index of women's participation to men's, 2009)

	Asians aged 15 or older, percent participating		index of women to men
	men	women	
Total, all activities	**100.0%**	**100.0%**	**100**
Personal care	100.0	100.0	100
Sleeping	100.0	100.0	100
Grooming	73.5	79.6	108
Household activities	59.7	82.2	138
Housework	20.2	45.9	227
Food preparation and cleanup	31.7	73.7	232
Household management	26.5	25.7	97
Caring for and helping household members	25.7	38.7	150
Caring for and helping household children	20.4	36.2	177
Work and work-related activities	59.9	43.2	72
Working	56.6	42.2	75
Education	14.7	12.9	88
Consumer purchases (store, telephone, Internet)	29.2	42.5	146
Eating and drinking	96.3	99.2	103
Socializing, relaxing, and leisure	96.1	94.4	98
Socializing and communicating	28.3	34.2	121
Watching television	78.4	75.3	96
Computer use for leisure (excluding games)	18.4	10.8	59
Reading for personal interest	20.6	24.9	120
Sports, exercise, recreation	28.6	23.0	80
Religious and spiritual activities	9.2	15.3	166
Volunteer activities	6.2	4.9	78
Telephone calls	13.0	16.4	126
Traveling	87.9	87.7	100

Note: The index is calculated by dividing percent of Asian women doing primary activity by percent of Asian men doing primary activity and multiplying by 100. Primary activities are those respondents identified as their main activity. Other activities done simultaneously, such as eating while watching TV, are not included. Asians are those who identify themselves as being of the race alone.

Source: Bureau of Labor Statistics, unpublished tables from the 2009 American Time Use Survey, Internet site http://www.bls.gov/tus/home.htm; calculations by New Strategist

Glossary

adjusted for inflation Income or a change in income that has been adjusted for the rise in the cost of living, or the consumer price index (CPI-U-RS).

American Community Survey An on-going nationwide survey of 250,000 households per month, providing detailed demographic data at the community level. Designed to replace the census long-form questionnaire, the ACS includes more than 60 questions that formerly appeared on the long form, such as language spoken at home, income, and education. ACS data are available for areas as small as census tracts.

American Housing Survey The AHS collects national and metropolitan-level data on the nation's housing, including apartments, single-family homes, and mobile homes. The nationally representative survey, with a sample of 60,000 homes, is conducted by the Census Bureau for the Department of Housing and Urban Development every other year.

American Indians Include Alaska Natives (Eskimos and Aleuts) unless those groups are shown separately.

American Time Use Survey Under contract with the Bureau of Labor Statistics, the Census Bureau collects ATUS information, revealing how people spend their time. The ATUS sample is drawn from U.S. households completing their final month of interviews for the Current Population Survey. One individual from each selected household is chosen to participate in ATUS. Respondents are interviewed by telephone about their time use during the previous 24 hours. About 40,000 households are included in the sample each year.

Asian Beginning with the 2000 census and in 2003 for government surveys, Asians can identify themselves as being Asian and no other race (called "Asian alone") or as being Asian in combination with one or more other races (called "Asian in combination"). The combination of the two groups is termed "Asian alone or in combination." In this book, the "Asian alone or in combination" population is shown whenever possible.

average hours per day On the time use tables, the average number of hours spent in a 24-hour day (between 4 a.m. on the diary day and 4 a.m. on the interview day) doing a specified activity. Estimates are adjusted for variability in response rates across days of the week. Average hours per day are shown in decimals. To convert decimal portions of an hour into minutes, multiply 60 by the decimal. For example, if the average is 1.2 hours, multiply 60 by 0.2 to get 12 minutes, so the average is 1 hour and 12 minutes. If the average is 0.05 hours, multiply 60 by .05 to get 3 minutes. If the average is 5.36 hours, multiply 60 by 0.36 to get 21.6, so the average is 5 hours and about 22 minutes.

baby boom U.S. residents born between 1946 and 1964.

baby bust U.S. residents born between 1965 and 1976, also known as Generation X.

Behavioral Risk Factor Surveillance System A collaborative project of the Centers for Disease Control and Prevention and U.S. states and territories. It is an ongoing data collection program designed to measure behavioral risk factors in the adult population aged 18 or older. All 50 states, three territories, and the District of Columbia take part in the survey, making the BRFSS the primary source of information on the health-related behaviors of Americans.

black Beginning with the 2000 census and in 2003 for government surveys, blacks can identify themselves as being black and no other race (called "black alone") or as being black in combination with one or more other races (called "black in combination"). The combination of the two groups is termed "black alone or in combination." In this book, the "black alone or in combination" population is shown whenever possible.

Consumer Expenditure Survey An ongoing study of the day-to-day spending of American households administered by the Bureau of Labor Statistics. The CEX includes an interview survey and a diary survey. The average spending figures shown are the integrated data from both the diary and interview components of the survey. Two separate, nationally representative samples are used for the interview and diary surveys. For the interview survey, about 7,500 consumer units are interviewed on a rotating panel basis each quarter for five consecutive quarters. For the diary survey, 7,500 consumer units keep weekly diaries of spending for two consecutive weeks.

consumer unit *(on spending tables only)* For convenience, the term consumer unit and household are used interchangeably in the Spending chapter of this book, although consumer units are somewhat different from the Census Bureau's households. Consumer units are all related members of a household, or financially independent members of a household. A household may include more than one consumer unit.

Current Population Survey A nationally representative survey of the civilian noninstitutional population aged 15 or older. It is taken monthly by the Census Bureau for the Bureau of Labor Statistics, collecting information from more than 50,000 households on employment and unemployment. In March of each year, the survey includes the Annual Social and Economic Supplement (formerly called the Annual

Demographic Survey), which is the source of most national data on the characteristics of Americans, such as educational attainment, living arrangements, and incomes.

disability The National Health Interview Survey estimates the number of people aged 18 or older who have difficulty in physical functioning, probing whether respondents could perform nine activities by themselves without using special equipment. The categories are walking a quarter mile; standing for two hours; sitting for two hours; walking up ten steps without resting; stooping, bending, kneeling; reaching over one's head; grasping or handling small objects; carrying a ten-pound object; and pushing/pulling a large object. Adults who reported that any of these activities was very difficult or they could not do it at all were defined as having physical difficulties.

dual-earner couple A married couple in which both the husband and wife are in the labor force.

earnings A type of income, earnings is the amount of money a person receives from his or her job. *See also* Income.

employed All civilians who did any work as a paid employee or farmer/self-employed worker, or who worked 15 hours or more as an unpaid farm worker or in a family-owned business, during the reference period. All those who have jobs but who are temporarily absent from their jobs due to illness, bad weather, vacation, labor management dispute, or personal reasons are considered employed.

expenditure The transaction cost including excise and sales taxes of goods and services acquired during the survey period. The full cost of each purchase is recorded even though full payment may not have been made at the date of purchase. Average expenditure figures may be artificially low for infrequently purchased items such as cars because figures are calculated using all consumer units within a demographic segment rather than just purchasers. Expenditure estimates include money spent on gifts for others.

family A group of two or more people (one of whom is the householder) related by birth, marriage, or adoption and living in the same household.

family household A household maintained by a householder who lives with one or more people related to him or her by blood, marriage, or adoption.

female/male householder A woman or man who maintains a household without a spouse present. May head family or nonfamily households.

foreign-born population People who are not U.S. citizens at birth.

full-time employment Thirty-five or more hours of work per week during a majority of the weeks worked.

full-time, year-round Fifty or more weeks of full-time employment during the previous calendar year.

General Social Survey A biennial survey of the attitudes of Americans taken by the University of Chicago's National Opinion Research Center, which conducts the GSS through face-to-face interviews with an independently drawn, representative sample of 1,500 to 3,000 noninstitutionalized people aged 18 or older who live in the United States.

generation X U.S. residents born between 1965 and 1976, also known as the baby-bust generation.

Hispanic Because Hispanic is an ethnic origin rather than a race, Hispanics may be of any race. While most Hispanics are white, there are black, Asian, American Indian, and even Native Hawaiian Hispanics.

household All the persons who occupy a housing unit. A household includes the related family members and all the unrelated persons, if any, such as lodgers, foster children, wards, or employees who share the housing unit. A person living alone is counted as a household. A group of unrelated people who share a housing unit as roommates or unmarried partners is also counted as a household. Households do not include group quarters such as college dormitories, prisons, or nursing homes.

household, race/ethnicity of Households are categorized according to the race or ethnicity of the householder only.

householder The person (or one of the persons) in whose name the housing unit is owned or rented or, if there is no such person, any adult member. With married couples, the householder may be either the husband or wife. The householder is the reference person for the household.

householder, age of Used to categorize households into age groups such as those used in this book. Married couples, for example, are classified according to the age of either the husband or wife, depending on which one identified him or herself as the householder.

housing unit A house, an apartment, a group of rooms, or a single room occupied or intended for occupancy as separate living quarters. Separate living quarters are those in which the occupants do not live and eat with any other persons in the structure and that have direct access from the outside of the building or through a common hall that is used or intended for use by the occupants of another unit or by the general public. The occupants may be a single family, one person living alone, two or more families living together, or any other group of related or unrelated persons who share living arrangements.

Housing Vacancy Survey Asupplement to the Current Population Survey, providing quarterly and annual data on rental and homeowner vacancy rates, characteristics of units available for occupancy, and homeownership rates by age, household type, region, state, and metropolitan area. The Current Population Survey sample includes 51,000 occupied housing units and 9,000 vacant units.

housing value The respondent's estimate of how much his or her house and lot would sell for if it were for sale.

iGeneration U.S. residents born in 1995 or later.

immigration The relatively permanent movement (change of residence) of people into the country of reference.

in-migration The relatively permanent movement (change of residence) of people into a subnational geographic entity, such as a region, division, state, metropolitan area, or county.

income Money received in the preceding calendar year by each person aged 15 or older from each of the following sources: (1) earnings from longest job (or self-employment); (2) earnings from jobs other than longest job; (3) unemployment compensation; (4) workers' compensation; (5) Social Security; (6) Supplemental Security income; (7) public assistance; (8) veterans' payments; (9) survivor benefits; (10) disability benefits; (11) retirement pensions; (12) interest; (13) dividends; (14) rents and royalties or estates and trusts; (15) educational assistance; (16) alimony; (17) child support; (18) financial assistance from outside the household, and other periodic income. Income is reported in several ways in this book. Household income is the combined income of all household members. Income of persons is all income accruing to a person from all sources. Earnings are the money a person receives from his or her job.

industry The industry in which a person worked longest in the preceding calendar year.

job tenure The length of time a person has been employed continuously by the same employer.

labor force Includes both the employed and the unemployed (people who are looking for work). People are counted as in the labor force if they were working or looking for work during the reference week in which the Census Bureau fields the Current Population Survey. The labor force tables in this book show the civilian labor force only.

labor force participation rate The percent of the civilian noninstitutional population that is in the civilian labor force, which includes both the employed and the unemployed.

married couples with or without children under age 18 Married couples with or without own children under age 18 living in the same household. Couples without children under age 18 may be parents of grown children who live elsewhere, or they could be childless couples.

median The amount that divides the population or households into two equal portions: one below and one above the median. Medians can be calculated for income, age, and many other characteristics.

median income The amount that divides the income distribution into two equal groups, half having incomes above the median, half having incomes below the median. The medians for households or families are based on all households or families. The median for persons are based on all persons aged 15 or older with income.

metropolitan statistical area A large population nucleus with adjacent communities having a high degree of social and economic integration with the core. The Office of Management and Budget defines the nation's metropolitan statistical areas. In general, they must include a city or urbanized area with 50,000 or more inhabitants and a total population of 100,000 or more. The county (or counties) that contains the largest city is the "central county" (counties), along with any adjacent counties that are socially and economically integrated with the central county (or counties). In New England, MSAs are defined in terms of cities and towns rather than counties.

millennial generation U.S. residents born between 1977 and 1994.

mobility status People are classified according to their mobility status on the basis of a comparison between their place of residence at the time of the March Current Population Survey and their place of residence in March of the previous year. Nonmovers are people living in the same house at the end of the period as at the beginning of the period. Movers are people living in a different house at the end of the period than at the beginning of the period. Movers from abroad are either citizens or aliens whose place of residence is outside the United States at the beginning of the period, that is, in an outlying area under the jurisdiction of the United States or in a foreign country. The mobility status of children is fully allocated from the mother if she is in the household; otherwise it is allocated from the householder.

National Ambulatory Medical Care Survey An annual survey of visits to nonfederally employed office-based physicians who are primarily engaged in direct patient care. Data are collected from physicians rather than patients, with each physician assigned a one-week reporting period. During the week, the physician or office staff record a systematic random sample of visit characteristics.

National Compensation Survey Conducted by he Bureau of Labor Statistics, this survey examines the incidence and detailed provisions of selected employee benefit plans in small, medium, and large private establishments, and state and local governments. Each year BLS economists visit a representative sample of establishments across the country, asking questions about the establishment, its employees, and their benefits.

National Health and Nutrition Examination Survey A continuous survey of a representative sample of the U.S. civilian noninstitutionalized population. Respondents are interviewed at home about their health and nutrition, and the interview is followed up by a physical examination that measures such things as height and weight in mobile examination centers.

National Health Interview Survey A continuing nationwide sample survey of the civilian noninstitutional population of the U.S. conducted by the Census Bureau for the National Center for Health Statistics. In interviews each year, data are collected from more than 100,000 people about their illnesses, injuries, impairments, chronic and acute conditions, activity limitations, and use of health services.

National Hospital Ambulatory Medical Care Survey Sponsored by the National Center for Health Statistics, it is an annual national probability sample survey of visits to emergency departments and outpatient departments at non-Federal, short stay and general hospitals. Hospital staff collect data from patient records.

National Household Education Survey Sponsored by the National Center for Education Statistics, it provides descriptive data on the educational activities of the U.S. population, including after-school care and adult education. The NHES is a system of telephone surveys of a representative sample of 45,000 to 60,000 households in the U.S.

Native Hawaiian and other Pacific Islander The 2000 census identified this group for the first time as a separate racial category from Asians. In most survey data, however, the population is included with Asians.

net migration Net migration is the result of subtracting out-migration from in-migration for an area. Another way to derive net migration is to subtract natural increase (births minus deaths) from total population change in an area.

nonfamily household A household maintained by a householder who lives alone or who lives with people to whom he or she is not related.

nonfamily householder A householder who lives alone or with nonrelatives.

non-Hispanic People who do not identify themselves as Hispanic are classified as non-Hispanic. Non-Hispanics may be of any race.

non-Hispanic white People who identify their race as white alone and who do not indicate an Hispanic origin.

nonmetropolitan area Counties that are not classified as metropolitan areas.

occupation Occupational classification is based on the kind of work a person did at his or her job during the previous calendar year. If a person changed jobs during the year, the data refer to the occupation of the job held the longest during that year.

occupied housing units A housing unit is classified as occupied if a person or group of people is living in it or if the occupants are only temporarily absent—on vacation, example. By definition, the count of occupied housing units is the same as the count of households.

outside principal cities The portion of a metropolitan county or counties that falls outside of the principal city or cities; generally regarded as the suburbs.

own children Sons and daughters, including stepchildren and adopted children, of the householder. The totals include never-married children living away from home in college dormitories.

owner occupied A housing unit is "owner occupied" if the owner lives in the unit, even if it is mortgaged or not fully paid for. A cooperative or condominium unit is "owner occupied" only if the owner lives in it. All other occupied units are classified as "renter occupied."

population versus participant measures On the time use tables, average time spent doing an activity is shown for either the population as a whole (such as all 25-to-34-year-olds) or only for those participating in an activity in the previous 24-hours, or diary day. Data referring to the population as a whole include every respondent, even those who did not engage in the activity on diary day. This type of calculation allows researchers to see how Americans prioritize the entire range of daily activities, but it results in artificially short amounts of time devoted to activities done infrequently (such as volunteering). Data referring to participant time show only the time spent on specific activities by respondents who reported doing the activity on diary day. They more accurately reflect the amount of time people spend doing specific activities when they do them.

part-time employment Less than 35 hours of work per week in a majority of the weeks worked during the year.

percent change The change (either positive or negative) in a measure that is expressed as a proportion of the starting measure. When median income changes from $20,000 to $25,000, for example, this is a 25 percent increase.

percentage point change The change (either positive or negative) in a value which is already expressed as a percentage. When a labor force participation rate changes from 70 percent of 75 percent, for example, this is a 5 percentage point increase.

poverty level The official income threshold below which families and people are classified as living in poverty. The threshold rises each year with inflation and varies depending on family size and age of householder. For more on poverty thresholds, go to Internet site http://www.census.gov/hhes/www/poverty/data/threshld/index.html

primary activity On the time use tables, primary activity is the main activity a respondent was doing at a specified time.

principal cities The largest cities in a metropolitan area are called the principal cities. The balance of a metropolitan area outside the principal cities is regarded as the "suburbs."

proportion or share The value of a part expressed as a percentage of the whole. If there are 4 million people aged 25 and 3 million of them are white, then the white proportion is 75 percent.

race Race is self-reported and can be defined in three ways. The "race alone" population comprises people who identify themselves as only one race. The "race in combination" population comprises people who identify themselves as more than one race, such as white and black. The "race, alone or in combination" population includes both those who identify themselves as one race and those who identify themselves as more than one race.

regions The four major regions and nine census divisions of the United States are the state groupings as shown below:

Northeast:

—New England: Connecticut, Maine, Massachusetts, New Hampshire, Rhode Island, and Vermont
—Middle Atlantic: New Jersey, New York, and Pennsylvania

Midwest:

—East North Central: Illinois, Indiana, Michigan, Ohio, and Wisconsin
—West North Central: Iowa, Kansas, Minnesota, Missouri, Nebraska, North Dakota, and South Dakota

South:

—South Atlantic: Delaware, District of Columbia, Florida, Georgia, Maryland, North Carolina, South Carolina, Virginia, and West Virginia
—East South Central: Alabama, Kentucky, Mississippi, and Tennessee
—West South Central: Arkansas, Louisiana, Oklahoma, and Texas

West:

—Mountain: Arizona, Colorado, Idaho, Montana, Nevada, New Mexico, Utah, and Wyoming
—Pacific: Alaska, California, Hawaii, Oregon, and Washington

renter occupied *See* Owner Occupied.

Retirement Confidence Survey Sponsored by the Employee Benefit Research Institute (EBRI), the American Savings Education Council (ASEC), and Mathew Greenwald & Associates (Greenwald), it is an annual survey of a nationally representative sample of 1,000 people aged 25 or older. Respondents are asked a core set of questions that have been asked since 1996, measuring attitudes and behavior towards retirement. Additional questions are also asked about current retirement issues.

rounding Percentages are rounded to the nearest tenth of a percent; therefore, the percentages in a distribution do not always add exactly to 100.0 percent. The totals, however, are always shown as 100.0. Moreover, individual figures are rounded to the nearest thousand without being adjusted to group totals, which are independently rounded; percentages are based on the unrounded numbers.

self-employment A person is categorized as self-employed if he or she was self-employed in the job held longest during the reference period. Persons who report self-employment from a second job are excluded, but those who report wage-and-salary income from a second job are included. Unpaid workers in family businesses are excluded. Self-employment statistics include only nonagricultural workers and exclude people who work for themselves in incorporated business.

sex ratio The number of men per 100 women.

suburbs *See* Outside principal city.

Survey of Consumer Finances A triennial survey taken by the Federal Reserve Board. It collects data on the assets, debts, and net worth of American households. For the 2007 survey, the Federal Reserve Board interviewed a representative sample of 4,422 households. To capture the effect of the Great Recession on household wealth, the Federal Reserve re-interviewed in 2009 the households that participated in the 2007 survey.

unemployed Unemployed people are those who, during the survey period, had no employment but were available and looking for work. Those who were laid off from their jobs and were waiting to be recalled are also classified as unemployed.

white The "white" racial category includes many Hispanics (who may be of any race) unless the term "non-Hispanic white" is used.

Bibliography

Bureau of Labor Statistics

Internet site http://www.bls.gov

—2009 Consumer Expenditure Surveys, Internet site http://www.bls.gov/cex/

—2009 American Time Use Survey, Internet site http://www.bls.gov/tus/home.htm

—Employee Tenure, Internet site http://www.bls.gov/news.release/tenure.toc.htm

—Labor Force Statistics from the Current Population Survey, Internet site http://www.bls.gov/cps/tables.htm#empstat

—*Monthly Labor Review*, "Labor Force Projections to 2018: Older Workers Staying More Active," November 2009, Internet site http://www.bls.gov/opub/mlr/2009/11/home.htm

Bureau of the Census

Internet site http://www.census.gov/

—2000 Census, *An Overview: The Asian Population 2000,* 2000 Census Briefs, Internet site http://www.census.gov/population/www/cen2000/briefs.htm

—2000 Census, *An Overview: The Black Population 2000,* 2000 Census Briefs, Internet site http://www.census.gov/population/www/cen2000/briefs.htm

—2000 Census, *An Overview: The Hispanic Population 2000,* 2000 Census Briefs, Internet site http://www.census.gov/population/www/cen2000/briefs.htm

—2007, 2008, and 2009 American Community Survey, Internet site http://factfinder.census.gov/servlet/DatasetMainPageServlet?_program=ACS&_submenuId=&_lang=en&_ts=

—2010 Census, *An Overview: Race and Hispanic Origin and the 2010 Census*, 2010 Census Briefs, Internet site http://2010.census.gov/2010census/data/

—2010 Census Factfinder, Internet site http://factfinder2.census.gov/faces/nav/jsf/pages/index.xhtml

—2010 Census, *State Population Distribution and Change: 2000 to 2010*, 2010 Census Briefs, Internet site http://2010.census.gov/2010census/data/

—American Housing Survey for the United States, Internet site http://www.census.gov/hhes/www/housing/ahs/ahs.html

—America's Families and Living Arrangements, 2010 Current Population Survey Annual Social and Economic Supplement, Internet site http://www.census.gov/population/www/socdemo/hh-fam/cps2010.html

—Families and Living Arrangements, Historical Time Series, Current Population Survey Annual Social and Economic Supplements, Internet site http://www.census.gov/population/www/socdemo/hh-fam.html

—Geographic Mobility: 2008 to 2009, Detailed Tables, Current Population Survey Annual Social and Economic Supplement, Internet site http://www.census.gov/population/www/socdemo/migrate/cps2009.html

—Health Insurance, Internet site http://www.census.gov/hhes/www/cpstables/032010/health/toc.htm

—Historical Income Tables, Current Population Survey Annual Social and Economic Supplements, Internet site http://www.census.gov/hhes/www/income/histinc/histinctb.html
—Historical Poverty Tables, Current Population Survey Annual Social and Economic Supplements, Internet site http://www.census.gov/hhes/www/poverty/histpov/histpovtb.html
—Housing Vacancy Surveys, Internet site http://www.census.gov/hhes/www/housing/hvs/hvs.html
—*Income, Poverty, and Health Insurance Coverage in the United States: 2009,* Current Population Report, P60-238, 2010; Internet site http://www.census.gov/hhes/www/income/data/incpovhlth/2009/index.htm
—National Population Estimates, Internet site http://www.census.gov/popest/national/asrh/
—Number, Timing, and Duration of Marriages and Divorces: 2004, Detailed Tables, Internet site http://www.census.gov/population/www/socdemo/marr-div/2004detailed_tables.html
—School Enrollment—Social and Economic Characteristics of Students: October 2009, detailed tables, Internet site http://www.census.gov/population/www/socdemo/school/cps2009.html

Centers for Disease Control and Prevention
Internet site http://www.cdc.gov
—Behavioral Risk Factor Surveillance System, Prevalence Data, Internet site http://apps.nccd.cdc.gov/brfss/
—HIV/AIDS, Internet site http://www.cdc.gov/hiv/surveillance/resources/reports/2008report/table2a.htm

Federal Reserve Board
Internet site http://www.federalreserve.gov/pubs/oss/oss2/scfindex.html
—"Surveying the Aftermath of the Storm: Changes in Family Finances from 2007 to 2009," Appendix tables, Internet site http://www.federalreserve.gov/pubs/oss/oss2/2009p/scf2009phome.html

National Center for Education Statistics
Internet site http://nces.ed.gov
—Digest of Education Statistics: 2010, Internet site http://nces.ed.gov/programs/digest/
—Projections of Education Statistics to 2019, Internet site http://nces.ed.gov/programs/projections/projections2019/tables.asp

National Center for Health Statistics
Internet site http://www.cdc.gov/nchs
—*Anthropometric Reference Data for Children and Adults: United States, 2003–2006*, National Health Statistics Reports, Number 10, 2008, Internet site http://www.cdc.gov/nchs/products/pubs/pubd/nhsr/nhsr.htm
—*Births: Preliminary Data for 2009*, National Vital Statistics Reports, Vol. 59, No. 3, 2010, Internet site http://www.cdc.gov/nchs/births.htm
—*Deaths: Preliminary Data for 2009*, National Vital Statistics Reports, Vol. 59, No. 4, 2011, Internet site http://www.cdc.gov/nchs/deaths.htm

—*Health, United States, 2010,* Internet site http://www.cdc.gov/nchs/hus.htm

—*Summary Health Statistics for U.S. Adults: National Health Interview Survey, 2009*, Series 10, No. 249, 2010, Internet site http://www.cdc.gov/nchs/nhis.htm

—*Summary Health Statistics for U.S. Children: National Health Interview Survey, 2009*, Series 10, No. 247, 2010, Internet site http://www.cdc.gov/nchs/nhis.htm

—*Summary Health Statistics for the U.S. Population: National Health Interview Survey, 2009*, Series 10, No. 248, 2010, Internet site http://www.cdc.gov/nchs/nhis.htm

—*United States Life Tables by Hispanic Origin*, Vital and Health Statistics, Series 2, No. 152, 2010, Internet site http://www.cdc.gov/nchs/deaths.htm

Survey Documentation and Analysis, Computer-assisted Survey Methods Program, University of California, Berkeley

Internet site http://sda.berkeley.edu/

—General Social Surveys, 1972-2010 Cumulative Data Files, Internet site http://sda.berkeley.edu/cgi-bin/hsda?harcsda+gss10

Index